# Human Resource Management in Organisations

## The theory and practice of high performance

**Izabela Robinson**, BA, MA, PhD is a senior lecturer at Northampton Business School, The University of Northampton. She teaches on a range of HRM programmes. Her research interests include international HRM and labour relations in post-socialist Poland. She is a Fellow of the CIPD and worked previously as a personnel manager in the printing, publishing and footwear industries.

The Chartered Institute of Personnel and Development is the leading publisher of books and reports for personnel and training professionals, students and all those concerned with the effective management and development of people at work. For details of all our titles, please contact the publishing department:

*tel* 020 8612 6204

*e-mail* publish@cipd.co.uk

The catalogue of all CIPD titles can be viewed on the CIPD website:

www.cipd.co.uk/bookstore

# Human Resource Management in Organisations

## The theory and practice of high performance

Izabela Robinson

Chartered Institute of Personnel and Development

Published by the Chartered Institute of Personnel and Development, 151 The Broadway, London, SW19 1JQ

First published 2006

Typeset by Fakenham Photosetting, Norfolk

Printed in Great Britain by Cromwell Press, Trowbridge, Wiltshire

British Library Cataloguing in Publication Data
A catalogue of this publication is available from the British Library

ISBN 1 84398 066 5
ISBN-13 978 1 84398 066 7

Chartered Institute of Personnel and Development,
151 The Broadway, London, SW19 1JQ
Tel: 020 8612 6200
E-mail: cipd@cipd.co.uk    Website: www.cipd.co.uk
Incorporated by Royal Charter    Registered Charity No. 1079797

# Contents

## Chapter 8 Managing and rewarding performance at work 215

### Kevin Lamb

# Figures and tables

# Acknowledgements

I would like to thank Joe and Rich for their support and encouragement.

I would also like to thank colleagues at Northampton Business School whose expertise and co-operation is reflected in the authorship of individual chapters.

Finally, I would like to thank the following for permission to reproduce copyright material;

Table 2 taken from *Organisational Dynamics* vol 13, no 1, p48 reproduced with permission from Elsevier; table 7 taken from *Strategic Human Resource Management*, reproduced with permission from Blackwell Publishing; table 14 taken from *The Fifth Discipline*, reproduced with permission from The Random House Group Ltd; figure 6 taken from *Human Resource Management* Anniversary edition reproduced with permission from Palgrave Macmillan; figure 11 taken from *Managing Service Quality* vol 14, no 2/3 p132 republished with permission from Emerald Group Publishing Ltd (http://www.emeraldinsight.com/msq.htm); figure 12 taken from *Strategic Human Resource Management*, reproduced with permission from Blackwell Publishing; figure 28 taken from *Organisation Theory* reproduced with permission from Oxford University Press; figure 29 taken from *The Mind of the Strategist*, reproduced with permission from McGraw-Hill Education; figure 31 taken from *Developing People and Organisations*, reproduced with permission from Elsevier; figure 33 taken from *Exploring Strategic Change* and figure 34 taken from *Exploring Corporate Strategy* reproduced with permission from Pearson Education; extracts pp44, 46, 47 taken from *Human Resource Management Journal* vol 3, no 3 p56 and vol 6, no3 p60 reproduced with permission from Blackwell Publishing; extracts p69 taken from *Human Resource Management* Anniversary edition reproduced with permission from Palgrave Macmillan; extracts pp106, 107, 206 from *Managing Service Quality* vol 13 no 1; extract p227 taken from *Management Decision* republished with permission from Emerald Group Publishing Ltd; extracts pp107, 113, 121 taken from *Strategic Human Resource Management*, reproduced with permission from Blackwell Publishing; extract p286 from *Inspiring Leadership*, reproduced with permission from Thomson Learning; extract pp313–4 abridged from *The High Performance Organisation* and *Understanding Change*, reproduced with permission from Elsevier; extracts pp207–9 from *The Fifth Discipline* reproduced with permission from The Random House Group Ltd; extract p102 taken from *Beyond Contract*, reproduced with permission from Faber; extract p271 taken from *Organisation Theory* reproduced with permission from Oxford University Press; extract p164 taken from *Industrial and Organisational Psychology* reproduced with permission from Blackwell Publishing.

# Guided tour

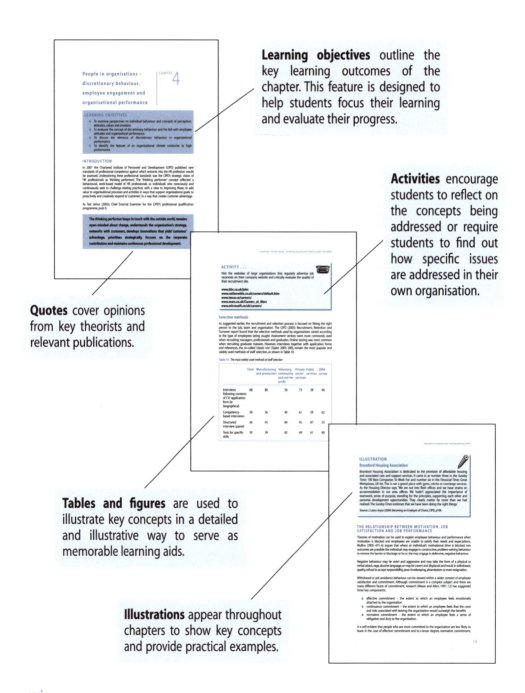

**Learning objectives** outline the key learning outcomes of the chapter. This feature is designed to help students focus their learning and evaluate their progress.

**Activities** encourage students to reflect on the concepts being addressed or require students to find out how specific issues are addressed in their own organisation.

**Quotes** cover opinions from key theorists and relevant publications.

**Tables and figures** are used to illustrate key concepts in a detailed and illustrative way to serve as memorable learning aids.

**Illustrations** appear throughout chapters to show key concepts and provide practical examples.

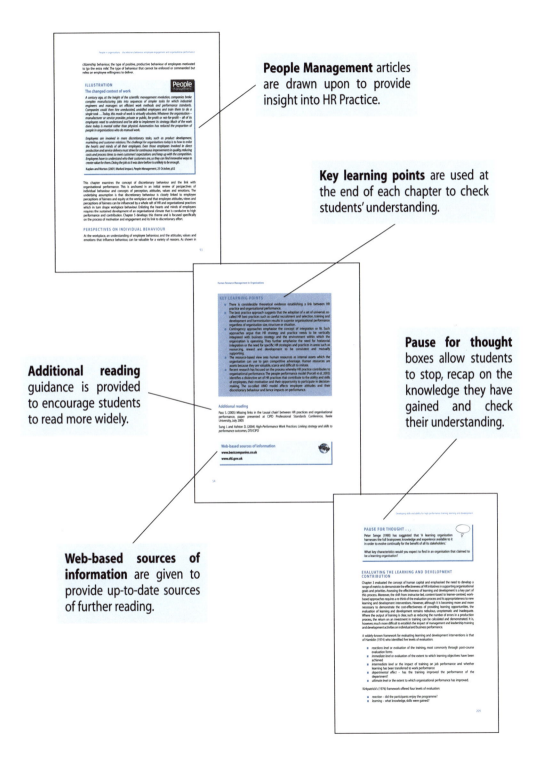

**People Management** articles are drawn upon to provide insight into HR Practice.

**Key learning points** are used at the end of each chapter to check students' understanding.

**Additional reading** guidance is provided to encourage students to read more widely.

**Pause for thought** boxes allow students to stop, recap on the knowledge they have gained and check their understanding.

**Web-based sources of information** are given to provide up-to-date sources of further reading.

# Introduction

The expression 'Our people are our greatest asset' may have suffered from considerable over(mis)use but there can be no doubting the sentiment that the effective resourcing and management of people within contemporary organisations remains a crucial factor of organisational survival, adaptation and success. Research evidence has, however, shown that there can be no one magic formula or set of 'off the shelf' prescriptions that can be applied in securing employee commitment to organisational goals. The effective management and motivation of people at work requires the development and adoption of a range of integrated policies and practices for the resourcing, development and reward of employees which builds upon organisational values and norms. Managers need to be aware of the nature and scope of factors which influence human behaviour at work and to have the competence to develop and implement effective and appropriate approaches to managing individuals, groups and themselves.

In short, organisations must find their own distinctive ways of unlocking the ability and potential of their employees. Nevertheless, there are certain key characteristics which set high-performing organisations apart. It is these key differentiating practices and activities which set high-performing organisations apart from others that this text seeks to explore and explain.

This book has been written for business and management students on generalist undergraduate programmes studying stand-alone modules in HRM/OB. It is also appropriate for students following a dedicated programme of study in HRM/OB. In particular, it is likely to be of value to third-year undergraduate students in enabling them to use prior knowledge and learning of the subject matter to develop their skills of analysis and evaluation more fully. Additionally, this book has been aimed more generally at postgraduate, professional and post-experience students who wish to expand their knowledge and understanding of the issues concerned with the management of people in organisations. It would be appropriate for postgraduate students following a stand-alone HRM/OB module or a more general degree programme such as MBA or DMS; for HR specialists following the CIPD Professional Development Scheme; and for non-specialists who need some understanding of the subject matter of the text – for example, accountants studying for professional qualifications.

This text deals with contemporary issues in human resource management and provides students with a sound understanding of the theoretical approaches to the management of people together with an appreciation of their application within different organisational contexts. The principal areas of HRM are covered – ie resourcing, reward, relations and learning and development – but links are also made to underpinning organisational behaviour and psychology aspects and the role of leadership. The text draws extensively upon case study material to identify and discuss developments within a variety of organisational contexts including the public sector, privatised utilities, SMEs and the not-for-profit sectors.

The book is structured in three parts. Part 1 analyses the changing context of employment and the theory and practice of HRM. Within this part, Chapter 1 summarises the impact of wider environmental forces on the functioning of organisations, on changing patterns of employment, and on attitudes to work. Against this backcloth of transformation and change in the world of work, Chapter 2 evaluates the extent to which the management of people impacts on the success of business strategy and examines the research evidence linking HR practice to organisational effectiveness. The reasons why theoretical linkages often fail to make the transition to organisational reality and the barriers to high performance are explored in Chapter 3.

Part 2 of the text focuses on the organisational architecture of high performance and the key areas differentiating high-performance organisations. Chapter 4 examines the concept of discretionary behaviour and the link with high performance. Chapter 5 develops this theme and focuses specifically on the process of employee motivation and engagement and the link with discretionary effort. Chapters 6, 7, 8 and 9 focus on the main areas of HRM and key contemporary developments and issues within these areas. Chapter 6 evaluates the resourcing process and the importance of employee retention. Chapter 7 explores the processes of training, learning and development in the enhancement of employee skills and abilities and the creation of a high-performance working environment in which employees are able to contribute to the full extent of their abilities. Chapter 7 evaluates the principles and models of performance management and strategies for recognising and rewarding high performance. Chapter 8 focuses on managing individual and collective relationships at work and the process of building commitment through involvement, participation, consultation and communication.

The final Part of the text focuses on the process of optimising and sustaining high performance. Chapter 10 evaluates the role of leadership, and Chapter 11 evaluates the process of organisational change and the HR role in managing effective change. Throughout the text, evidence-based research is combined with up-to-date examples of organisational practice.

This book has been designed to be easy to read and follow: its chapters are dedicated to specific areas, and the content of each chapter is interspersed with a variety of activities and illustrations. Each chapter begins with a set of learning objectives and ends with a summary of the key learning points in order to focus learning and understanding. Throughout each chapter a range of features are incorporated to further assist learning and understanding. Illustrations of organisational practice are provided to bring the material covered to life. Specific questions and activities for individual and group exercises and discussions are given so that the individuals and groups may explore the material more fully and test understanding. 'Pause for thought' themes and questions are provided to encourage reflection in relation to specific aspects of the material covered. At the end of each chapter, suggestions for additional reading and web-based sources of information are provided. The website associated with the text represents an additional source of information and advice (www.cipd.co.uk/tss).

# PART 1

# THE CHANGING CONTEXT OF EMPLOYMENT

# The changing world of work

## INTRODUCTION

The employment relationship is pivotal to the study of managing people in organisations. However, the relationship between an organisation and the people it employs does not occur in a vacuum. It is shaped by a wide range of environmental factors – economic factors, social and demographic trends, the political and legal context, technological developments all influence the process and practice of managing people. Moreover, these wider factors are not static and stable but subject to change and volatility. Ted Johns (2005: xi) describes the world of work 20 years ago as a 'relatively … uneventful place'. His observations are reproduced fully below because they neatly summarise the massive transformation that has occurred in the world of work and provide an appropriate backdrop for this chapter.

> *Until about twenty years ago, the world of work was (relatively speaking) an uneventful place. Change of all kinds was slow or non-existent; technological innovation, where it occurred at all, was incremental rather than revolutionary; products enjoyed long life cycles; many people had what they believed to be jobs for life, with slow but steady occupational progression; customers were passive and in many instances were compelled to endure products, services and utilities supplied by monopolies; organisations were characterised by central control and universally applied, rule-based systems.*

*These were the typical features of such organisations in those days;*

- *Hierarchical control through a rigid chain of command with minimal delegation and jealously guarded authority barriers*
- *Fragmented, directive and mechanistic problem-solving with an emphasis on serial solutions (What did we do last time?) rather than imaginative, 'off-the-wall', creative thinking and innovation*
- *Single-function specialisms with departmental boundaries, hostile stereotyping and careers concentrated in a single profession thus nurturing a narrowness of intellect, self-absorption and a readiness to treat other parts of the same organisation, even customers, as if they were enemies*
- *Individualism rather than teamwork, reflected in the design of incentive systems and the encouragement of competitive behaviour rather than co-operation*
- *Job descriptions written as lists of tasks and responsibilities, with no reference to 'added value' except perhaps at very senior levels*
- *Reactive, procedure-bound systems where performance improvement was almost entirely attributable to the learning/experience curve rather than the deliberate implementation of change*

*All these corporate characteristics were exhibited against a background of 'slack in the environmental soup'; sluggish or non-existent competition, allowing organisations to laze along, carrying superfluous employees. These employees may have felt comfortable about the fact that they thought they had a job for life, but in practice many were massively under-utilised and under-developed in terms of their potential and their capabilities.*

*As a case in point, take the TV factory at Hirwaun in South Wales. In 1981, run as a joint venture between GEC (now Marconi) and Hitachi, the factory achieved a one-day record output of 1,750 TV sets with 2,200 employees. By 1986, with Hitachi running the business on its own, Hirwaun was routinely churning out 2,400 TV sets, 500 hi-fi units and 500 video recorders every day with a workforce of only 1,000 employees. Many of these people, moreover, were the same people who had worked there in 1981.*

*That world has (by and large) gone. Technological change can cause established products to disappear virtually overnight; product life cycles in some instances can be measured in months rather than years; the 'job for life' seems to have been replaced by a concern for 'employability' and transferable skills; customers have become aggressive and litigious; erstwhile monopolies now regularly confront competition; globalisation has meant that in the UK we have continuous access to products and*

*services that have originated in other parts of the world where labour and manufacturing costs are substantially lower; for some skills there is a global labour market and work (especially customer contact activity, many 'back office' functions and computer software design) can migrate to countries like India. As a result organisations have to function differently.*
(T. Johns et al (2005) **Managing People**, CIPD: xi–xiii)

Starting from the premise that the world of work has experienced massive transformation, this chapter looks backwards and forwards. It starts by summarising the key, interrelated factors that have contributed to the creation of a workplace that is very different from that which existed previously. It then moves to consider the effects of wider environmental forces on the functioning of organisations, on changing patterns of employment and on attitudes to work. However, this chapter also looks forward in order to evaluate the nature and scope of trends that are likely to shape the world of work in the future and the different HR scenarios that may emerge.

**Table 1**  *General factors in PEST analysis*

| Political | Economic | Socio-cultural | Technological |
|---|---|---|---|
| Government stability | Inflation rates | Population demographics | Government investment policy |
| Taxation policy | Interest rates | Income distribution | Speed of change and adoption of new technology |
| Foreign trade regulations | Levels of unemployment | Social mobility | Rates of obsolescence |
| Legislation – eg taxation, employment | Currency fluctuations and exchange rates | Lifestyle changes | Levels of expenditure in R&D |
| Government ownership of industry | Money supply | Attitudes to work and leisure | |

## THE DRIVING FORCES OF ENVIRONMENTAL CHANGE

A useful way of identifying, categorising and evaluating the impact of environmental factors on an organisation has been through the use of frameworks such as PEST, which groups environmental influences into four principal categories; Political, Economic, Socio-cultural and Technological. Table 1 lists some of the main factors that could be included in a PEST analysis.

However, it is important to recognise that environmental factors will have different potential implications for different organisations in different sectors and markets. A PEST analysis enables the organisation to identify structural drivers of change which, when combined together, are likely to affect the structure of an industry sector or market. A comprehensive review of the environmental factors and forces of change is outside the scope of this chapter. However, since the 1980s several important developments have combined to create a working environment that is substantially different from that existing previously. These developments and their consequences are briefly reviewed in the next sections.

## ACTIVITY . . .

Conduct a PEST analysis for your organisation. What are the key drivers for change in the external environment in which your organisation operates?
What are the implications of these drivers, or combinations of drivers, for the management of people?

## Political change

Government economic and labour policies over the last two decades have been characterised by a liberal economic model of free market capitalism reflected in an ideology of 'enterprise culture', responsiveness to markets and customers and a 'rugged individualism' (Guest 1990: 31). Over the last two decades national governments have swung to the political right and have supported an economic model of the 'commercial enterprise' or a privately owned firm operating in a free market economy (Legge 2005: 119). The logic of this model suggests that those organisations that succeed in an enterprise culture need to be lean, fit, customer-driven, quality-focused and competitive to deal with the rigours of the marketplace.

The concept of 'enterprise culture' and the model of the 'commercial organisation' have had particular significance for public sector organisations. The 1980s and 1990s saw the large-scale privatisation of state-owned industries and public utilities and the introduction of internal markets in the public sector – eg 'opting out' of schools, 'trust' status for hospitals, competitive tendering in local government and purchaser–provider relationships in the NHS.

The government's strategy for public sector improvement has been set out in the document *Reforming our Public Services – Principles into Practice*, which emphasises four key aspects of reform – setting national standards within a framework of accountability, devolving responsibility for delivery to local levels, introducing greater flexibility in meeting customer needs, and expanding public services to provide greater customer choice. Implicit within such proposals are: a greater awareness of 'customers' and the deliberate application of management practices from competitive industry; increased reliance on outsourcing; the widespread application of performance management systems; fostering a positive and receptive climate of change; breaking down barriers between public sector organisations to provide a seamless service from a variety of agencies; new styles of leadership in managing complex partnership and stakeholder groups; the development of greater levels of employee empowerment; and the reform of pay systems and terms and conditions of employment to allow greater flexibility to reflect local needs and priorities.

## Economic internationalisation and globalisation

In recent years it has been argued that there has been a 'globalisation' of economic activity. Some organisations have always operated across national and international boundaries through, for example, exporting, licensing or foreign direct investment (FDI) (Hendry 1994: 17). However, in recent years political and economic developments have significantly altered the nature, scope and intensity of international trade. The dismantling of the Communist system in Central and Eastern Europe, political and economic transformation in China, and rapid industrialisation in Latin America and the Pacific Rim countries have opened up the flow of trade and resulted in an intensification of competition in product markets.

In essence, globalisation suggests that the world has become a single marketplace where goods, services, capital and people are able to move freely and quickly in response to global supplies and global demands (Parker 1998: 37). Globalisation also reflects an increase in the number of multinational corporations (MNCs) and the scale of their activities. MNCs are key actors in globalisation. As Harris *et al* (2003: 2) point out, the world's 1,000 largest companies produce 80 per cent of the world's industrial output, and around 60 per cent of international trade involves transactions between two related parts of multinationals.

## Socio-cultural change

Socio-cultural change can take many overlapping forms. There have, for example, been major changes in population demographics which can be seen in an increasingly diverse and ageing society. Between 1971 and 2003, the number of people aged 65 and over rose by more than 28 per cent, while the number aged 16 and under fell by 18 per cent (*Social Trends* 35). There has also been a steady increase in the participation of women in the labour force, and women now comprise 46 per cent of total employment. Such trends together with wider social changes relating to rising levels of divorce and a growth in single parent families carry considerable implications for the provision of health, education and social and welfare services.

Another aspect of socio-cultural change relates to changes in people's attitudes and values. Leisure activities have become more important in people's lives and the notion of 'lifestyle' has become a central concept of the so-called consumer society and is reflected in spending patterns. People as consumers have much greater choice and power.

Wider societal influences also impact on work and workplace change, which in turn affect employee attitudes towards their work. For example, evidence points to generational differences in attitudes towards work and the emergence of a more demanding workforce as a result of such generational differences. Taylor (2005) suggests that the attitudes of the so-called Generation Y carry important consequences for organisations seeking to recruit and retain young people. He identifies attitudes such as opposition to intolerance, resistance to tight systems of control and support for better work–life balance as resulting in less organisational loyalty, lower acceptance of managerial prerogative and a greater tendency to question and challenge.

## Technological change

Technological change has of course made globalisation possible and feasible. Technological innovations in telecommunications, digital electronics, computers, satellite systems and artificial intelligence have made it possible for information and innovations to rapidly cross national boundaries. The Internet is the ultimate symbol of 'boundarylessness' – it is unrestricted, accessible, operates night and day across the world, and provides a knowledge-based window to the world (Parker 1998: 582). Technological advances have likewise accelerated the speed with which companies can operate in global markets.

Technological developments have also fuelled growth in customer demands for higher-quality products, shorter delivery times and greater customisation of products. It is no longer sufficient to sell a product or service. In order to compete in certain markets superior customer service is essential. For example, the deregulation of the UK financial services industry in the 1980s resulted in intense competition and the entry of a large number of new players – eg supermarkets, retail outlets and overseas banks. In this context some banks began to distinguish themselves on their ability to offer exceptional levels of service through 24-hour banking by telephone or online.

### PAUSE FOR THOUGHT . . .

Reflect upon the political, economic, social and technological trends identified above. Are there any additional trends that you can identify?

## THE IMPACT AND CONSEQUENCES OF ENVIRONMENTAL CHANGE

To varying degrees, the combined pressures of globalisation, technological change and intensified competition have created opportunities for economic growth and business development but have also presented challenges for organisations operating in mature economies that have experienced slower growth. Environmental factors have thus had macro- and micro-level effects and have placed a strong pressure on institutions and organisations, both public and private, to increase their level of competitiveness.

## Structural change

Over the past 20 years the British economy has experienced major structural change evidenced by a dramatic decline in manufacturing industry and a corresponding growth in the service sector. The number of people employed in the manufacturing sector has reduced by a half since 1970, and public sector employment has reduced by some 30 per cent since 1979. During this time the service sector grew from around 10 million in 1970 to over 20 million in 2000, with the fastest growth in the financial and business services sector (Marchington and Wilkinson, 2005: 39). Alongside shifts in the national economic landscape have come shifts in occupational structure and a growth in management and professional occupations and a corresponding decline in skilled and semi-skilled manual jobs. Structural shifts in industrial sectors and labour markets have shaped and been shaped by political and legislative influences.

## Organisational change

At the micro or organisational level, the effects of the external environment have put pressure on companies to constantly monitor costs and improve levels of productivity to respond to threats from overseas competitors who may be able to keep costs to a minimum because of more efficient manufacturing processes or cheaper labour costs. Organisational change, driven by wider environmental pressures, has carried with it significant implications for the management of people. Radical organisational restructuring programmes evidenced in downsizing, de-layering and re-engineering have marked a shift from large, bureaucratic, centralised hierarchies to leaner, flatter, decentralised, networked organisations that are able to respond more quickly to wider environmental changes.

Environmental pressures for increased flexibility and responsiveness have been supported by technological advances to create entirely new forms of work organisation. Telephone call centres have grown dramatically over the last decade fuelled by demand for 24-hour banking, information and leisure services. It is estimated that there are some 4,500 call centres in the UK employing 400,000 people or around 2 per cent of the workforce. By 2008 it is predicted that call centres will employ 600,000 people (IDS, 2002). Call centres cover a wide range of services including technical support, mail order, customer surveys, ticket sales and marketing.

The servicing of customers through call centres represents substantial cost savings to organisations through a rationalisation of work processes and the use of information technology. However, the design of jobs in calls centres owes a great deal to scientific management and critical studies have branded call centres as electronic sweatshops (Frenkel *et al*, 1998), as electronic Taylorism (Kinnie *et al*, 2000), assembly lines in the head (Taylor and Bain, 1999) and as female ghettos (Batt, 2002). Call centre work is fragmented, closely monitored, tightly controlled, highly routinised, low-skilled, stressful, poorly paid and characterised by antisocial shift patterns. Low levels of job satisfaction in call centres reflect low levels of job control, inadequate training and high levels of monitoring.

A recent IDS Report (2002) of 133 call centres employing 106,000 staff found average turnover rates of 24.5 per cent (an increase of 22 per cent over 2001). The same report found average annual pay rates to be £12,400. Other studies have identified high levels of turnover and absence as a form of exit from working conditions viewed as unpleasant and stressful. Moreover, call centre work cannot be disembodied from the provider of such services and the way in which call centre employees express their feelings towards customers impacts on the perceived quality of the service provided. The report found that a significant number of organisations had introduced a number of initiatives aimed at improving staff retention. These included improved recruitment and selection techniques; the introduction of incentive schemes, flexibility of working and career progression programmes; increased training and development activities and improved communications mechanisms; and improvements to the work environment. However, few mentioned job design initiatives or any significant changes to the work itself.

## PAUSE FOR THOUGHT . . .

Given the findings of research studies into the nature of work and work organisation in call centres and the consequences for employee retention, what do you think should be the key features of people management in call centre environments?

## Flexibility

In line with wider restructuring, flexibility in work organisation and design has been seen as crucial in increasing organisational responsiveness, reducing costs and improving the level and quality of service. The concept of the flexible firm (see Figure 1) distinguishes between different groups of core and peripheral employees. The core comprises key employees on whom the organisation depends and who are crucial to organisational success. Core employees are likely to be employed on a relatively permanent basis and be eligible to receive investment in the form of training and development and career planning. Peripheral employees fall into two distinct groups. One group may be employed on relatively permanent contracts similar to the core but perform jobs requiring low levels of skills, autonomy and discretion and are thus subject to high levels of labour turnover

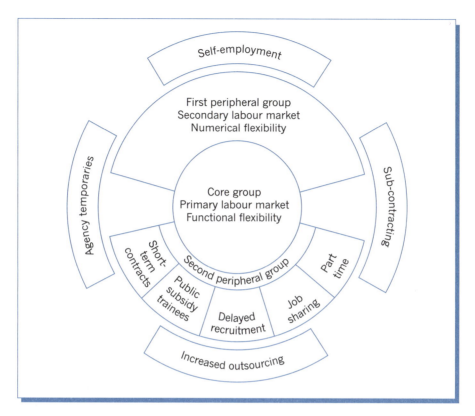

**Figure 1** *The flexible firm*
*Source: J. Atkinson (1984) Manpower strategies for flexible organisations, Personnel Management, August*

and wastage. In this case flexibility stems from being able to control the overall headcount and, depending on business requirements, not replace employees that leave.

The second peripheral group comprises those employed on a variety of non-standard contractual arrangements which provide spatial, temporal and numerical flexibility – eg job-share, fixed-term contracts, temporary staff, annualised hours. The core/periphery model is predicated on the view that production systems need to adapt to a changed economic environment and that in order to respond best to changes, employers need a workforce that can be flexible and adaptable to new pressures and demands.

The outer circle of the core/peripheral model of the flexible firm highlights the use of sub-contracting and outsourcing as additional features of flexibility in work organisation and design. Increasingly, activities and services that were previously regarded as the organisation's responsibility to manage and provide are being purchased from external suppliers. The growth of outsourcing has been particularly marked in the public sector where activities such as cleaning, transport, security and maintenance have been contracted out to private sector providers.

Although many organisations continue to use in-house call centres, outsourcing or off-shoring is becoming a major feature of the call centre industry. Communication and information technology makes it feasible to locate call centres anywhere in the world and there have been a number of well-publicised examples of the transfer of call centre work to countries such as India where labour costs are lower.

The HR function has seen many of its own areas of activity subject to outsourcing, and there have been a number of well-publicised examples of HR outsourcing and shared services. In 2000, BP Amoco outsourced all of its HR administration to Exult, a US-based company, as part of a five-year contract worth £370 million. Exult took over the administration of almost all of BP Amoco's HR function, including compensation and benefits, payroll, relocation, policy and legal compliance, which were provided through two service centres. Exult also established an intranet system to provide information on performance management, training administration and career planning.

## ACTIVITY . . .

What forms of flexibility of working have been introduced by your organisation? Compare your list with that of a colleague working in a different sector.

What are the advantages and disadvantages of non-standard forms of working – for the organisation and for employees?

The rationale behind outsourcing and off-shoring is that it enables the organisation to focus on its core activities while allowing peripheral activities to be performed by specialist providers. Advances in technology and employee acceptance of technology have facilitated such arrangements and provided the mechanisms for its delivery. Straightforward cost considerations are another driver in that support functions, especially with off-shoring, can be provided more cheaply by external providers.

However, there are legal implications with outsourcing because such arrangements often fall within the Transfer of Undertakings (Protection of Employment) (TUPE) Regulations 1981, which require that the rights of employees are safeguarded when their employment is transferred from one employer to another. There are also a range of issues relating to issues of control, the quality assurance of the product or service outsourced and the commitment and quality of external staff. To work successfully, shared services require clear, unambiguous objectives, effective partnership and robust monitoring processes.

**ACTIVITY . . .**

Imagine that you head up the HR function in a local authority that has decided to outsource some of its support roles, including those within the HR function. The contract is expected to run for 10 years with review clauses at three and six years.

Comment on what you see as the possible problems of an outsourcing strategy for the authority and suggest how these might be overcome.

Outline your strategy for recruiting and selecting an appropriate partner for providing the authority with shared services.

## CHANGE AND CONTINUITY IN THE WORLD OF WORK – AN EVALUATION OF THE EVIDENCE

There can be no doubt that the world of work has changed and continues to change. However, the precise nature and scope of change can be open to different interpretations. Emphasising the radical nature and impact of change obscures threads of continuity. This section thus seeks to unpack some of the hyperbole and misconceptions concerning the world of work and to evaluate the evidence both for change and continuity in work organisation. In particular, it draws on the findings of longitudinal studies funded by ESRC which, over a five-year period, sought to gather factual evidence in relation to changes in the world of work.

The ESRC Future of Work research study has highlighted significant changes in employment relations, labour markets, work–life balance and the nature of work organisation. However, it has also found evidence of continuity in contemporary workplaces. The ESRC Working in Britain Survey (2000) points to relative stability in the workplace and challenges commonly held views of widespread flexibility and radical developments in non-standard forms of working. Full-time working is still the norm and has accounted for 60 per cent of the rise in employment since 1993. There has been a growth in permanent employment, rather than a contraction: 92 per cent of workers are employed on permanent contracts, compared to 88 per cent in 1982.

The proportion of temporary jobs in relation to total employment amounts to 6.5 per cent, a figure much lower than commonly perceived. The level of self-employment grew throughout the 1980s but has barely changed over the last decade, while the proportion of self-employment in relation to total employment has fallen from 12.4 per cent in 1983 to 11.3 per cent in 2002. The latest research evidence does not therefore support the view that a larger number of people are working for shorter periods with a wider number of employers. Neither is there evidence that the types of jobs being created are predominantly part-time and temporary.

Many people still regard their job as part of a career with distinct promotion prospects, and the concept of having a career at work is not confined to those in managerial or professional grades (Taylor 2000b: 12). The concept of the 'portfolio worker' remains the exception and portfolio workers are more likely to be the casualties of corporate restructuring than a new breed of entrepreneur. There has, however, been significant growth in the use of interim managers in employment, within both private and public sectors.

There is, therefore, limited evidence that the flexible firm exists as a practical reality or that organisations are concentrating on their core functions and sub-contracting other activities to save costs and reduce overheads. As Taylor (2000a: 7) puts it,

> **The evidence simply does not sustain the view that we are witnessing the emergence of a 'new' kind of employment relations seen in the 'end of the career' and 'the death of the permanent job for life'. The shift away from permanent and full-time jobs to temporary, short-term or part-time work is exaggerated.**

Where significant change has been noted, this relates to job tenure, the use of IT at the workplace and changing attitudes to work. Job tenure, or the length of time spent in a job, does vary between occupations and jobs. In low-skilled occupations where employment is sensitive to cyclical changes in the economy, tenure is lower. It is higher in skilled occupations. Such variations provide evidence that the UK labour market is beoming segmented into 'primary' sectors of 'good jobs' (skilled, relatively secure) and 'secondary' sectors of 'bad' jobs (unskilled, low-paid, insecure).

Female activity rates have increased and the proportion of women in the labour force accounts for 46 per cent of total employment. However, labour markets remain heavily segmented with women concentrated in the service sector and in lower-level jobs. The proportion of women in managerial, executive and board-level roles has increased only marginally.

The use of computers and other forms of IT at work has advanced significantly. In 2000, two thirds of women and men reported that new technologies were 'essential' to the accomplishment of their work compared with 35 per cent (women) and 28 per cent (men) in 1997 (Taylor 2000a: 16). Workers are now required to have more complex and advanced IT skills. There has also been a marked deterioration in worker satisfaction as a result of the hours worked and growing levels of stress at work. This is explored more fully in the next section.

## CHANGING ATTITUDES TO WORK

Work remains central to the lives of many people, to the extent that many indicate that they would continue to work even if they had the economic resources not to. Work provides a sense of identity and purpose, the opportunity for social interaction and the means to gain recognition and reward. Although attitudes to work can be attributed partly to psychological differences between individuals, they are likewise shaped by the organisational context within which work is performed and by management practice. Attitudes to work are thus influenced by the degree to which any organisation regards its employees as an asset to be invested in, as a resource to be developed, or as a commodity to be exploited.

Evidence as to the quality of working life is mixed and generalisations are difficult. For example, research by Guest and Conway (2001) reported that job satisfaction within the private sector rose between 1998 and 2001. However, research by the Policy Studies Institute (2000) found that the proportion of people who felt completely satisfied with their work fell from 52 to 45 per cent between 1992 and 2000.

The ESRC Working in Britain Survey (2000) found that work intensification, greater management control and surveillance and long hours were key factors that contributed to lower levels of job satisfaction and personal commitment to the organisation, especially among those with higher levels of education. 46 per cent of men and 32 per cent of women reported frequently working longer hours because their jobs had become more demanding. The CIPD's (2003) Living to Work Report also found evidence of work intensification and an increase in the number of hours worked. It showed that the number of people working in excess of 48 hours a week had more than doubled since 1998, and that those working in excess of 60 hours a week had risen by a third. 25 per cent of 30–39-year-olds worked 75 or more hours a week.

Work intensification and longer working hours have contributed to reduced levels of job satisfaction and made work more stressful. As Taylor (2000c: 9) puts it,

> **Today's world of work is much less satisfying to employees than the one they were experiencing 10 years ago.**

The concept of empowerment suggests that employees at all levels in the organisation are responsible and accountable for their actions and should be given the responsibility and authority to make decisions about their work. Empowerment implies the ability to communicate, to learn, to exercise initiative, to solve problems, to work independently or in teams. However, empowerment must be analysed within a broader context of organisational practice. The reality for many employees has been a widening gap between the rhetoric of empowerment and the reality of work intensification, increased organisational stress and insecurity at work. The effects of change, organisational restructuring and increased insecurity invariably generate a tendency to 'play it safe', to 'keep your head down' – hardly empowered behaviours. Moreover, as Wilkinson (2001) suggests, employees empowered to take decisions are sceptical and unwilling to use their discretion if they feel constantly under the scrutiny of managers.

Few organisations have created conditions that are conducive to empowerment, and much of the evidence suggests that organisations have adopted a piecemeal ad hoc approach to empowerment rather than taking an integrated and holistic approach (Wilkinson, 2001). The ESRC (2000) Future of Work research likewise suggested that lower levels of job satisfaction in turn impacted on levels of organisational loyalty and commitment but found little evidence that high-performance work practices were being introduced to enhance human capital, create partnerships at work, improve the learning and skills of employees or generate higher levels of commitment (Taylor, 2000a) (see Chapter 3).

A number of indicators point, in particular, to lower levels of job satisfaction by public sector employees. For example, despite the existence of strong absence management policies, absence levels in the public sector are considerably higher than in the private sector. The CIPD Annual Survey of Absence found average absence levels within the public sector of 10.5 per cent compared with an average level of 6.8 per cent in the private sector (CIPD, 2005). Stress levels in the public sector are also higher, with the highest levels reported in the NHS and local government (CIPD Living to Work Report, 2003).

Lower levels of job satisfaction by public sector employees can be attributed to a variety of causes. Public sector organisations have experienced considerable change. As outlined earlier, most state-run corporations have been privatised (telecommunications, utilities) and state-run services (eg the NHS, the educational system) have been required to operate along more commercial lines. Restructuring and the introduction of market-driven reforms have prompted far-reaching changes in employment and management practice, and public sector work is increasingly carried out under some form of sub-contracting or franchising arrangement.

Despite market-driven reforms, however, public sector decision-making remains inherently political, and managerial decision-making and employment practice is subject to a wide variety of legal, political and economic constraints and influenced by a multiplicity of stakeholders. Government influence, the legal framework of public policy and public scrutiny of the quality of public sector service delivery have increased in intensity as a result of the introduction of league tables publicising poorly-performing schools, hospitals and local authorities. Customer expectations of public sector services have also been transformed so that customers expect high-quality services and standards which are 'joined up' across different agencies and public bodies. There are additional expectations that public sector services should be responsive and utilise appropriate forms of electronic delivery. Contextual and structural change has thus contributed to initiative overload and 'change fatigue'.

## The psychological contract

It is important to recognise the impact of organisational change on the employment relationship and that patterns of workplace change affect different people in different ways.

A relevant concept in discussing attitudes to work in the context of changing labour markets is that of the psychological contract. The term 'the psychological contract' refers to the implied, unwritten expectations that employees have of the organisation in terms of their contribution and what they can expect in return. Briner and Conway (2004: 43) have demonstrated that there are different types of psychological contract. Relational contracts are 'broad, open-ended exchanges of relatively intangible things such as employee loyalty in return for longer-term job security'. Transactional contracts are more specific and involve 'the exchange of much more explicit and tangible factors such as the amount of pay in return for a specified level of staff performance'.

---

### THE CONTENTS OF THE PSYCHOLOGICAL CONTRACT

Examples of the implicit or explicit mutual promises made by employees and organisations

Employees promise to:
- work hard
- uphold the company reputation
- maintain high levels of attendance and punctuality
- show loyalty to the organisation
- work extra hours when required
- develop new skills and update old ones
- be flexible – eg by taking on a colleague's work
- be courteous to clients and colleagues
- be honest.

Organisations promise:
- pay commensurate with performance
- opportunities for training and development
- opportunities for promotion
- recognition for innovation or new ideas
- feedback on performance
- interesting tasks
- an attractive benefits package
- respectful treatment
- reasonable job security
- a pleasant and safe working environment.

Source: R. Briner and N. Conway (2004) Promises, promises, *People Management*, 25 November

---

In the context of large-scale change it becomes more difficult to deliver the promises, commitments and expectations that lie at the heart of the psychological contract. The critical issue becomes how change affects discretionary behaviour and the choices individuals make about how they work.

Herriot and Pemberton (1995) have argued that the psychological contract for many employees has changed fundamentally. Whereas the traditional psychological contract was based on long-term commitment, security, steady progression through the organisational hierarchy, the 'new' psychological contract is more transactional and based on short-term flexible arrangements and the offer of employability. Research (eg Coyle-Shapiro and Kessler, 2000) has shown that when employees perceive that the organisation has breached their psychological contract, or their expectations about work and progression, they feel less committed to the organisation, experience lower levels of motivation and are less willing to share information and engage in discretionary behaviour. Briner and Conway (2004: 43) suggest that although staff are told ever more clearly what is expected of them, employers are unable to say what they will give in return. The result is that employees perceive the exchange to be inequitable.

## WORLD-CLASS HIGH-PERFORMANCE ORGANISATIONS

It is progressively being acknowledged that in order to compete effectively in an increasingly turbulent economic environment, organisations cannot rely on cutting costs to the bone and competing in a global market on the basis of low-cost goods and services. To meet competitive challenges, organisations need to innovate and differentiate their goods and services. What is important is continuous improvement and effective change management. In other words, organisations need to generate ways of adding value in order to obtain competitive advantage – ie to do something that nobody has done before. So what are the characteristics of world-class high-performing organisations? What are the features that distinguish high-performing organisations?

Research evidence suggests that high-performance organisations demonstrate significant differentiators. For example, the work of Purcell *et al* (2003) has highlighted differentiators such as the 'big idea' or a set of aspirational values supported by strategies, systems and practices and people-focused leadership by which front-line managers ensure that performance-enhancing HR policies and practices are implemented. Such organisations adopt empowered rather than control structures and aim to create an environment focused on sharing information, creativity and innovation. In such an environment, teamworking, networking and initiatives to harness the specialist knowledge and skills of employees are widespread. These represent critical success factors, sources of competitive advantage and the ingredients which turn employers into 'brands' and 'talent magnets' and which stimulate employees to engage in discretionary behaviour (Whittaker and Johns, 2004: 33).

The mechanisms that enable organisations to elicit high performance and commitment from their people thus go beyond the establishment of an infrastructure of systems and processes of legal/ethical compliance. What makes organisations such as Tesco, Nationwide, First Direct world-class is not the background presence of HR policies and practices but the way in which people absorb and demonstrate an aspirational culture and set of values. Adding value is a key preoccupation for many high-performing organisations. As Kaplan and Norton (Marked impact, *People Management*, 25 October 2001:52) put it,

> **The challenge for organisations today is how to enlist the hearts and minds of all their employees. Even those employees involved in direct production and service delivery must strive for continuous improvement in quality, reducing costs and process time to meet customer expectations and keep up with the competition. Doing the job as it was done before is unlikely to be enough.**

The following illustrations are provided as examples of high-performance organisations and factors that differentiate their approach to managing and leading people. They provide practical examples of the link between the ways that people are managed, developed and led, and organisational performance.

## ILLUSTRATION

### Richer Sounds

*Richer Sounds* is Britain's largest hi-fi and home cinema retailer, employing 450 people in 43 stores with a turnover of £100 million. It was founded in 1978 by Julian Richer who outlines his business philosophy in his book entitled *The Richer Way* (2001). Richer argues that it is possible to achieve strong central control and empowerment, and that effective leadership is about achieving the right balance between control and motivation. Staff are set clear standards. All employees are engaged in continuous improvement through learning. Reward systems are aligned to behaviours that the organisation values and wishes to encourage, such as innovation and outstanding customer service. To emphasise the importance of customer satisfaction to business success, staff are given a degree of freedom to use their initiative to ensure that customer needs are met. Bureaucracy is kept to a minimum so that prompt action 'delights' the customer.

Source: J. Richer (2001) *The Richer Way*

## ILLUSTRATION

### Semco

*Semco* is a Brazilian manufacturing company which makes marine pumps, food-processing equipment and air-conditioning units. In his books *Maverick* (1993) and *The Seven-Day Weekend* (2003), Ricardo Semler describes how he took over a traditional manufacturing company and introduced pioneering forms of worker participation and workplace democracy. Within Semco there are only four grades of staff, no dress codes, no segregated parking or dining, no job titles, no job specifications or other formalities common to large organisations. Managers and employees are empowered to set their own production quotas, re-design products and formulate marketing plans. Workers set their own working hours and salaries, and all financial information is openly discussed. They are responsible for product quality, for implementing improvements and for appraising the performance of managers. Between 1994 and 2001, Semco's annual revenue grew from $35 million to $160 million. As Ricardo Semler puts it,

*We've taken a company that was moribund and made it thrive, chiefly by refusing to squander our greatest resource, our people. Semco has grown sixfold despite withering recession, staggering inflation and chaotic national economic policy. Productivity has increased nearly sevenfold. Profits have risen fivefold. And we have had periods of up to 14 months in which not one worker has left us. We have a backlog of more than 2,000 job applications.*

Source: R. Semler (1993) *Maverick*, published by Century: reprinted by permission of The Random House Group Ltd

## ILLUSTRATION

### Tesco

*Tesco* is the UK's biggest private sector employer and retailer, who recently unveiled half-year figures showing that pre-tax profits jumped by 28 per cent to a record £804 million to August 2004. Tesco has consistently demonstrated expertise in boosting productivity while putting people and customers first. Tesco's profit share reward scheme allows employees to share in the success of the business as the share price has grown by over 30 per cent since 1999. Tesco states its core purpose is 'to create value for customers to earn their lifetime loyalty. We drive this through our values – no one tries harder for the customer – and treat people how we like to be treated.' Tesco's personnel director, David Fairhurst, said that Tesco's

*'magic formula' is illustrated by the equation $L^2 (c+e) + r = s + p$; listening a lot to our customers and employees + responding accordingly = sales and profitability. To make the*

*formula work, organisations must also learn to raise employee engagement through effective line leadership.*

Source: *People Management,* 30 September 2004: 11

## ILLUSTRATION
### Timpson

*Timpson* is a chain of shoe repair and key-cutting shops with nearly 2,000 employees in 568 branches and annual sales of £96 million. Timson aims for its outlets to be part of the community they are serving, and the company has adopted a radical employee empowerment strategy which allows employees (within certain limits) to order stock and settle customer complaints. Staff are encouraged to provide help and information, yellow pages are kept at every branch, and staff never refuse customer requests for change for meters or the use of toilets or phones. As John Timpson says of customer service 'Each problem gives us a chance to amaze you.'

Source: quoted in J. Leary-Joyce (2004) *Becoming an Employer of Choice,* CIPD

## ILLUSTRATION
### Kwik-Fit Financial Services

*Kwik-Fit Financial Services* (KFFS) won the CIPD *People Management* Award in 2005 for innovative HR practices in transforming the company. KFFS was set up in 1995 selling insurance policies based on leads from Kwik-Fit auto repair centres. In 2001, following a series of takeovers and poor financial results, employee morale was low and the company had a turnover rate of 52 per cent and a vacancy rate of 21 per cent.

On joining the company, Keren Edwards, HR director, made the decision to advertise jobs quarterly instead of weekly in order to 'protect the brand'. She then persuaded the company to increase pay rates by 19 per cent over three years. Supported by a new MD, initiatives were put in place to change the culture to one of employee involvement in generating ideas for innovation and improvement.

The results have been a doubling of profits and a reduction in turnover to 34 per cent in an industry that often experiences rates in excess of 100 per cent. In addition to winning the CIPD award, KFFS came in at number 15 in the *Sunday Times* 100 Best Companies To Work For listing. As Edwards puts it, 'We're constantly stunned by what people are capable of when you give them the freedom and resources.'

Source: *People Management,* 10 November 2005: 30

**ACTIVITY . . .**

Each year the *Sunday Times* publishes a list of the 100 Best Companies To Work For. The process of producing the list starts with a nomination. This is followed by a random survey of selected employees and a company questionnaire. Many workplaces are also visited so that the atmosphere of the policies in action can be assessed. Companies featured in the top 100 listing regularly outperform the FTSE All-Share Index. As Leary-Joyce (2004: 1) suggests, 'Over the past five years, the best companies would have earned an investor a compounded annual return of 12.1 per cent, compared with a 5.8 per cent decline in the FTSE All-Share Index as a whole.'

Visit the Best Companies website (www.bestcompanies.co.uk) for case studies of ranked companies in the top 100 list and what makes them great places to work. Measure your own organisation against the Best Companies Employee Survey as a gauge of internal employee satisfaction.

## FUTURE WORKPLACE AND HR SCENARIOS

Making predictions about future labour market characteristics and trends provides considerable scope for formulating future scenarios. Continuity is as relevant as change, and given the gradual and incremental change in labour markets over the last 20 years, it would be reasonable to expect such changes to continue. As a result we might expect to see a steady increase in the growth of non-standard employment, a continuing de-industrialisation of the UK economy and shift from manufacturing to service sector employment, and changes in the demographic composition of the labour force. Public sector employment has also declined significantly in recent years. Structural changes in employment are likely to become embedded as Britain becomes a predominantly service- and information-based economy.

Self-employment, flexible and part-time working offer personal freedom to combine work with other commitments, but the downside is that a greater proportion of low-paid low-skilled jobs are undertaken by women, school-leavers, students and older workers. Future change in this scenario might mean that some types of work – eg low-level customer-facing jobs such as supermarket check-out operators and some call centre functions – disappear and are replaced by automated systems. More conspicuous change might relate to the nature of work itself as a result of technological change and the development of Internet technologies.

The casualisation of jobs in sectors such as retail and hotel and catering is likely to result in strengthened political pressures for a higher national minimum wage. Long-term careers in large organisations are likely to decline as employees are forced to move between companies. Forthcoming decades are also likely to see pressures on the labour market because of an ageing population, with consequent demands to lift the retirement age. The past decade has also seen the UK labour market move from labour surplus to labour shortage and a reduction in structural unemployment. Future increases in the employment rate will depend on organisations' making better use of this potential reserve of labour supply. For service, professional and knowledge-based organisations the management of intellectual capital will become more important than management compliance. Becoming an employer of choice and building a high-trust high-performance culture, making the organisation a great place to work with supportive and effective managers will increase the commitment of all employees.

Emmott (2004: 14) argues that the biggest contribution that futurology can make to helping managers is by constructing persuasive models of the present. He summarises the key findings from a recent survey of HR professionals within 2,000 workplaces as follows:

- The use of *flexible labour* – such as agency, temporary, casual or freelance – has already spread to every type of employer. But the further use of flexible labour is approaching a limit and is slowing down.
- Career opportunities are enjoying a revival. Most workplaces are attempting to offer *internal career paths*, and not just at management level.
- An extensive use of *HRM practices*, amounting to a high-performance 'strategy', can be identified in about one in three workplaces.
- Extensive use of ICT, amounting to a '*high-tech strategy*', can so far be attributed to about one in five workplaces.
- Many workplaces are recruiting *women* into jobs formerly held by men, and [men into jobs formerly held by women].
- A 'high benefits strategy' to strengthen recruitment and retention, incorporating both significant *fringe benefits* and *family-friendly practices*, can be identified in about one in five workplaces.

## KEY LEARNING POINTS

- The employment relationship is shaped and influenced by changes in the environment within which the organisation operates.
- Key driving forces of organisational change have included a political agenda of free market capitalism, economic internationalisation and globalisation, changes in social attitudes, structures and demographics and by technological developments.
- To varying degrees, combined environmental pressures for increased flexibility and responsiveness have led to the creation of new forms of work organisation such as call centres, outsourcing, off-shoring and shared services.
- Patterns of workplace change have impacted on levels of employee satisfaction, and the concept of the psychological contract is useful in discussing attitudes to work in the context of changed labour markets.

■ It is increasingly being recognised that in order to compete effectively in a turbulent environment, organisations need to differentiate themselves from competitors. Examples of high-performance work organisations demonstrate that approaches to the management of people represent a competitive differentiator.

## Additional reading

Bunting M. (2004) *Willing Slaves: How the overwork culture is ruling our lives*, London, HarperCollins

Conway N. and Briner R. (2005) *Understanding psychological contracts at work. A critical evaluation of theory and research*, Oxford, Oxford University Press

Garrett N., Jacques T. and Wynne B. (2002) *Managing Human Resources in Call Centres*, Oxford, Chandos Publishing

Guest D. and Conway N. (2002) *Pressure at Work and the Psychological Contract*, London, CIPD

Kinnie N. (2000) Rules of engagement, *People Management*, Vol.6, No.12, pp34–5

Pickard J. (2000) Centre of attention, *People Management*, Vol.6, No.14, p30

Porter M. and Ketels H. (2003) UK competitiveness: moving to the next stage, DTI Economic Paper No.3, ESRC

## Web-based sources of information

**www.cca.org.uk/** call centre association

**www.cca.org.uk/documents/Questionnaire.pdf** standard for best practice for call centres, self-evaluation assessment

**www.hse.gov.uk/research/rrpdf/rr169.pdf** health and safety Report 169, the psychological risk factors in call centres, an evaluation of work design and well-being

**www.statistics.gov.uk/socialtrends35/** contains a wide range of statistics on aspects of contemporary British society and how this has changed

**www.pm.gov.uk/output/com** office of Public Services Reform

**www.dti.gov.uk/work-lifebalance.com**

**www.leeds.ac.uk/esrcfutureofwork**

## REFERENCES

Atkinson J. (1984) Manpower strategies for flexible organisations, *Personnel Management*, August, pp28–31

Batt R. and Moynihan L. (2002) The viability of alternative call centre production models, *Human Resource Management Journal*, Vol.12, No.4, pp14–34

Briner R. and Conway N. (2004) Promises, promises, *People Management*, 25 November, pp42–3

CIPD (2003) *Living to Work?* Survey Report, October

CIPD (2005) Absence Management Survey of Policy and Practice, July

Cook L. and Martin J. (2005) *Social Trends* 35, available at **www.statistics.gov.uk/social trends35/**

Coyle-Shapiro J. and Kessler I. (2000) Consequences of the psychological contract for the employment relationship, *Journal of Management Studies*, Vol.37, No.7, pp903–30

Emmott M. (2004) Britain's real working lives, *People Management*, 30 June, pp14–15

ESRC (2000) Working in Britain Survey, available at **www.esrc.ac.uk**

Frenkel S., Korczynski M., Shire K. and Tam M. (1998) Beyond bureaucracy? Work organisation in call centres, *International Journal of Human Resource Management*, Vol.9, No.6, pp957–79

Guest D. (1990) Human resource management and the American dream, *Journal of Management Studies*, Vol.27, No.4, pp378–97

Guest D. and Conway N. (2001) *Public and Private Sector Perspectives on the Psychological Contract*, CIPD Research Report, London, CIPD

IDS Report 864, September 2002

Harris H., Brewster C. and Sparrow P. (2003) *International Human Resource Management*, London, CIPD

Hendry C. (1994) *Human Resource Strategies for International Growth*, London, Routledge

Herriot P. and Pemberton C. (1995) *New Deals*, Chichester, Wiley

Johns T., Robinson I. and Weightman J. (2005) *Managing People*, CIPD Revision Guide

Kaplan R. and Norton D. (2001) Marked impact, *People Management*, 25 October, pp52–7

Kinnie N., Purcell J. and Hutchinson S. (2000) Managing the employment relationship in telephone call centres, in Purcell K. (ed.) *Changing Boundaries*, Bristol, Bristol Academic Press

Leary-Joyce J. (2004) *Becoming an Employer of Choice*, London, CIPD

Legge K. (2005) *Human Resource Management. Rhetoric and realities*, anniversary edition, Basingstoke, Palgrave

Marchington M. and Wilkinson A. (2005) *Human Resource Management at Work*, 3rd edition, London, CIPD

Parker B. (1998) *Globalization and Business Practice. Managing Across Boundaries*, London, Sage

*People Management* (2004) 30 September

*People Management* (2005) 10 November

Purcell J., Kinnie N., Hutchinson S., Rayton B. and Swart J. (2003) *Understanding the People and Performance Link: Unlocking the black box*, CIPD Research Report, London, CIPD

Richer J. (2001) *The Richer Way*, London, Richer Publishing

Semler R. (1993) *Maverick*, London, Random House

Semler R. (2003) *The Seven-Day Weekend*, London, Random House

Taylor R. (2000a) *Britain's World of Work – Myths and Realities*, ESRC Future of Work Programme Seminar Series

Taylor R. (2000b) *Managing Workplace Change*, ESRC Future of Work Programme Seminar Series

Taylor R. (2000c) *Diversity in Britain's Labour Market*, ESRC Future of Work Programme Seminar Series

Taylor S. (2005) *People Resourcing*, London, CIPD

Taylor P. and Bain P. (1999) An assembly line in the head: the call centre labour process, *Industrial Relations Journal*, Vol.30, No.2, pp101–17

Whittaker J. and Johns T. (2004) Standards deliver, *People Management*, 30 June, pp32–4

White M. (2000) *Working in Britain in the Year 2000*, Policy Studies Institute

Wilkinson A. (2001) Empowerment, in Redman T. and Wilkinson A. (eds) *Contemporary Human Resource Management*, Harlow, FT/Prentice Hall

# The link between people management and organisational performance

## CHAPTER 2

## LEARNING OBJECTIVES

- To examine the research evidence linking HR practice to organisational effectiveness
- To assess the meaning and characteristics of best practice, configurational, contingency, and resource-based approaches to HRM
- To critically review the theoretical links between HRM and organisational performance

## INTRODUCTION

The relationship between HR practice and organisational performance is a topical and ongoing concern. It is against a background of changes in the world of work that research emphasising the importance of effective people management acquires particular significance. As the business environment becomes increasingly competitive and complex, knowledge and understanding of the contribution of people and other intangible assets to organisational performance have become critical success factors.

Organisations that want to succeed need to switch from business models that see people as costs to be minimised to assets that need to be nurtured and developed. What remains uncertain, however, is the issue of what organisations need to do in order to get the best out of the people they employ. What employment practices work? Why do some approaches work in some environments but not in others? Understanding how to add value for customers and the capacity to innovate are crucial differentiators of competitive advantage. Both depend on the effective management of people.

This chapter evaluates the extent to which people management and development policies impact on the success of business strategy. A critical evaluation is provided of research studies that have focused on establishing and assessing the contribution of HR practice to organisational performance. This is followed by a discussion of the work of Purcell *et al* (2003) in unlocking the so-called 'Black Box' and investigating the processes whereby HR practices impact on organisational performance.

## RESEARCHING THE LINK BETWEEN PEOPLE AND ORGANISATIONAL PERFORMANCE

There has been a great deal of research focused on establishing the precise nature of the link between the way people are managed and the effect this has on organisational effectiveness. As Guest (1997) suggests, the dominant HRM issue in the 1990s was focused on demonstrating that there is a positive link between HRM and performance. (For a review of the studies linking HRM and business performance and an account of the underpinning methodologies, see Richardson and Thompson, 1999.)

## CONCEPTUALISING THE LINK BETWEEN PEOPLE AND ORGANISATIONAL PERFORMANCE

Although expressed in different ways by different authors, the fundamental theoretical framework guiding research activity is illustrated in Figure 2. The essential point is that HRM strategies and systems (for recruitment, selection, training, development, pay) produce employee behaviours that are focused on key business priorities and which in turn impact on organisational financial indicators.

Conceptually, the link between the management of people and organisational effectiveness and success can be categorised under three principal theoretical approaches:

- *the best practice approach* which suggests that the application of a universal set of HR practices results in superior organisational performance
- *the contingency approach* which argues that HR strategy and practice need to be integrated and responsive to business strategy and the environment within which the organisation is operating

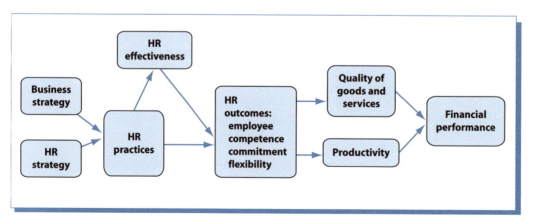

**Figure 2** *Model of the link between HRM and performance*
Source: D. Guest, J. Michie, M. Sheehan, N. Conway and M. Metochi (2000) *Effective People Management*, London, CIPD, p5

■ *the resource-based view* (RBV) which sees human resources as internal assets which organisations can effectively exploit to gain competitive advantage.

## BEST PRACTICE APPROACHES

The best practice or universal approach has its roots in the so-called 'excellence' movement (eg Peters and Waterman, 1982; Peters, 1987) which advocated the existence of a number of basic underlying philosophies that resulted in the successful management of people and in turn led to improved work performance and to organisational success. The logic of the argument was that people were the most valuable resource of any organisation and that training and developing them, adequately rewarding them, involving them in organisational policy-making, especially at the customer-interface level, resulted in enhanced motivation and organisational performance.

In their seminal work *In Search of Excellence* (1982), Peters and Waterman studied 62 US companies with outstandingly successful performance and identified eight basic attributes of excellence which appeared to account for their success. These attributes included a bias for action, closeness to the customer, innovation and risk-taking as an accepted practice, treating staff as a source of quality and productivity, having and communicating well-defined philosophies, staying close to what they knew and did well, simple structural forms and systems, and operational decentralisation but strong centralised control over the few, important core values.

More recently, research equating organisational performance with people management practice has been highlighted in the work of Pfeffer (1998). Pfeffer has argued that people are at the heart of business success and that seven HR policies are common to high-performing organisations irrespective of sector, size, country, product market, industry or workforce. Pfeffer's Seven Best HR Practices are summarised in the box below.

---

### PFEFFER'S SEVEN BEST HR PRACTICES

■ employment security
■ careful recruitment and selection
■ teamworking and decentralised management
■ high pay with an incentive element linked to company performance
■ extensive training
■ narrow status differentials
■ developed communications mechanisms and information sharing.

Source: J. Pfeffer (1998) *The Human Equation: Building profits by putting people first*, Harvard Business School Press

# BUNDLES OF HR PRACTICES

The concept of universal best practice HR is supported by the so-called 'configurational' or 'bundling' approach which emphasises the need for particular sets of people management practices to be internally consistent, mutually supportive and reinforcing (MacDuffie, 1995; Huselid, 1995). A series of studies has suggested a link between what have been termed 'high-performance work practices' (Huselid, 1995; Delaney and Huselid, 1996) and organisational performance.

Configurational approaches emphasise the need for HR policy and practice to be *horizontally integrated* or mutually supportive and reinforcing. This internal coherence avoids unnecessary duplication of HR activities which may be 'negatively synergistic' (Delery, 1998: 293), ie activities which may be costly to implement and operate but bring no added value to the organisation (eg over-designed selection systems).

Configurational approaches argue that organisations stand to gain potentially attractive pay-offs when adopting integrated clusters or bundles of HR practices. However, studies have shown considerable diversity in the HR practices that make up so-called HR bundles. Huselid (1995) identified 13 HR practices factored around two key dimensions. The first dimension, 'employee skills and organisational structures', included practices such as formal job design, selectivity in recruitment and selection, formal training, information-sharing, programmes for employee involvement, and profit- and gain-sharing schemes. The second dimension focused on 'employee motivation' and included practices such as promotion policies and formal performance appraisal linked to pay.

In their research, Delery and Doty (1996: 825) concluded that some HR practices always had a positive effect on performance, but found support principally for three HR practices in supporting organisational performance – namely, results-oriented appraisal, profit-sharing and employment security. The variety in the number and type of practices falling under the high-performance work practice umbrella led Becker and Gerhart (1996: 784) to conclude that

> **studies of so-called high-performance work systems vary significantly as to the practices included and sometimes even as to whether a practice is likely to be positively or negatively related to high performance.**

## PAUSE FOR THOUGHT . . .

Reflect on the features and characteristics of the best practice approach. Is it possible, do you think, to identify HR practices which result in employee competence, commitment and flexibility, and which improve financial performance, quality and productivity? Can you relate this framework to your own organisation?

## Quantifying the contribution of HR practices

Configurational or 'bundles' approaches are often concerned with establishing a quantifiable link between specific HR practices and organisational performance. Based on large-scale surveys of top US companies, Huselid (1995) compared HR practices with data on economic and market performance. He used company market value as the key indicator of business performance and found that firms with significantly above-average scores on an index of high-performance work practices provided an extra market value of between £10,000 and £40,000. Huselid's work underscored the importance of 'fit' or integration of HR practice. It was only practices that were integrated, cohesive and mutually supportive that brought positive benefits. As Huselid (1995: 644) put it, 'all else being equal, the use of high-performance work practices and good internal fit should lead to positive outcomes for all types of firms.'

The work of US academics has been supplemented by other studies. Bae *et al* (2003) examined the impact of high-performance work practices on organisational performance in 700 companies in the Pacific Rim countries of Korea, Taiwan, Singapore and Thailand and found a positive HR-performance link despite cultural and organisational variations. Huang's (2001) study of 315 Taiwanese firms also lends support to the best practice approach and suggests that high-performance work practices can significantly improve organisational performance in newly industrialised economies.

In the UK, studies have covered a range of organisations and industrial sectors and have also focused on providing hard evidence that people management is the most important factor in determining organisational performance. The Sheffield Effectiveness Programme study (Patterson *et al*, 1997) examined market environment, organisational characteristics and management practice within 100 medium-sized UK manufacturing firms over a ten-year period and concluded that people management was not only critical to business performance but was more important than an emphasis on quality, technology, corporate strategy or research and development in influencing the bottom line. The study found that HR practices explained 18 per cent and 19 per cent of variations in productivity and profitability respectively between organisations. By comparison, strategy accounted for 2 per cent, and research and development for 8 per cent of variations. An emphasis on quality accounted for less than 1 per cent.

The research linked the following key HR practices to improvements in productivity and profitability:

- acquisition and development of skills (assessed by the sophistication of induction, training, section and appraisal processes)
- job design (assessed by the degree of job variety, responsibility, skill flexibility and team work)

The study also found that workforce skills were an important predictor of future productivity and that positive employee attitudes and motivation could be sustained and developed through favourable reward systems, harmonisation and involvement. The researchers concluded that people management was not just about traditional HR practices such as recruitment, appraisal and training but ensuring that all aspects of employee satisfaction – eg the need for growth and development, security, work relationships, work–life balance – were addressed. In other words, HR strategies and practices needed to be mutually reinforcing. Research by Guest *et al* (2000) has also contributed to confirming the link between progressive HR practice and employee involvement, satisfaction, commitment, productivity and financial performance within a larger sample of organisations.

## PAUSE FOR THOUGHT . . .

Reflect on the research evidence focused on quantifying and measuring the HR contribution. Can you identify any drawbacks with this approach? Does it, for example, leave the HR function vulnerable to outsourcing based solely on an evaluation of what people management practices exist and how much these cost?

## Shortcomings of best practice and configurational approaches

Best practice and configurational approaches have been influential in highlighting the key role of human resources in organisational performance. Nevertheless, they can be criticised on conceptual, methodological and practical grounds.

Pfeffer's approach and that of the 'excellence' writers generally has been criticised on the grounds of advocating a universalist approach to the management of people rather than tailoring HR practice to the organisation's specific situation and environment. As Marchington and Wilkinson (2005: 95) suggest, a best practice approach suggests that organisations have the 'luxury' of taking a long-term perspective, whereas in reality, institutional pressures may shape the HRM agenda more in some situations than in others.

More pragmatically, there are a large number of organisations who do not adopt best practice or implement high-performance work practices but who are nevertheless successful. This raises the issue of what constitutes success or superior performance in order to be able to compare meaningfully performance measures at individual and organisational level (Truss, 2001: 1146). The best practice approach fails to take account of an organisation's specific situation and environment and ignores potentially significant differences between organisations, sectors and countries. It overlooks how specific situational factors might prevent the introduction of certain practices or influence the adoption of others. As Marchington and Wilkinson (2005: 95) suggest, a high-commitment best practice approach is easier to adopt in situations where labour costs represent a low proportion of controllable costs than in situations where labour costs are high and where it might be difficult to increase pay rates or offer training.

Although there may be general agreement on standard HR practices that are sensible and appropriate (eg structured selection interviews) there is less agreement on what constitutes best practice within different organisational contexts. Some studies have focused on specific sectors and have used performance measures relevant to that sector (eg Arthur, 1992, analysed scrap rates in US mini steel mills; West et al, 2002, analysed mortality rates in hospitals; Appelbaum et al, 2000, focused on three very different manufacturing plants – ie steel, apparel and medical electronic instruments). These are more valuable because they allow for greater precision in identifying the HR practices that are likely to be influential. However, as suggested earlier, the variety of HR practices is an area of concern and there is considerable diversity in relation to the composition of HR bundles that contribute to organisational performance, and inconsistency in relation to how many HR practices make up the bundle, what they are, and which elements matter most.

Research which seeks to provide hard, statistical evidence for the link between HR practice and organisational performance suffers from methodological constraints. The underlying assumption behind such approaches is that value can only be added in financial terms. Adopting an accounting terminology and attempting to quantify the people management contribution conforms to a prevailing accountancy view of how organisations and organisational processes should be managed. It overlooks the problem of causality – ie are organisations successful in financial terms because of the HR practices they utilise, or do they adopt sophisticated HR practices because they are successful? Despite the increasing sophistication of research and statistical analysis suggesting causality between people management and organisational performance, there is no established link. Statistical correlations do not prove causality and other variables may impact on organisational performance.

The quantitative approach is thus too simplistic and can undermine the people contribution because the effectiveness of people management practices on organisational performance is difficult to measure. People are not passive, compliant assets and human behaviour cannot be readily predicted. Feelings, attitudes, opinions, emotions and behaviours cannot be easily quantified, reliably counted and uniformly measured.

Hard measures, such as statistical correlations between aspects of people management practice and profit, shareholder value and revenue growth, have the advantage that they appear objective and can often be expressed simply to suggest a direct and causal relationship between HR practice and revenue growth.

However, the methodology for putting numbers behind people assets is questionable and incompletely developed. The measures and samples used are variable, and as a result it is difficult to draw general conclusions. The selection of the measures used is also subject to qualitative interpretation in that judgement may be required as to which criteria are relevant. Lists of practices have been developed on the basis of individual preference, by looking at what other researchers have used or by constructing groupings of practices on the basis of factor analysis and then attempting to impose some post-hoc rationalisation for their selection (Marchington and Wilkinson, 2005: 91).

There are also practical problems in collecting reliable and meaningful information. The validity and reliability of information gathered through questionnaires can be affected by the self-awareness and honesty of respondents, and attitude surveys can be misleading if poorly designed. A further problem may be that the methodology for working out how different people management practices impact on organisational performance is only possible within large organisations with a wealth of different practices to analyse and measure (such as in the Sears case example below). It may also be possible that the costs of collecting and analysing certain sets of information may not be justified by the benefits in the shape of improved performance.

## ILLUSTRATION

### Sears Group

At the Sears Group in the USA, over a period of some years, a great deal of data was collected by task forces concerning employee development and teamworking, customer need and satisfaction and revenue growth, sales per square foot and other financial measures. Central was the way that the company sought to capture 'soft issues' such as staff satisfaction using hard measurements. This was done through the use of questionnaire surveys. Correlations were then made between changes in the P&D (personnel and development) indicators and improvements in the financial performance of different business units (ie benchmarking). The analysis allowed the company to make the following statement: 'A 5-point improvement in employee attitudes will drive a 1.3-point improvement in customer satisfaction, which in turn will lead to a 0.5 per cent improvement in revenue growth.'

Source: S. Taylor (2005) *People Resourcing*, CIPD, pp424–5

## CONTINGENCY APPROACHES

Contingency approaches emphasise that there can be no one, best, universal way of organising and managing people because of the large number of variables or situational factors that influence organisational performance, and that some degree of fit or integration with the company's environment, business strategy, history and other HR practices needs to be achieved (Baird and Meshoulam, 1988). Studies advocating contingency approaches argue that the particular sets of practices an organisation adopts must fit with other organisational factors if they are to be effective in raising organisational performance.

Contingency approaches thus advocate the *vertical integration* of HR strategy and practice with business strategy in a way that reflects the specific features of the environment within which the organisation is operating. They likewise advocate the *horizontal integration* of specific HR strategies and practices in areas such as resourcing, learning and development, performance management and remuneration, in order to ensure that these are mutually consistent and mutually supportive. Improved business performance comes when HR strategies support the organisation's choice of competitive strategy and are internally consistent. HRM is thus integrated into the strategic planning process, as illustrated in Figure 3 on page 40.

Porter (1985) has argued that organisations have three generic strategic options – price-based, differentiation and focus. A price leadership strategy is the 'no frills' approach such as that adopted by the retail outlets Aldi and Netto. These stores are very basic, the merchandise is limited, and prices are very low. Another example is the airline easyJet in which cost reduction underpins all aspects of the operation. A differentiation strategy seeks to provide products or services that are different from those offered by competitors to specific groups who are prepared to pay more for a product (eg designer clothes, perfume). A focused strategic approach is aimed at a small niche market where a premium price may be charged for exceptional quality (eg Ferrari cars, Haagen Daz ice cream). An organisation's choice of competitive strategy provides the context for a range of operational policies and practices including the approach taken to managing people.

Miles and Snow (1984) built upon Porter's generic strategies to define three basic types of strategic behaviour which call for different HR policies and practices as illustrated in Table 2 on pages 41–3. Defenders have a limited product line and compete on the basis of cost efficiencies. In this scenario jobs are likely to be closely prescribed and reflect scientific management principles of work organisation and management control. Training and development opportunities are likely to be limited and focused on the development of job-related skills. Pay levels are likely to be at or below market rates. Prospector organisations are focused on identifying new product and market opportunities and compete through product innovation. They are likely to use a range of HR practices similar to best practice or high-performance activities identified earlier. Analysers operate in two domains: they have certain operations that are stable where they operate routinely but they also aim to emulate more creative competitors and operate innovatively.

In a similar vein Schuler and Jackson (1987) have argued that different marketing strategies require specific employee behaviours. For example, an innovation strategy rests on behaviours such as collaboration, creativity, a willingness to learn and experiment, and a readiness to take risks. A quality enhancement strategy calls for relatively predictable behaviours with some degree of co-operative and collaborative behaviour. A cost-reduction strategy requires low-risk repetitive behaviour with a focus on quantity of output rather than quality.

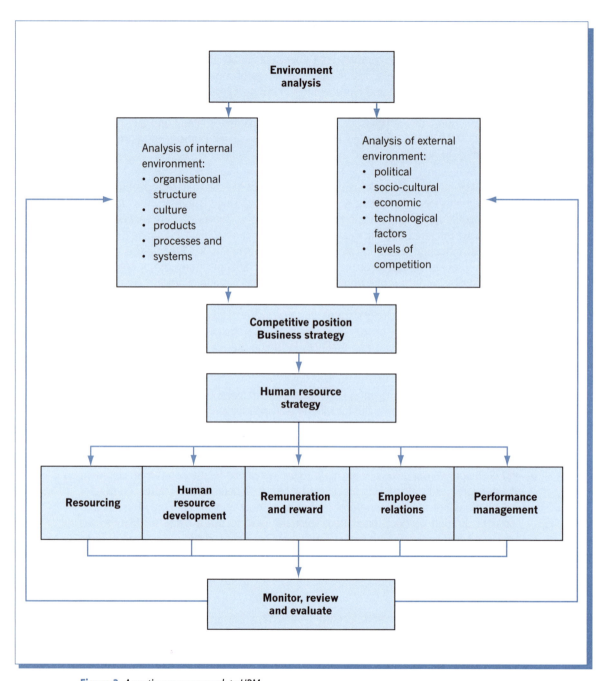

**Figure 3** *A contingency approach to HRM*

Table 2 *Miles and Snow's model of business strategies and HRM systems*

| Organisational/ Managerial characteristics | Type A (Defender) | Type B (Prospector) | Type C (Analyser) |
|---|---|---|---|
| Product market strategy | Limited, stable product line Predictable markets Growth through market penetration Emphasis = deep | Broad, changing product line Changing markets Growth through product and market development Emphasis = broad | Stable and changing product line Predictable and changing markets Growth mainly through market development Emphasis = deep and focused |
| Research and development | Limited – mostly to product improvement | Extensive – emphasis on 'first to market' | Focused – emphasis on second to market |
| Production | High volume, low cost Emphasis on efficiency and process engineering | Customised and prototypical Emphasis on effectiveness and product design | High volume, low cost, some prototypical Emphasis on process engineering and product development |
| Marketing | Limited mostly to sales | Focused heavily on market research | Utilises extensive marketing campaign |
| Organisational structure | Functional | Divisional | Functional and matrix |

**Table 2**  *continued*

| Organisational/ Managerial characteristics | Type A (Defender) | Type B (Prospector) | Type C (Analyser) |
| --- | --- | --- | --- |
| Control process | Centralised | Decentralised | Mostly centralised but decentralised in marketing and brand management |
| Dominant coalition | CEO Production Finance | CEO Product R&D Market research | CEO Marketing Process engineering |
| Business planning sequence | Plan–Act–Evaluate | Act–Evaluate–Plan | Evaluate–Plan–Act |
| Basic strategy | Building human resources | Acquiring human resources | Allocating human resources |
| Recruitment/selection | Little recruitment above entry level Selection based on weeding out undesirable employees | Sophisticated recruitment at all levels Selection may involve pre-employment psychological testing | Mixed recruitment and selection strategies |
| Staff planning | Formal, extensive | Informal, limited | Formal, extensive |
| Training and development | Skill-building Extensive training programmes | Skill identification and acquisition Limited training | Skill-building and acquisition Extensive training |

**Table 2** *continued*

| Organisational/ Managerial characteristics | Type A (Defender) | Type B (Prospector) | Type C (Analyser) |
|---|---|---|---|
| Performance appraisal | Process-oriented (eg based on critical incidents) Identification of training needs Individual, group performance evaluations Time–series comparisons | Results-oriented procedure Identification of staffing needs Division/corporate performance evaluations Cross-sectional comparisons | Mostly process-oriented procedure Identification of training and staffing needs Individual/group/division performance evaluations Mostly time–series, some cross-sectional comparisons |
| Compensation | Oriented towards position in hierarchy Internal consistency Total compensation heavily oriented towards cash and driven by superior/ subordinate differentials | Oriented towards performance External competitiveness Total compensation heavily oriented towards incentives and driven by recruitment needs | Mostly oriented towards hierarchy, some performance considerations Internal consistency and external competitiveness Cash and incentive compensation |

Source: R. Miles and C. Snow (1984) Designing strategic human resource systems, *Organisational Dynamics*, Vol.13, No.1, pp36–48

## Evidence to support contingency approaches

Empirical evidence in relation to the existence and benefits of 'fit' are mixed. In a study of 30 mini mills in the US steel industry, Arthur (1992) explored differences in HR practices among otherwise similar firms and found that mills following a cost reduction strategy almost always adopted a command-and-control approach whereas those mills seeking to achieve product or quality differentiation adopted a bundle of high-performance work practices. Arthur (1992) concluded that variations in workplace industrial relations were related to differences in business strategy.

Studies by Delery and Doty (1996) in US banks and Youndt *et al* (1996) in 97 manufacturing plants also found support for the Miles and Snow typology. More recently, Eaton's (2000) study of 14 US nursing homes provided an alternative to the high-performance models borrowed from industry and found distinct variations in systems of work, care organisation, HRM and management values linked to different management philosophies and strategies of care provision.

However, Truss *et al*'s (1997: 67–8) study of eight UK organisations found no evidence of an integrative link between business and HR strategies. The firms studied showed a one-way link where business strategy informed HR practice, but not vice versa. Sanz-Valle *et al*'s (1999) study of 200 Spanish companies demonstrated significant associations between certain human resource practices and business strategy. This study adopted Schuler and Jackson's (1987) categorisation of business strategies – ie innovation, quality and cost – and found that certain differences in HR practice between the organisations studied could be attributed to the business strategy adopted. These included the provision of training and development, career development and promotion opportunities, levels and type of remuneration and arrangements for employee participation.

The study (Sanz-Valle *et al*, 1999: 666) found that

firms that spent less money on training were those which followed a cost leadership strategy; their main concern was to reduce costs in different areas and their employees basically carried out autonomous repetitive tasks. Companies with an innovation strategy invested more money due to the fact that they needed to develop not only the knowledge and skill of their personnel, but also attitudes in order to encourage creativity, flexibility, propensity to take risks and the co-operation that this strategy requires to be implemented with success. Firms with a quality strategy also needed

> **to invest in training in order to stimulate co-operation and obtain the continuous improvement that quality implies.**

However, the study also found that some HR practices did not vary with business strategy. The majority of firms in the sample preferred internal recruitment and used similar selection techniques regardless of the business strategy adopted. Moreover, certain practices were found to directly contradict Schuler and Jackson's assumptions: for example, firms with a quality strategy were found to have more hierarchical payment systems than those with an innovation strategy.

Sanz-Valle *et al* do not explain the reasons behind the variations found but the implication can be drawn that while some HR practices do not vary with strategy, a range of situational factors can act as constraints or enhancements of HR practices. This view is supported by Cassell *et al*'s (2002) research into the use and effectiveness of HRM practices within UK SMEs which found that rather than being driven by a strategic focus the adoption of HR practices within SMEs was fundamentally driven by triggers such as skills shortages, a decrease in output or productivity or issues of individual performance in the context of current business priorities. As Cassell *et al* (2002: 680) put it,

> **rather than taking a coherent strategy-based approach to the implementation of HRM, [key managers] are taking a more 'pick and mix' contingency approach.**

**ACTIVITY . . .**

Can you identify organisations operating in the same sector that have different strategies and different HR practices? What are these differences? How valuable is a contingency approach in explaining these differences?

## Shortcomings of contingency approaches

The strengths of a contingency approach lie in its emphasis on the coherence and consistency of HR policies and practices based on a long-term integrated HRM philosophy. However, contingency approaches have limitations. Firstly, contingency approaches can be criticised for their determinism. The underlying assumption is that HR strategies can be selected depending on the organisation's business strategy but this line of theorising overlooks the problematic nature of the concept of strategy.

Contingency and best fit approaches imply a view of strategy as a rational, linear, objective process in which senior managers make rational and informed decisions based on an analysis of the environment in which the organisation is operating (Marchington and Wilkinson, 2005: 108–9). However, alternative views of strategy see it as an emergent process in which strategy evolves in a fragmented way as a result of internal decisions and external events. Contingency approaches are based on so-called classical views of strategy as a planned, rational, top-down process. As a result they are largely normative and static – ie focused on what should be rather than what is, and lacking a focus on change (Marchington and Wilkinson, 2005: 110). They tend to portray HR in a reactive way as concerned with the efficient implementation of preconceived and rational strategy which marginalises the potential HR contribution to strategy development.

More prosaically, contingency approaches overlook the fact that many organisations do not have a clearly defined business strategy, while an emphasis on the importance of synergy between various elements of the HR systems questions how compatible contingency approaches are with the concept of flexibility in skills and behaviours needed for different competitive scenarios (Wright and Snell, 1998). The key question becomes how organisations reduce the lag between the adoption of new strategies and appropriate HR practices.

Secondly, contingency approaches marginalise the turbulence of the environment within which organisations are required to operate and oversimplify the challenges of managing people. The challenges posed by external environmental pressures is graphically illustrated by Snape *et al*'s (1993: 56) analysis of British building societies:

> **While the intensification of competition presented building societies with an incentive to develop a strategic HRM approach to the management of their staff, these same competitive pressures placed cost control at a premium and the pressures and uncertainties of the new environment meant that the implementation of a consistent HRM approach was difficult.**

Contingency approaches thus underplay the multifaceted reality of organisational life and overlook the inherent contradictions and tensions involved in achieving fit and coherence in HR practice. The empowerment of certain groups of workers may result in loss of security for other groups; an emphasis on teamworking may be undermined by the differentiation and reward of individual performance under a performance-related pay scheme; segmentation of the workforce with a core of strategically important employees employed on more favourable terms may reduce the commitment and opportunities available to other, peripheral groups.

Truss' (2001) study of Hewlett Packard demonstrates how a more hostile and competitive environment can mean that even highly successful organisations with a strong tradition of utilising high-performance work practices may find it difficult to achieve complementarity in HR practice, and may have to pursue multiple approaches in meeting the needs of organisational stakeholders. As Boxall (1996: 60) puts it,

> **The managers of firms are typically engaged in a process of managing the 'strategic tension' between ends and means in an external environment characterised by risk, change, complexity and ambiguity and an internal environment characterised by bounded rationality, endemic co-ordination problems, inertial tendencies and political trade-offs.**

## ACTIVITY . . .

Contingency studies have been criticised for their methodological constraints. As Legge (2005: 154) puts it, 'A lack of longitudinal in-depth case studies in the American work, combined with a penchant for small-scale low-response-rate surveys, gives only fragile empirical support – if that – for a weighty prescriptive infrastructure.'

Obtain a copy of any of the contingency studies referred to in this section and critically evaluate the research design used and the conclusions reached. On the basis of the data collected, is it possible to generalise the findings to a wider sample of organisations? How can case studies be made more credible and robust?

## RESOURCE-BASED APPROACHES (RBV)

The resource-based view (RBV) shifts the emphasis away from the external environment and the organisation's position within its competitive environment to a focus on how competitive advantage might be achieved through innovative exploitation of distinct internal resources or capabilities. Originating with the work of Penrose (1959), this approach has been extended and developed to emphasise human and other intangible resources as a source of sustainable competitive advantage which enables the organisation to take advantage of market opportunities or deal with threats in a way that competitors are unable to do (Barney, 1991).

The issue of sustainability is important because although a firm's resources may have added value in the past, changes in customer preferences, industry structures or technology can reduce their value in the future (Barney, 1995: 51). Competitive advantage stems from an organisation's ability to build distinctive 'core' competencies which are superior to those of rivals.

RBV thus emphasises a long-term perspective and the organisation's ability to develop and sustain distinctive, core competencies over time. The resource-based view is thus closely linked to concepts such as the 'learning organisation' and 'knowledge management' (discussed in Chapter 7) and the organisation's ability to learn collectively and to harness that learning in a way that continuously enables the organisation to adapt to its environment.

According to the resource-based approach, resources are a source of competitive advantage when they are valuable, hard to imitate and non-substitutable. Resources can be rare when they are unequally distributed and difficult to obtain and not all competitors possess them. Resources can be valuable when they have a significant impact on the bottom line. Resources can be inimitable when they cannot be readily substituted – eg automated or copied by competitors.

The practical application of the RBV approach is helped by the distinction between *human capital advantage* and *human process advantage* (Boxall, 1996) which clarifies *what* it is that can be uniquely and exceptionally valuable about human resources and *how* managers might obtain, develop and retain resources that are valuable (Boxall and Purcell, 2003: 85). In other words, is it the skills, abilities and capabilities of people that exist within an organisation at any given time (the stock of human capital) or is it the ways, systems and processes used to manage this stock of human capital that constitute a source of competitive advantage?

> **Human capital advantage is concerned with 'recruiting and retaining outstanding people, through capturing a stock of exceptional human talent, latent with productive possibilities'**
>
> **(Boxall, 1996: 66–7).**

The concept of 'human capital' is predicated on the notion of people as an organisational resource or asset. It is fundamentally about measurement and has led to the development of a range of metrics and reporting measures designed to quantify the contribution of people to organisational success. These measures are discussed in Chapter 3.

> **Human process advantage can be understood as 'a function of causally ambiguous, socially complex, historically evolved processes such as learning, co-operation and innovation'**
>
> **(Boxall, 1996: 67).**

Human process advantage puts the spotlight on the actual link between processes that connect inputs (HR practices) and outputs (financial performance). This is often referred to as the 'Black Box' or the nature of the connection between HR practice and organisational performance. The work of Purcell *et al* (2003) has focused on unlocking the 'Black Box' and providing direct evidence of the processes whereby HR practices influence the variables that contribute to organisational success. This is discussed fully in *Unlocking the black box* below.

Both human capital and organisational processes can generate exceptional value and competitive advantage, but they are likely to do so more powerfully if they are dovetailed together in a mutually supportive and self-reinforcing way (Boxall, 1996). In other words, it is not enough for an organisation to be able to recruit people with talent and ability; it needs to have in place processes, systems and practices to ensure that people work effectively.

Successful organisations combine, in unique ways, values, routines and policy-practice which affect both individuals and collective activities (Purcell *et al*, 2003: 14). It is this 'social complexity' which is so hard to imitate. Individual HR policies and practices can be easily replicated but it is the mix of these policies and practices together underpinned by embedded values that differentiates organisations.

As Holbeche (2005) argues, high-performance organisations develop and change by making changes in carefully integrated and mutually supporting practices that are contextually appropriate. Organisations may of course also squander or fail to productively utilise their human resources (Boxall and Purcell, 2003: 86). They may recruit highly talented managers but fail to offer them opportunities to extend their talents, with the result that they may become disillusioned and leave the organisation or stay and become dis-engaged.

## PAUSE FOR THOUGHT ...

Can you think of any examples from your own experience of a mismatch between human capital and its utilisation? What were the consequences – for the organisation? For the individual?

## Limitations of the RBV approach

The RBV approach offers a compelling conceptual basis for the link between people and organisational performance. It avoids the prescription of best practice approaches and the reactivity of contingency models. Nevertheless, it too has limitations and shortcomings. Principally, RBV approaches have been criticised for emphasising idiosyncrasy and exaggerating differences between organisations operating within the same sector. As Boxall and Purcell (2003: 81) suggest, although high-performance firms may have distinctive features, they may also need similar resources to meet standard customer expectations. By focusing on internal resources and capabilities in building competitive advantage, RBV approaches marginalise the impact of the external environment and wider competitive pressures. An organisation may invest in building both human capital and organisational processes but external pressures may serve to undermine them.

As Truss' (2001) study of Hewlett Packard demonstrates, a more hostile environment resulted in tougher work targets and work intensification while previous benefits such as stability of employment, high pay and career development opportunities were eroded. Inconsistencies between policy intentions and practice were not lost on employees and contributed to a strong disconnect between the rhetoric expressed by the HR department and the reality experienced by employees (Truss, 2001: 1143). Truss' study highlights the impact and importance of the informal organisation in the process and implementation of HR policies.

## UNLOCKING THE BLACK BOX – MOVING TO REAL STRATEGIC BUSINESS CONTRIBUTION

The resource-based approach has been developed through the work of Purcell *et al* (2003) who have focused on the so-called 'Black Box' dilemma and gathered empirical evidence on the processes that link HR practice to organisational performance.

This study was based on 12 case-study organisations covering a range of sectors and industries including manufacturing, retail, finance, professional services, IT and the NHS, spanning a period of three years. Its purpose was to unlock the 'Black Box' of performance and to provide direct evidence of the link between HR practice and organisational performance. Purcell *et al*'s (2003) work represents a significant step forward in that it moves away from the input/output models and a focus on counting HR practices and provides insight into how and why HR practices influence organisational performance.

The theoretical framework underpinning Purcell *et al*'s study is illustrated in Figure 4.

Purcell *et al*'s (2003) people performance model identifies a distinctive set of HR practices and approaches (ranging from careful recruitment and selection and learning and development to teamworking and involvement activities) that feed into three generic practices which affect employee attitudes and hence their discretionary effort and performance.

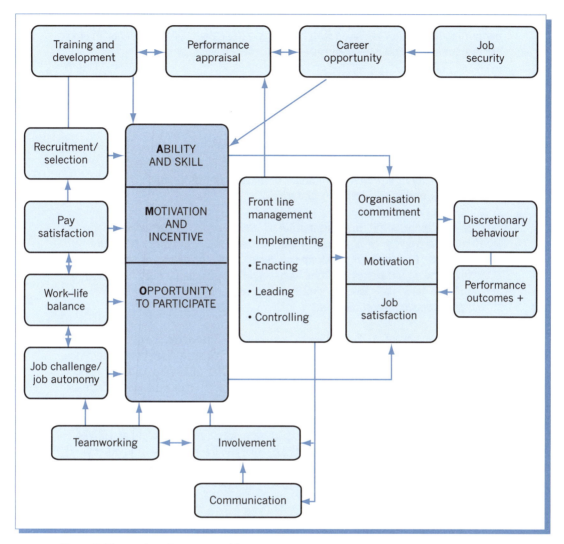

**Figure 4** *The people performance model*
Source: J. Purcell, N. Kinnie, S. Hutchinson, B. Rayton and J. Swart (2003) *Understanding the People and Performance Link: Unlocking the black box*, CIPD Research Report, London, CIPD, p7

These generic approaches are similar to those used by Appelbaum (2000) and include the *Ability* and skill of employees, their level of *Motivation*, and *Opportunity* to participate in decision-making. The so-called *AMO* model sees discretionary behaviour and hence high performance as a function of the ability, motivation and the opportunity employees have to make individual/team choices over the way in which the job is done and the speed, care and innovation that goes into its delivery. In other words, high performance comes when

51

people possess the necessary knowledge and skills, when they have the motivation to perform, and when they are given the opportunity to use their skills and talents. The logic of the argument is explained by Purcell *et al* (2003: 6) as follows:

*The assumption in A (Ability) is that people will want to apply for jobs in an organisation (recruitment), have their attributes recognised (selection) and be willing to learn new skills and behaviours (training and development).*

*In M (Motivation) the assumption is that people can be motivated to use their ability in a productive manner because they will respond to various extrinsic and intrinsic rewards and stimuli.*

*In O (Opportunity) the assumption is that people will provide good customer service, or high-quality work beyond the satisfactory level and will wish to engage in problem-solving or wider involvement schemes, given the opportunities to do so. They need the opportunity both to use or practise their skills and to contribute to collective efforts at the team, section and organisation level.*

The crucial function of AMO policies is therefore to engender employee attitudes of commitment, motivation and satisfaction which in turn influence discretionary behaviour and effort. This is supported by Appelbaum *et al* (2000: 201) who in their study of manufacturing firms found that the core characteristics of so-called High Performance Working Practices (HPWPs) – ie providing the opportunity for participation, skill enhancement, and incentives to increase motivation – were positively related to employee commitment and job satisfaction. The explanation was that the effects of HPWPs on commitment and satisfaction were mediated by trust and intrinsic rewards. In other words, HPWPs served to establish a greater level of trust between employees and managers and increased employee experiences of their work as intrinsically rewarding, challenging and meaningful.

Purcell *et al* (2003) identified a range of HR policies and practices required to mobilise the AMO ingredients. These included recruitment and selection, training and development, career opportunities, involvement in decision-making, teamworking, appraisal, pay, job security, job challenge/autonomy and work–life balance. These performance-related HR policies helped develop attitudes and feelings of satisfaction, commitment and motivation and encouraged the use of discretionary behaviour. Certain HR policies and practices (ie career progression, job influence and challenge, training, performance appraisal, teamworking, involvement, work–life balance) were particularly influential.

Crucially, however, the study found that performance-related HR policies were not enough to deliver superior performance. Such practices contributed to human capital advantage but this needed to be combined with human process advantage to lead to genuine competitive differentiation. In high-performing organisations there were found to be two common and crucial ingredients: firstly, a strong, inclusive culture built around a 'Big Idea' which expressed what the organisation stood for and what it was trying to achieve, and its relationship with its customers, employees and other stakeholders; and secondly, front-line management who were able to implement and bring policies to life.

Even in the most standardised organisations managers will have some discretion as to how they put HR practices into operation and employees are more likely to demonstrate discretionary behaviour if their managers behave in ways that stimulate and encourage this kind of behaviour. HR policies may be comprehensive and well designed but they may not get implemented in the way intended. Purcell *et al*'s (2003) research illustrates the importance of how HR practices are actually put into practice by managers and how these practices are perceived by employees (see Chapter 4).

## ILLUSTRATION

### Nationwide Building Society

The idea of 'mutuality' as a key value deeply influences the way the Society manages relationships with its customers and its employees. Nationwide's commitment to mutuality back in 1995 resulted in the development of a new business strategy to improve customer services and streamline operations, and has enabled the Society to develop a unique position in the financial services market place. By putting the customer first, rather than the shareholder, the Society is able to operate on narrower margins and reduced planned profit so that customers receive long-term benefits by way of improved rates and better services. This focus on customer-based performance driven through people, products and processes led to a group-wide campaign launched in 2002 called PRIDE (Putting the people first, Rising to the challenge, Inspiring confidence, Delivering better value, Exceeding expectations). The Society has used a wide range of HR policies to support the long-term strategy of mutuality. In terms of recruitment and selection, internal applicants are preferred for cultural reasons. Reward is based on collective as well as individual performance.

What is particularly interesting in this case are the additional drivers of attitudinal outcomes, especially people's sense of having opportunities to be involved, to know about plans and prospects (communication), the perceived openness of the Society in allowing concerns to be raised and generally the behaviour of front-line managers. HR practices are not concrete policies enshrined and defined in a manual. They are management behaviours and are a clear indication of the values of 'mutuality' in action.

Purcell *et al* (2003), *Understanding the People Performance Link: Unlocking the black box*, CIPD, pp17–19

## KEY LEARNING POINTS

- There is considerable theoretical evidence establishing a link between HR practice and organisational performance.
- The best practice approach suggests that the adoption of a set of universal, so-called HR best practices such as careful recruitment and selection, training and development and harmonisation results in superior organisational performance regardless of organisation size, structure or situation.
- Contingency approaches emphasise the concept of integration or fit. Such approaches argue that HR strategy and practice needs to be vertically integrated with business strategy and the environment within which the organisation is operating. They further emphasise the need for horizontal integration or the need for specific HR strategies and practices in areas such as resourcing, reward and development to be consistent and mutually supporting.
- The resource-based view sees human resources as internal assets which the organisation can use to gain competitive advantage. Human resources are assets because they are valuable, scarce and difficult to imitate.
- Recent research has focused on the process whereby HR practice contributes to organisational performance. The people performance model (Purcell *et al*, 2003) identifies a distinctive set of HR practices that contribute to the ability and skills of employees, their motivation and their opportunity to participate in decision-making. The so-called AMO model affects employee attitudes and their discretionary behaviour and hence impacts on performance.

## Additional reading

Pass S. (2005) Missing links in the 'causal chain' between HR practices and organisational performance, paper presented at CIPD Professional Standards Conference, Keele University, July 2005

Sung J. and Ashton D. (2004) *High-Performance Work Practices: Linking strategy and skills to performance outcomes*, DTI/CIPD

## Web-based sources of information

**www.bestcompanies.co.uk**

**www.dti.gov.uk**

## REFERENCES

Appelbaum E., Bailey T., Berg P. and Kalleberg A. (2000) *Manufacturing Advantage. Why High Performance Work Systems Pay Off*, Ithaca and London, ILR Press

Arthur B. (1992) The link between business strategy and industrial relations systems in American steel minimills, *Industrial and Labor Relations Review*, Vol.45, No.3, pp488–507

Bae J., Chen S., Wan T., Lawler J. and Walumbwa F. (2003) Human resource strategy and firm performance in Pacific Rim countries, *International Journal of Human Resource Management*, Vol.14, No.8, pp1308–32

Baird L. and Meshoulam I. (1988) Managing two fits of strategic human resource management, *Academy of Management Review*, Vol.13, No.1, pp116–28

Barney J. (1991) Looking inside for competitive advantage, *Academy of Management Executive*, Vol.9, No.4, pp49–61

Becker B. and Gerhart B. (1996) The impact of human resource management on organizational performance: progress and prospects, *Academy of Management Journal*, Vol.39, No.4, pp779–801

Boxall P. (1996) The strategic HRM debate and the resource-based view of the firm, *Human Resource Management Journal*, Vol.6, No.3, pp59–75

Boxall P. and Purcell J. (2003) *Strategy and Human Resource Management*, Basingstoke, Palgrave

Cassell C., Nadin S., Gray M. and Clegg C. (2002) Exploring human resource management practices in small and medium-sized enterprises, *Personnel Review*, Vol.31, No.6, pp671–92

Delaney J. and Huselid M. (1996) The impact of human resource management practices on perceptions of organizational performance, *Academy of Management Journal*, Vol.39, No.4, pp949–69

Delery J. (1998) Issues of fit in strategic human resource management: implications for research, *Human Resource Management Review*, Vol.8, No.3, pp289–309

Delery J. and Doty D. (1996) Modes of theorizing in strategic human resource management: tests of universalistic, contingency and configurational performance predictions, *Academy of Management Journal*, Vol.39, No.4, pp802–35

Eaton S. (2000) Beyond 'unloving care': linking human resource management and patient care quality in nursing homes, *International Journal of Human Resource Management*, Vol.11, No.3, pp591–616

Guest D. (1997) Human resource management and performance: a review and research agenda, *International Journal of Human Resource Management*, Vol.8, No.3, pp263–76

Guest D., Michie J., Sheehan M., Conway N. and Metochi M. (2000) *Effective People Management*, London, CIPD

Holbeche L. (2005) *The High Performance Organization: Creating dynamic stability and sustainable success*, Oxford, Elsevier

Huselid M. (1995) The Impact of HRM practices on training, productivity and corporate financial performance, *Academy of Management Journal*, Vol.38, No.3

Huang T. (2001) The effects of linkage between business and human resource management strategies, *Personnel Review*, Vol.30, No.2, pp132–51

Legge K. (2005) *Human Resource Management: Rhetoric and realities*, anniversary edition, Basingstoke, Palgrave.

MacDuffie J. (1995) Human resource bundles and manufacturing performance: organisational logic and flexible production systems in the world auto industry, *Industrial and Labor Relations Review*, Vol.48, No.2

Marchington M. and Wilkinson A. (2005) *Human Resource Management at Work*, London. CIPD

Miles R. and Snow C. (1984) Designing strategic human resource systems, *Organizational Dynamics*, Vol.13, No.1, pp36–52

Patterson M., West M., Lawthorn R. and Nickell S. (1997) *The Impact of People Management Practices on Business Performance*, London, IPD

Penrose E. (1959) *The Theory of the Growth of the Firm*, New York, Wiley

Peters T. (1987) *Thriving on Chaos*, New York, Harper & Row

Peters T. and Waterman R. (1982) *In Search of Excellence, Lessons from America's best run companies*, New York, Harper & Row

Pfeffer J. (1994) *Competitive Advantage through People: Unleashing the power of the workforce*, Boston, Harvard Business School Press

Pfeffer J. (1998) *The Human Equation*, Boston, Harvard Business School Press

Porter M. (1985) *Competitive Advantage: Creating and sustaining superior performance*, New York, Free Press

Purcell J., Kinnie N., Hutchinson S., Rayton B. and Swart J. (2003) *Understanding the People and Performance Link: Unlocking the black box*, CIPD Research Report, London, CIPD

Richardson R. and Thompson M. (1999) *The Impact of People Management Practices on Business Performance: A literature review*, London, CIPD

Sanz-Valle R., Sabater-Sánchez R. and Aragón-Sánchez A. (1999) Human resource management and business strategy links: an empirical study, *The International Journal of Human Resource Management*, Vol.10, No.4, pp655–71

Schuler R. and Jackson S. (1987) Linking competitive strategies with human resource management practices, *The Academy of Management Executive*, Vol.1, No.3, pp209–19

Snape E., Redman T. and Wilkinson A. (1993) Human resource management in building societies: making the transformation?, *Human Resource Management Journal*, Vol.3, No.3, pp44–61

Taylor S. (2005) *People Resourcing*, 3rd edition, London, CIPD

Truss C., Gratton L., Hope-Hailey V., McGovern P. and Stiles P. (1997) Soft and hard models of human resource management: a reappraisal, *Journal of Management Studies*, Vol.34, No.1, pp53–73

Truss C. (2001) Complexities and controversies in linking HRM with organizational outcomes, *Journal of Management Studies*, Vol.38, No.8, pp1121–49

West M., Borrill C., Dawson J., Scully J., Carter M., Anelay S., Patterson M. and Waring J. (2002) The link between the management of employees and patient mortality in acute hospitals, *International Journal of Human Resource Management*, Vol.13, No.8, pp1299–310

Wright P. and Snell S. (1998) Toward a unifying framework for exploring fit and flexibility in strategic human resource management, *Academy of Management Review*, Vol.23, No.4, pp756–72

Youndt M., Snell S., Dean J. and Lepak D. (1996) Human resource management, manufacturing strategy, and firm performance, *Academy of Management Journal*, Vol.39, No.4, pp836–66

# Translating theory into practice – an appraisal of HR practice

## LEARNING OBJECTIVES

- To evaluate the take-up of progressive HR practices within organisations
- To assess the reasons why theoretical links between people management and organisational performance fail to make the transition to organisational practice
- To discuss the barriers to high-performance working
- To discuss the nature and scope of the HR role in organisations
- To evaluate the concept of human capital and assess the nature, scope and value of tools, techniques and metrics for evaluating HR effectiveness

## INTRODUCTION

The previous chapter reviewed a range of research studies which have established a link between HR practice and organisational performance. While theoretical approaches can be criticised on conceptual and methodological grounds, they nevertheless paint a compelling picture of the economic and business case for good people management. The precise nature of the link remains unclear although Purcell *et al*'s (2003) work has provided insight into the so-called 'Black Box' problem or the what, why and how practices that influence organisational performance and business outcomes.

However, although the conceptual link between people management and organisational performance is well established, the empirical links are less secure. Theoretical developments are not translated into organisational practice and there is a large gap between the rhetoric of HRM and its practical implementation within organisations. The phrase 'people are our greatest asset' may have entered the management lexicon, but there is little evidence to suggest that research findings are having a significant influence within organisations or that business leaders are putting people management issues on a level with other business decisions.

Evidence suggests no increase in the adoption by organisations of progressive HRM practices. In other words, the idea of people as an organisation's greatest asset is not borne out by the reality of organisational practice. As Pfeffer and Sutton (2000: ix) put it,

> **Why is it that so many managers know so much about organisational performance, say so many smart things about how to achieve performance, and work so hard, yet are trapped in firms that do so many things they know will undermine performance?**

Several explanations can be offered for the pervasive and enduring gap between academic research and business practice. However, one explanation for the limited take-up of progressive HR practices by organisations can be attributed to the role and credibility of the HR function. A CIPD (2003) survey of over 1,000 HR practitioners from a variety of sectors reported a growth in the numbers employed in HR, higher levels of influence for the HR function compared with senior colleagues and a key role for HR in achieving business outcomes. However, the survey also reported a gap between HR strategies and their application; between HR strategies on paper and in practice, with HR practitioners more involved in the planning and development of strategy than its implementation. As one survey respondent (CIPD, 2003: 24) put it,

> **Anyone can read a book or policy document which gives the answers to 'how' to do something or 'how' to resolve an issue. HR needs to think more of the 'why' and then be able to lead on managing change.**

One third of HR practitioners reported their primary role as being strategic business partners, while the majority were inclined to see the function as operational rather than strategic. In other words, although the HR role is evolving and changing in line with changes in business priorities, the function still has some considerable way to go in establishing its strategic business credentials and making a real strategic contribution. As the CIPD (2003: 9) survey suggests, HR needs to become significantly more business-focused and strategic in the future.

The challenge for HR professionals appears to lie in the ability to communicate a clear and consistent message about the value of people and to develop effective tools and understanding to demonstrate the contribution of people to organisational effectiveness. Research by Purcell *et al* (2003) and others has demonstrated the ways in which effective HR policies and practices can deliver bottom-line performance and HR practitioners need to do more to drive such a strategic contribution.

This chapter evaluates trends in the take-up of high-performance progressive HR working practices within organisations and examines the reasons why theoretical linkages fail to make the transition to organisational reality. In particular, the analysis focuses on the HR role and the credibility of the HR function and HR practitioners in supporting business goals and making a contribution to organisational performance. There is, of course, much more to the effective management of people than the HR role, and issues relating to the creation of an environment that supports high performance are discussed in Chapters 4 and 5. Here, however, the analysis focuses specifically on the HR role and contribution. The final part of the chapter evaluates the concept of human capital and discusses a range of metrics in measuring the contribution of people to organisational success.

## THE TAKE-UP OF PROGRESSIVE HR PRACTICE IN ORGANISATIONS

As Chapter 2 outlined, high-performance working practices (HPW) reflect aspects of work organisation that result in improved organisational performance. Although discrepancies were noted within research studies of the precise aspects of HR practice that result in enhanced organisational performance, a consensus nevertheless appears to be emerging (EEF/CIPD, 2003: 7) of the common characteristics of HPW:

- appropriate selection and recruitment processes
- comprehensive induction programmes
- sophisticated and wide coverage of training
- coherent performance management systems
- flexibility of workforce skills
- job variety and responsibility
- teamworking
- frequent and comprehensive communication to employees
- use of quality improvement teams
- harmonised terms and conditions
- market-competitive pay
- use of rewards related to individual and/or group performance
- policies to achieve an appropriate work–life balance.

As Purcell *et al* (2003) have suggested, HPW practices improve organisational performance through three causal routes – by increasing employee skills and abilities; by promoting positive attitudes, increasing motivation and promoting discretionary behaviour; and by providing employees with opportunities at work to make full use of their skills and abilities

Few organisations, however, are applying high-performance HR practices. The Workplace Employee Relations Survey (WERS) (Cully *et al*, 1998) analysed the take-up of 16 core HR practices clustered around appraisal and reward, involvement and participation, training and development, status and security, and found that only 20 per cent of over 2,000 organisations sampled had half or more of these practices in place, and that only 2 per cent had ten or more in place. Guest *et al*'s (2000a) study, which centred on the nature and distribution of HR practices and covered over 800 different organisations in the UK, found a relatively low take-up of high-commitment HR practices. The research focused on 18 typical HR practices (eg recruitment and selection, training and development, appraisal, flexibility, job design, two-way communications, employment security, harmonisation) and found that only 1 per cent of organisations had more than three quarters of these practices in place and applying to most workers, and that 20 per cent of organisations made extensive use of less than one quarter of typical HR work practices.

Moreover, few organisations reported any plans to introduce high-commitment HR practices in the future. Guest *et al*'s (2000b) subsequent study of the 1998 Workplace Employee Relations Survey, covering 2,000 workplaces and over 28,000 workers, confirmed a positive link between greater use of HR practices and a range of outcomes such as productivity, labour costs, quality and financial performance. However, it found that the adoption of core HR practices was generally low, and that only 41 per cent of private sector workplaces and 70 per cent of public sector organisations represented were using more than half of the HR practices analysed.

A survey by the Engineering Employers Federation (EEF) in conjunction with the CIPD in 2003 analysed workplace initiatives which encapsulated some form of HPW, and found that while manufacturers were embracing some aspects of HPW, half of the firms studied had done so moderately, minimally, or not at all. The majority of firms used basic practices such as output monitoring and individual performance appraisals. The take-up of more imaginative initiatives such as employee involvement, individual/team incentives and profit-based pay was significantly lower.

The evidence thus points to a low adoption of progressive high-performance working practices across British industry. Moreover, even if organisations implement a wide range of HR practices it does not necessarily follow that these are embedded or effective. Studies have highlighted inconsistency, fragmentation and a 'pick and mix' approach to the implementation of HR practices (Truss *et al*, 1997).

## ACTIVITY . . .

Compare your organisation (or an organisation you are familiar with) against the list of HPW practices shown above.

To what extent has your organisation adopted high-performance working?

What have been the reasons for the adoption/non-adoption of progressive HR practices?

What scope exists within your organisation for the introduction of HPW?

## EXPLORING THE GAP BETWEEN RESEARCH EVIDENCE AND ORGANISATIONAL REALITY

Several explanations may be offered as to why theoretical and conceptual linkages between the management of people and organisational performance fail to make the transition to implementation and practice. The EEF/CIPD survey (2003: 20) identified a number of specific reasons for the non-adoption of HPW practices within manufacturing organisations. These were:

- *alternative strategies* – organisations might adopt alternative strategies such as increased outsourcing, new technology, improved recruitment and training which might be viewed as cheaper and better able to deliver results in the short term
- *system inertia* – the introduction of HPW requires change and may be resisted because organisations may get locked into their initial choice of practices and the switch to HPW may require investments in new production and distribution technologies with additional costs. More generally, the organisation may be resistant to change
- *mistrust* between management and employees can inhibit the introduction of HPW especially where poor employee relations exist or where there is a legacy of mistrust following redundancy exercises
- *costs* – there are additional costs involved in the introduction of HPW, particularly as such initiatives take time to design, implement and require time to become effective.

Wider situational factors that might inhibit the adoption or widespread implementation of HPW relate to the level and standing of HRM in the UK context, structural and cultural factors within organisations, and the 'ambiguous' role of the HRM function. Inevitably, these factors overlap, but their specific features are discussed below.

### The structure of financial markets

Sisson and Storey (2000: 9) have suggested that key features of the UK business system and the structure of UK financial markets have created an environment which is inhospitable to treating people as the key to success. Their analysis highlights the following features as significant;

- an overwhelming emphasis on shareholder value as the key business driver, as opposed to the interests of other stakeholders
- institutional share ownership by investment trusts and pension funds which encourages a focus on short-term profitability
- the relative ease of take-over which reinforces pressure on short-term profitability but also encourages expansion by acquisition and merger rather than by internal growth
- a premium on 'financial engineering' as a core organisational competence and domination of financial management over other functions.

In the UK national context, management performance is focused to meet annual, even quarterly, reporting targets which emphasise immediate returns and cause managers to resort to opportunistic, fire-fighting, reactive solutions. Such approaches inhibit the development of a long-term vision conducive to the adoption of high-performance HR practice. As Storey and Sisson (1993:76) put it,

> **short-term reporting periods tend to put pressure on managers to have recourse to opportunistic quick-fix agreements, firefighting solutions and Tayloristic job design methods which are built on command-and-control rather than the more time-consuming and consensus-seeking methods.**

Nationally, the effects can be seen in a traditional lack of investment in training and development in UK society and industry (Keep, 1989; Handy, 1987; Constable and McCormick, 1987). At the organisational level, this approach works against many HRM and HPW initiatives which are geared to a positive return over a longer time horizon. Marchington and Wilkinson (2005: 145–6) suggest that trends towards restructuring, delayering and devolvement within UK organisations have reduced the importance of HR issues at the expense of 'harder', production-oriented priorities.

## Occupational management labour markets

Features of the UK business system outlined above are reflected in the number of accountants in senior positions within British industry. The occupational structure of British senior managers has emphasised financial competence and the accountancy profession has been a recognised route into senior management. This has resulted in the dominance of accountancy logic and accountancy-driven management control systems (Storey and Sisson, 1993:76).

A dominant accounting terminology has served to undermine the contribution of people to organisational success as people management practices are difficult to quantify and measure.

However, organisational socialisation processes and power relations in organisations can serve to constrain and limit management education and professionalism.

## The informal organisation

The metaphor of an iceberg (see figure 5) is frequently used to contrast the formal and informal aspects of the functioning of organisations and to emphasise the importance of informal elements on behaviour at work.

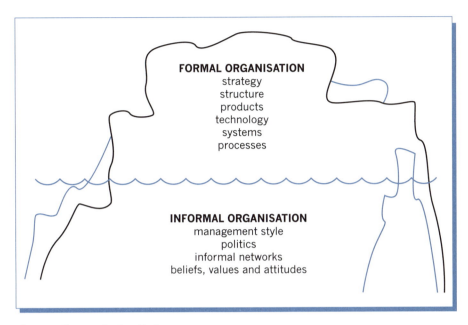

**Figure 5** *The organisational iceberg*

The formal structure of any organisation incorporates explicit elements which arise from the interactions and relationships of individuals and groups within the organisation such as hierarchy, strategy, structure, rules and regulations and lines of authority. However, the organisation is likewise based on more covert, 'hidden' systems of social relations, power and influence which can constrain and undermine formal, overt policies and systems.

People are unpredictable and have diverse needs, attitudes and motivations, and the informal organisation can serve to satisfy the social and psychological needs of employees outside the formal, official structure. The informal organisation can likewise influence attitudes towards change and may fuel employee scepticism stemming from past change initiatives. The informal organisation thus exerts an important influence on employee behaviour, and a lack of congruence between employee and organisational values, goals, relationships and norms of behaviour can serve to undermine or even de-rail wider organisational initiatives. The workings of the informal organisation can be an important factor in the ownership of initiatives such as HPW and the degree to which these become accepted and embedded.

## Power and politics in organisation

Organisational politics and issues of power, influence, co-operation and conflict form a part of the fabric of the informal organisation and represent an essential aspect of the functioning of the organisation. Pfeffer (1993: 204–5) defines power as

> [the] potential ability to influence behaviour, to change the course of events, to overcome resistance, and to get people to do things that they would not otherwise do. Politics and influence are the processes, the actions, the behaviours through which this potential power is utilized and realized.

Organisations are replete with political rivalries, departmental splits and functional conflicts that may make it difficult to translate corporate goals into specific workplace practices. Internal political issues can thus be critical in explaining why decision-makers choose to or choose not to implement HPW practices. They can also help to explain why organisations choose to implement particular sets of HR practices which are subsequently changed with the appointment of a new Chief Executive. However, even if senior decision-makers elect to adopt specific HR practices, it does not follow that these will be enacted or implemented by lower levels of management.

Purcell *et al*'s (2003) study highlighted the key role of front-line managers in influencing the relationship between the management of people and business performance. Front-line managers were identified as having a crucial role in implementing HR policies, practices and values. As Purcell *et al* (2003: x) put it,

> It is not enough to have performance-enhancing HR policies and practices – what also matters is the way they are implemented. Managers have discretion in the way they practice good people management in the sense of, for example, communicating, solving problems, listening to employee suggestions, providing coaching and guidance, treating employees fairly, and showing respect.

Front-line managers are defined as managers in the first line responsible for work groups comprising 10 to 25 people. Such managers are normally placed at the first level in the organisational hierarchy and are accountable to higher levels of management (Hutchinson and Purcell, 2003: 4). Front-line managers were identified as having a major role in the extent to which HR policies were implemented and embedded. As the Tesco example below illustrates, the way that store managers interpreted and applied standardised policies had a key impact on store performance.

## ILLUSTRATION

### Tesco

At Tesco, Purcell *et al* researched section managers in four stores in similar demographic areas and found that differences in store performance could be explained by differences in management behaviour. Tesco is a highly centralised organisation with standardised policies and procedures and processes, and each store is governed by the company routine handbook which provides detailed information on how every task is to be performed. This, in turn, provides a guide to management behaviour. Yet there were considerable variations. Store C in the study had a very controlling style of management and significantly also was the worst performing store. Although there was a heavy standardisation of routines and processes, local store managers were clearly able to exercise discretion in how they put policies into practice, which in turn had a marked impact on store performance.

Adapted from S. Hutchinson and J. Purcell (2003) Bringing policies to life: the vital role of front line managers, pp18–19

Notwithstanding the key impact of front-line managers on managing people, the devolution of HR responsibilities to front-line managers has left many unprepared, under-supported, poorly trained and having to choose between conflicting goals (Hutchinson and Purcell, 2003: 41). Devolvement has served to accelerate a focus on the short term by increasing the workloads of middle managers with a resulting emphasis on meeting targets that will affect their own performance. Such targets are invariably production-oriented rather than people-centred. As Marchington and Wilkinson (2005: 146) put it,

> **Without explicit proactive support from senior managers, and recognition and rewards for their work in the HR area, it is easy to understand why line managers do not take this part of their job seriously.**

Pressures on front-line managers

> **'You never get anything completed. There's so much to do, covering areas . . . doing the work of my team.'**

Responses of front-line managers

**'It feels like a treadmill at times. I have a lot of staffing issues, trainees and absentees ... It's about keeping your head above water.'**

S. Hutchinson and J. Purcell (2003) Bringing policies to life: the vital role of front line managers, pp18–19

In addition to a lack of skills and competences, Marchington and Wilkinson (2005: 144–5) suggest that the respective power bases of line managers and HR specialists can also be influential in the degree and extent of adoption of HR practices. Where HR work is held in disdain or where the status of the HR function is perceived to be peripheral to the functioning of the organisation, HR issues can become marginalised.

## ACTIVITY . . .

To what extent has your organisation devolved responsibility for HR issues to front-line managers?

What activities have been devolved?

How effectively do front-line managers perform their HR responsibilities?

How might you persuade a sceptical front-line manager to take his or her HR role more seriously?

## THE HR ROLE AND FUNCTION

A final factor in the application of HR theory into organisational practice can be attributed to the ambiguous role of the HR function within organisations. The HR function has been described as a 'Cinderella' function which has traditionally found it difficult to demonstrate a unique contribution to organisational success. This has contributed to a vicious circle, illustrated in Figure 6, from which it has proved difficult for the HR function to break out (Legge, 2005: 68).

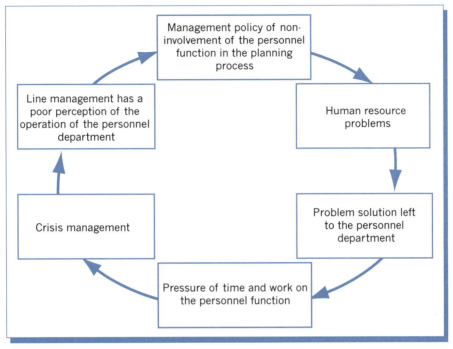

**Figure 6** *A vicious circle in personnel management*
Source: K. Legge (2005) *Human Resource Management: Rhetoric and realities*, p69

## PAUSE FOR THOUGHT . . .

Three professionals – an architect, an accountant and an HR manager – were discussing which (apart from the obvious one) was the oldest profession. The architect said: 'Well, of course it's architects because, if you remember your Bible, God created Heaven and Earth, and of course that's essentially an architectural job.' 'Ah,' said the accountant, 'but before he created the world, God created order out of chaos, and surely that's the essence of accountancy – so accountants must be the oldest profession.' 'Wrong!' said the HR manager. 'Where do you think the chaos came from?' (Legge 2005: 48)

What is your view? Does the HR function suffer from a lack of authority and status within organisations? If it does, why does it?

## ILLUSTRATION

### HR role and influence

'Anyone can read a book or policy document which gives the answer to "how" to do something or "how" to resolve an issue. HR needs to think more about the "why" and then be able to lead in managing change.'

'Give me one month and I'll make a good business person into a good HR person; too often you'd need an eternity to reverse the trick.'

'HR professionals need to understand business realities and create practical and pragmatic solutions to advise on best practice, meet legal requirements and be seen as an integral part of the business.'

– Respondents to CIPD (2003) HR survey *Where We Are, Where We're Heading*

'We hear ad nauseam about why aren't HR directors on the main board, and my answer to that would be, because not enough of them have the ability to prove the case that HR can contribute.'

'I think HR are probably the worst practitioners … They are the worst at developing their people, they are the worst at managing their people, their people are usually the most dissatisfied in the organisation, and they are the worst at doing the administration. So they are usually pretty poor. But they have grand ideas.'

– Respondents to Guest *et al* (2001) *Voices from the Boardroom* research report, CIPD

## ILLUSTRATION

### Thornton's scraps HR director post

Thornton's has scrapped its HR director post because the chief executive believes it is a 'luxury' the company cannot afford. Peter Burdon, chief executive of Thornton's, said the company dropped the post to save costs and that he would now take on much of the role, supported by a senior HR manager. 'We have been undergoing a cost review and concluded that the HR director was a luxury we could not afford. I have always taken a deep interest in HR,' said Burdon. Although he has no HR qualifications, Burdon said he had been managing people for 22 of his 24 years in business, which gave him the experience required for the job. 'The university of life is the best way of learning to manage people,' he said.

*People Management*, 15 July 2004, p9

The role played by HR professionals has evolved over time and continues to evolve and respond to changing business pressures and concerns. The roots of the HR function can be traced back to a welfare function concerned with improving the working conditions and well-being of employees. At the beginning of the twentieth century, many large organisations (eg Cadbury, Lever Brothers), often driven by strong moral and religious convictions, employed female welfare workers to look after the physical and social needs of women working on production lines. The Welfare Workers Association was established in 1913 and from this stemmed the professional body representing personnel practitioners. The welfare role subsequently broadened to incorporate responsibility for a range of employment issues including health and safety, wages and training, and in 1934 the Welfare Workers Association became the Institute of Labour Management, reflecting the broader and more formalised role of the personnel function. In 1946 the Institute of Personnel Management was formed reflecting the increased professionalism of the function. In 1994 this became the Institute of Personnel and Development and in 2000 the Chartered Institute of Personnel and Development.

There are a number of categorisations of the personnel/HR role reflecting different environmental and situational conditions (see Legge, 1978; Tyson and Fell, 1986; Storey, 1992). Ulrich (1998: 38) identified four distinct roles for HR professionals:

1   *Partner in strategy execution* – according to Ulrich, HR should be held responsible for defining the organisation's 'architecture' and ensuring fit between architecture and culture, competencies, rewards, governance, work processes and leadership.
2   *The administrative expert* role was concerned with improving efficiency by doing things quickly and more cost-effectively.
3   *The employee champion* role involved ensuring that employees felt committed to the organisation and its goals and involved training and developing line managers to get the best out of people, monitoring levels of employee morale, consulting on work processes.
4   *The change agent* role involved HR professionals in creating an appropriate culture and specifically mapping how to move from the present culture to the desired culture.

Ulrich developed his categorisation as a response to developments in the HR function, but his categorisation – in particular, his 'business partner' role – has been very influential in shaping the HR role. His original argument was that all four roles were to some extent business partners but within organisations there has been a selective adoption of his categorisation with 'business partner' emerging as the dominant model. The trend has been to equate the term 'business partner' with Ulrich's 'strategic partner' role to the exclusion of other roles. The *People Management* Guide to Recruitment Consultancies (2005: 16) reported that the number of advertisements seeking HR business partners had increased by 30 per cent in 2004, with an increasing number of organisations advertising for 'strategic' business partners.

However, the precise meaning of term 'strategic business partner' remains unclear and can vary from organisation to organisation. Moreover, the shift in organisations to the business partner model has not been accompanied by any significant new training and development activity for the function (Pickard, 2004: 30) and HR professionals and the strategic partners themselves are often unclear about the new role and what it involves.

The CIPD (2003) HR survey of over 1,000 HR practitioners from a range of industries and sectors found that only one in three HR practitioners saw his or her current role as that of strategic business partner, although many had aspirations to become more strategic. As the survey report (2003: 11) put it,

> **One third of practitioners currently see their primary role as being strategic business partners, one in four see themselves as change agents and fewer than 24 per cent as administrative experts. In terms of preferred roles, nearly three in five aspire to be business partners, while 23 per cent see their current role as business player – ie acting as coach, architect and facilitator; only 15 per cent see this as their preferred role ... possibly because they feel it would take them too far away from their HR moorings.**

A large number of HR professionals felt poorly equipped for a more strategic role, and the survey found a sizable gap between organisations' expectations of HR partners and partners' skills and knowledge. Key development needs were identified as business knowledge and strategy tools and skills of influencing and political astuteness.

## ILLUSTRATION

### Business partners at Royal Mail

Royal Mail has introduced the business partner role since the arrival of Tony McCarthy, group director of people, 18 months ago. Under his stewardship the organisation has adopted the Ulrich shared service model. Each of Royal Mail's regions will be represented by a business partner.

There are six capabilities of a business partner:

- *People and organisational development* – advising on HR interventions that would improve business performance

- *Leadership* – delivering results and building strong relationships
- *Personal credibility* – behaviours necessary for delivering projects in complex environments
- *Consulting* – in a shared service environment, the organisation is reliant on business partners delivering
- *Organisational design and development* – dealing with cultural change
- *Business knowledge* – understanding the commercial environment

Perfect partners, *People Management* Guide, April 2005, p19; **www.peoplemanagement. co.uk/recguide**

Ulrich (2005) recently adapted his HR role categorisation to five roles. The revised categories included employee advocate and human capital developer which replaced employee champion; functional expert which replaced administrative expert; strategic partner which incorporated the partner in strategy and change agent role; and leader. The revised categorisation is illustrated in Table 3 on page 74.

In the modified categorisation Ulrich stresses the employee advocate and human capital developer rules as forming the centre-piece of HR. However, the CIPD (2003) HR survey found that few senior HR practitioners saw themselves in such roles or aspired to such roles in the future. Over-emphasis on the strategic partner role appears to have had serious consequences for employee relations.

Research by Francis and Keegan (2005) highlighted the adoption by organisations of a range of HR initiatives to shift responsibility for HR issues in areas such as absence management, grievance-handling, coaching and counselling to line managers in order to free up HR practitioners to become more 'strategic'. Such initiatives included shared service centres, IT-driven changes to integrate HR activities, centralisation of HR administration, administrative templates and support packs for line managers to handle recruitment and discipline. The consequences of this shift have been problems related to loss of employee trust, costs to employee well-being and disenchanted practitioners and truncated careers. As Francis and Keegan (2005: 27) put it,

**The profession needs to reflect seriously on the consequences of devolving transactional tasks to line managers while locating HR advisers in distant service centres. As HR practitioners vanish from the shop floor, employees may lose trust and confidence in the HR function to advocate their needs.**

Table 3  *Evolution of HR roles*

| Mid-1990s | Mid-2000s | Evolution of thinking |
|---|---|---|
| Employee champion | Employee advocate (EA) Human capital developer (HC) | EA focuses on the needs of today's employee; HC developer focuses on preparing employees to be successful in the future |
| Administrative expert | Functional expert | HR practices are central to HR value. Some HR practices are delivered through administrative efficiency (eg technology, process redesign), and others through policies, menus and interventions |
| Change agent | Strategic partner | Being a strategic partner has multiple dimensions: business expert, change agent, strategic HR planner, knowledge manager, and consultant |
| Strategic partner | Strategic partner | As above |
| | Leader | Being an HR leader requires functioning in each of these four roles; however, being an HR leader also has implications for leading the HR function, collaborating with other functions, setting and enhancing the standards for strategic thinking, and ensuring corporate governance |

Source: Ulrich and Brockbank (2005) Role call, *People Management*, 16 June, p26

## ACTIVITY . . .

How would you categorise the HR role within your organisation? Which of Ulrich's role categorisations apply, and why? Do you see the need for the HR function to be performing roles outside those they are currently performing?

## THE CONCEPT OF HUMAN CAPITAL

The growing body of theoretical evidence demonstrating links between HR policy and practice and improved organisational performance have been accompanied by an emphasis on HR metrics or tools whereby the value and return on investment of an organisation's human assets can be measured and evaluated.

As suggested earlier, HR is unique among business functions in that it is hard to quantify the contribution made to the bottom line and this poses a distinct set of problems for financial reporting. The development of effective metrics that provide a robust measure of how HR adds value and the ability to measure the contribution of HR practice to organisational success represents a central concern for HR practitioners. This final section evaluates the concept of human capital, appraises a range of measurement tools and techniques and evaluates the extent to which organisations are undertaking external and internal reporting of HR issues.

The term 'human capital' is used to describe the organisation's human resources and the contribution they make to the organisation. Scarborough and Elias (2002: 9) define human capital as 'the competencies which employees apply to the production of goods and services for an employer'.

The distinction was made in Chapter 2 between human capital advantage and human process advantage, to the effect that human capital advantage clarifies what it is that is uniquely and exceptionally valuable about human resources, and human process advantage is focused on how managers might obtain, develop and retain valuable resources (Boxall and Purcell, 2003: 85). Human capital falls under the human capital advantage umbrella and refers to the stock of skills, experiences, competencies and knowledge assets in an organisation. Fundamentally, human capital is about measurement.

The concept of people as an organisational resource has its roots in the economic theory of human capital. The logic of human capital theory suggests that increasing the stock of human capital requires investment now for future returns. Thus investment in training and development can enhance the stock of an organisation's human capital just as an investment in technology can enhance physical capital. Equally, both can depreciate and become obsolete through neglect and lack of investment. The concept of human capital is relevant at both a macro, national level as well as a micro, organisational level and has implications for external and internal measurement and reporting.

## External reporting of human capital

As suggested earlier, the accountancy profession and accounting controls have been a prominent feature of British industry, and financial measures are pre-eminent indicators of organisational performance. Companies are by law required to produce an annual report and accounts in which they provide information about their financial and business performance. The financial statements that need to be included in published accounts include the profit and loss account (a summary of income and expenditure), balance sheet (a summary of the company's financial position at the end of the accounting year showing assets and liabilities) and a cash flow statement (showing how money has been raised to finance the business and how it has been spent).

There is, however, rarely any systematic accounting for 'hidden' intangible assets such as the knowledge of employees, the replacement costs of IT systems or the return on investment in training and development. As Scarborough and Elias (2002) suggest, management and accounting practices are insufficiently developed to enable human capital to be properly reflected in management decision-making and external reporting.

There is thus often a gap between the value of an organisation's tangible assets as shown on the balance sheet and its stock market value. Libert *et al* (2000) suggest that in 1978 the average book value represented 95 per cent of market value; ten years later the figure was 28 per cent. Today it is estimated that 80 per cent of stock market value is driven by assets that don't appear on the balance sheet – ie people, brand, knowledge and relationships. Companies such as Glaxo Wellcome and Microsoft are worth many times their balance sheet value. In a rapidly changing business environment, it is increasingly intangible factors – people, ideas, reputation – which underpin the best-performing businesses. Successful companies recognise that investing in these intangible aspects of their business is essential to their ability to create world-class, high-value-added products and services.

Human capital reporting was a key recommendation of the DTI sponsored 'Accounting for People' Task Force which highlighted the critical nature of the people element in the so-called intangible assets of growing organisational value. As Denise Kingsmill (2003), the Chair of the task force put it,

> **We need to develop a business culture that recognises that a company's investment in human capital is at least as important as its investment in plant and machinery. This means finding ways in which it can be measured and reported for the benefit of all the company's stakeholders.**

However, although the task force identified generic measures (eg absence levels, turnover figures) it stopped short of recommending any specific sets of measures for how organisations should gather and report information on human capital, with the result that there remains considerable uncertainty about the meaning of human capital management and how human capital-related information can be turned into practical measures for demonstrating how people management and development impacts on business performance.

In May 2004 the DTI launched plans to make an operational and financial review (OFR) a statutory requirement for company reporting from April 2006. However, the OFR remit was subsequently scaled down and quoted companies will now be required to produce a simpler, scaled-down 'business review'. Companies will still be required to provide information on employees and social and environmental matters where this is material to the business, but business reviews are likely to be less descriptive and more flexible. It is left to companies to decide what information to provide about employment and employees.

Intellectual capital can be crucial for an organisation yet it is generally excluded from external reporting because it is difficult to measure and there is no framework for assigning a value to human capital that would enable organisations to measure and account for changes and movements in human capital. Scarborough and Elias' (2002) study highlights the paradox of human capital; that the very features that make human capital so crucial to organisations are the same features that inhibit evaluation.

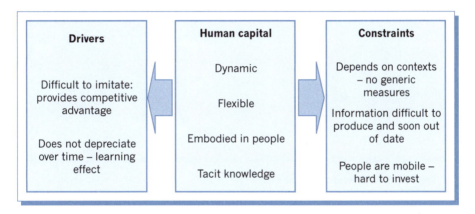

**Figure 7** *The paradox of human capital management*
Source: H. Scarborough and J. Elias (2002) *Evaluating Human Capital*, p5

## ILLUSTRATION

### Managing intellectual capital at Skandia

Skandia is a multinational insurance and financial services company based in Sweden with total assets of $35 billion and employing around 11,000 people worldwide. Since 1991 Skandia has developed a range of measures to assess its human capital. These measures include how customers are handled, how operational processes, business development and logistics are handled and measures of employee professional insights, applied experience and organisational learning.

Skandia has a Director of Intellectual Capital whose role is to develop and apply a systematic approach to valuing intangible assets. Leif Edrinsson reports to the Chief

Executive and is a member of the executive board. Skandia uses a balanced scorecard for measuring performance on financial and intellectual capital and have developed a model of intellectual capital (Figure 8).

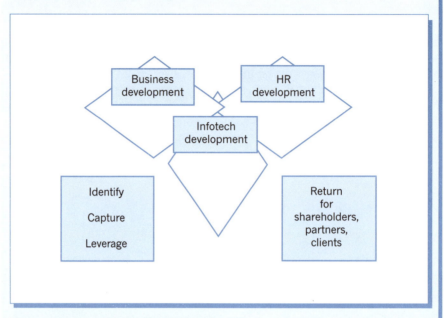

**Figure 8** *Skandia model of intellectual capital*

Skandia also includes a statement on human capital in its report and accounts. Visit the Skandia website to learn more about this organisation's approach to valuing and measuring its human capital assets:
**www.Skandia .com**
**www.fpm.com/script/UK/Jun93/930602.htm**

## Internal measures of human capital

Meaningful information also depends on the development of effective internal mechanisms to collect, analyse and evaluate human capital data.

### *The Balanced Scorecard*

The balanced scorecard (Kaplan and Norton, 2001) is one of the best-known techniques for aligning human capital to organisational performance. The underpinning rationale is that every organisation has multiple stakeholders or groups of individuals whose interests and requirements need to be satisfied for the organisation to be successful.

**Table 4** *The balanced scorecard*

| Element | Measures |
| --- | --- |
| Financial | Cash flow, return on capital, profitability |
| Customer | Market share, customer retention |
| Internal business processes | Quality, productivity, product cycle time |
| Learning and innovation | Percentage revenue from new products, research and development success rate |

Source: R. Kaplan and D. Norton (2001) Marked impact, *People Management*, 25 October, p54

Thus the requirements of investors are satisfied through financial performance and measured through profitability, return on capital, cash flow and market value. The requirements of customers are satisfied through the provision of a quality product or service and can be measured through market share, customer retention and customer attitudes. The requirements of employees are met through making the organisation a great place to work and can be measured through employee turnover, absence, retention and productivity.

The balanced scorecard is not specifically focused on human capital measurement but on the development of different measures in each area that meet the needs of the business over a period of time. It can thus be tailored to meet the specific needs of the organisation and represents a useful device for monitoring performance against a range of defined standards in a way that combines an evaluation of intangible assets and human capital with more conventional financial measures.

## HR scorecard

As highlighted in Chapter 2, best practice and configurational approaches have been concerned with establishing a quantifiable link between specific HR practices and organisational performance. Such approaches have advocated the use of HR-based measurement systems linked to the organisation's strategic aims and values. Becker *et al* (2001) draw on the experiences of a number of leading US companies to identify a range of processes which can be used to manage human resources as a strategic asset and measure the people contribution to business success. The consultancy firm Watson Wyatt have developed a Human Capital Index to evaluate the relationship between a range of HR practices such as recruitment and selection, reward, flexibility and communications and shareholder value (**www.watsonwyatt.com**).

## HR audits and benchmarking

HR audits are concerned with assessing the services provided by HR. Ulrich (1997) suggests that HR services can be clustered into six areas – namely: staffing, training and development, appraisal, rewards, organisational governance and communication – and

**Table 5**  *HR practice measures*

| Domain of HR activity | Possible measures |
|---|---|
| Staffing | Number of recruitment programmes, acceptance per offer ratio, time to fill vacancies, percentage of internally filled vacancies, cost of filling vacancies |
| Training and development | Number of training days and training programmes held per year, cost per trainee hour, percentage of employees involved in training, percentage of employees with development plans, percentage of payroll spent on training, payroll expense per employee, efficiency of training administration |

Adapted from D. Ulrich (1999) Measuring human resources: an overview of practice and a prescription for results, in R. Schuler and S. Jackson (eds) *Strategic Human Resource Management*, pp462–82

that measures can be identified for each area. Table 5 illustrates the types of measures that can be used in the areas of staffing and training and development.

Benchmarking is based on comparing specific HR policies and practices with those of other organisations either in the same sector or outside. Benchmarking might include retention and turnover rates, recruitment costs per new recruit, average days lost through absence, costs of the HR function as a percentage of total costs, ratio of HR staff to full-time employees.

## ACTIVITY . . .

Since 1984 the Saratoga Institute has been gathering information on different HR benchmarks against which subscribers can compare themselves. Visit the Saratoga Institute website for a demonstration of the Workforce Diagnostic System:

**www.pwcservices.com/saratoga-institute/workforce_diagnosis.html**

## ILLUSTRATION

**People management**

### People strategy toolkit for RBS

The Royal bank of Scotland Group (RBS) has launched an online toolkit for its HR staff, designed to measure the effectiveness of the organisation's people strategy and its impact on business performance. The RBS Human Capital Toolkit was rolled out earlier this month to more than 1,000 HR staff. It offers an extensive range of resources including surveys, measurements, research, benchmarking and reporting on all people management issues.

'This is a real tool to support the business,' said Greg Aitken, head of research and measurement at RBS. 'The point of human capital strategy is to understand the way we manage our people and the ultimate impact that has on the business.' HR staff can get information not only by business division, but also by sex, age and ethnicity. The toolkit also offers benchmarking in dozens of different areas and against a variety of competitor organisations. Along with the rollout of the toolkit, RBS has set up a Human Capital Board, which will prioritise initiatives to ensure the organisation gets the most out of its investment in people.

*People Management*, News, 27 January 2005, p9

## THE EXTENT AND USE OF HR MEASUREMENT

The implications of a human capital perspective for organisations is that employees are seen as an asset to be maximised rather than as a cost to be controlled and minimised. However, research evidence would suggest that few organisations understand the true worth of human capital, that the measures used are ill defined and that their application varies considerably between organisations.

Purcell *et al*'s (2003) study found that organisations undertook very little external reporting on human capital issues and focused instead on internal issues, with the balanced scorecard as the most commonly used measure. Scarborough and Elias' (2002) study of 10 UK-based firms from a variety of sectors found a similar picture and concluded that systems for evaluating and reporting human capital were 'rudimentary or non-existent' (Scarborough and Elias, 2002: 4). A summary of the approaches to human capital by the organisations studied is shown in Table 6 on pages 82–4.

As Table 6 illustrates, there are a number of diverse measures and approaches to human capital management. Scarborough and Elias (2002) suggest that high-performing successful organisations are not obsessed with measurement and that successful organisations create self-reinforcing loops that they act upon.

**Table 6** *Summary of approaches to human capital management*

| Company | Systems and practice | Impacts | External drivers | Internal drivers |
|---|---|---|---|---|
| Marks & Spencer | Mapping capabilities through skills survey | Skills mapping shows how employee skills support business plans | Downturn in late 1990s, drop in share price | Renewed emphasis on strategic planning |
| AutoCo | Records of capabilities profile of engineering population Performance review system Employee satisfaction index | Used to measure 'balanced scorecard' objectives Not used to evaluate the success of HR practices | | Changes within the HR function itself – 'getting smarter' HR as strategic partner to top management |
| Tesco | 'Balanced scorecard' (KPIs) on people People Insight Unit | Impact on the strategic planning process Annual people plan Skill profiles a basis for talent spotting | Highly competitive Focus on building customer loyalty | |
| Xerox | Total quality management approach Competence systems vary for different workforce populations Analysis of exit costs | HR function focused on creating value for the customer Performance profiles linked to career progression | Firm's loss of patent | |
| Norwich Union Insurance | Balanced Scorecard Transparent systems for career development and reward Training frameworks Brand values | Support reward and development Link into wider strategic goals: profit, morale and service | Merger between CGU and Norwich Union | |

**Table 6** *continued*

| Company | Systems and practice | Impacts | External drivers | Internal drivers |
|---|---|---|---|---|
| Motorola | Targeted on their leadership population – Learning Leadership and performance team 'Talent web' and use of IT Leadership assessment model | Leadership supply Supports system of reward and development | 'War for talent' | |
| Shell | Define basic, higher-level and leadership competencies Linked to formal assessment and used to identify skill gaps Emphasis on corporate values Balanced scorecard Focus on building talent | Improve leadership capacity Deliver the firm's talent promises Implements people strategy | Long-term development Growth and performance the major drivers More rigorous measurement systems a response to competitive pressures | Complements corporate social responsibility goals |
| BT | Overcoming reliance on headcount numbers In key areas review skill capability Brightstar programme Balanced scorecard linked to performance-related pay | | | Decade of downsizing Shift to learning v training linked to career ownership development Greater internal mobility |

**Table 6** *continued*

| Company | Systems and practice | Impacts | External drivers | Internal drivers |
|---|---|---|---|---|
| BAE Systems | Performance-centred Leadership competence-based system provides effective leadership supply for top 650 management population<br>Improves identification and retention of talent<br>Links to training and development outcomes | Provided coherence to leadership planning | Merger with Marconi | Strategic shift from engineering to systems<br>Development of corporate HR strategy has given HR strategic role |
| CityCo | Less systematic approach to evaluating human capital<br>Performance of certain individuals measured through revenue benchmarks | Bonuses for retaining staff | Some consultants pay attention to HRM | |

Source: H. Scarborough and J. Elias (2002) *Evaluating Human Capital*, pp51–2

As they put it (Scarborough and Elias, 2002: x),

> **Measures are less important than the activity of measuring – of continuously developing and refining our understanding of the productive role of human capital within particular settings. By embedding such activities in management practices, and linking them to the business strategy of the firm, firms may yet be capable of developing a more coherent and ultimately strategic approach to one of the most powerful, if elusive, drivers of competitiveness.**

## KEY LEARNING POINTS

- Despite research evidence suggesting a positive link between the management of people and organisational performance, there is limited evidence of the adoption of HPW or progressive HR practices within British organisations.
- There are several underlying reasons why theoretical links between HR practice and organisational performance fail to make the transition to organisational reality, and one reason relates to the ambiguity of the HR role.
- Different categorisations of the HR role have been proposed which reflect different situational and environmental conditions. Particularly influential has been Ulrich's (1998) concept of 'business partner', which has become the dominant organisational model. However the term 'business partner' remains contested and there is evidence that the widespread focus on business partnership has adversely affected employee relations
- The development of measures to establish the contribution of people to organisational success is crucial in demonstrating the value-added of people as an organisational resource but the methodology of human capital is problematic and under-developed.

### Additional reading

Davenport T. (1999) *Human Capital*, San Francisco, Jossey Bass

Edvinsson L. and Malone M. (1997) *Intellectual Capital*, London, Piatkus

Fitz-Enz J. (2000) *The ROI of Human Capital*, New York, Amacon

CIPD, *Human Capital Reporting*, **www.cipd.co.uk/guides**

Kaplan R. and Norton D. (2000) *The Strategy-Focused Organisation*, Boston, Harvard Business School Press

Likierman A. (2005) How to measure the performance of HR, *People Management*, 11 August, pp44–5

Manocha R. (2005) Grand totals, *People Management*, 7 April, pp27–31

Mayo A. (2001) *The Human value of the Enterprise*, London, Nicholas Brealey

*Personnel Today* (2002) Delivering HR strategy, 24 September, pp25–30
**www.personneltoday@rbi.co.uk**

Pfeffer J. (1997) Pitfalls on the road to measurement: the dangerous liaison of human resources with the ideas of accounting and finance, *Human Resource Management*, Vol.36, Fall 1997, pp357–65

Whiteley P. (2000) Intellectual investments, *Personnel Today*, 7 November, p12

**Web-based sources of information**

**www.sveiby.com**

**www.watsonwyatt.com**

**www.mayolearning.com**

**www.humanvalue.net**

**www.hcindex.com**

**www.accountingforpeople.gov.uk**

## REFERENCES

Becker B., Huselid M. and Ulrich D. (2001) *The HR Scorecard. Linking People, Strategy and Performance*, Boston, Harvard Business School Press

Beckett H. (2005) Perfect partners, *People Management*, 16 April, pp16–23

Boxall P. and Purcell J. (2003) *Strategy and Human Resource Management*, Basingstoke, Palgrave

CIPD (2003) HR Survey. *Where we are, Where we're heading*, Report, October

Constable J. and McCormick R. (1987) *The Making of British Managers*, London, British Institute of Managers

Cully M., Woodlands S., O'Reilly A., Dix G., Millward N., Bryson A. and Forth J. (1998) *The 1998 Workplace Employee Relations Survey: First Findings*, London, DTI

EEF/CIPD (2003) *Maximising Employee Potential and Business Performance: The role of high-performance working*, London, EEF/CIPD

Francis H. and Keegan A. (2005) Slippery slope, *People Management*, 30 June, pp26–31

Guest D., Michie J., Sheehan M., Conway N. and Metochi M. (2000a) *Effective People Management*, London, CIPD

Guest D., Michie J., Sheehan M., Conway N. (2000b) *Effective People Management: Initial fndings of the Future of Work study*, London, CIPD

Guest D., King Z., Conway N., Michie J., Sheehan-Quinn M. (2001) *Voices from the boardroom*, Research Report, London, CIPD

Handy C. (1987) *The Making of Managers*, London, MSC/NEDO/BIM

Hutchinson S. and Purcell J. (2003) *Bringing Policies to Life: The vital role of front-line managers in people management*, Executive Briefing, London, CIPD

Kaplan R. and Norton D. (2001) Marked impact, *People Management*, 25 October, pp52–7

Keep E. (1989) A training scandal?, in Sisson K. (ed.) *Personnel Management in Britain*, Oxford, Blackwell, pp177–202

Kingsmill D. (2003) Accounting for People Consultation Paper, 20 May, **www.accountingforpeople.gov.org**

Legge K. (1978) *Power, Innovation and Problem-Solving in Personnel Management*, London, McGraw-Hill

Legge K. (2005) *Human Resource Management, Rhetorics and Realities*, anniversary edition, London, Palgrave

Libert B., Samek S. and Boulton R. (2000) *Cracking the Values Code: How successful businesses are creating wealth in the new economy*, Harper Business

Marchington M. and Wilkinson A. (2005) *Human Resource Management at Work*, 3rd edition, London, CIPD

*People Management*, 15 July, 2004, p9

*People Management*, 27 January 2005, p9

Pickard J. (2004) One step beyond, *People Management*, 30 June 2004, pp27–31

Pfeffer J. (1993) Understanding power in organizations, in Mabey C. and Mayon-White B. (eds) *Managing Change*, 2nd edition, London, Paul Chapman Publishing, pp201–11

Pfeffer J. and Sutton R. (1999) *Knowing-Doing Gap: How smart companies turn knowledge into action*, Boston, Harvard Business School Press

Purcell J., Kinnie N., Hutchinson S., Rayton B. and Swart J. (2003) *Understanding the People and Performance Link: Unlocking the black box*, CIPD Research Report, London, CIPD

Scarborough H. and Elias J. (2002) *Evaluating Human Capital*, CIPD Research Report

Sisson K. (ed.) (1994) *Personnel Management A comprehensive guide to theory and practice in Britain*, 2nd edition, Oxford, Blackwell

Sisson K. and Storey J. (2000) *The Realities of Human Resource Management*, Buckingham, Open University Press

Storey J. (1992) *Developments in the Management of Human Resources*, Oxford, Blackwell

Storey J. and Sisson K. (1993) *Managing Human Resource and Industrial Relations*, Buckingham, Open University Press

Truss C., Gratton L., Hope-Hailey V., McGovern P. and Stiles P. (1997) Soft and hard models of human resource management: a reappraisal, *Journal of Management Studies*, Vol.34, No.1, pp53–73

Tyson S. and Fell A. (1986) *Evaluating the Personnel Function*, London, Hutchinson

Ulrich D. (1998) HR with attitude, *People Management*, 13 August, pp36–9

Ulrich D. (1999) Measuring human resources: an overview of practice and a prescription for results, in Schuler R. and Jackson S. (eds) *Strategic Human Resource Management*, pp462–82

Ulrich D. and Brockbank W. (2005) Role call, *People Management*, 16 June, p26

PART 2

# THE ORGANISATIONAL ARCHITECTURE OF HIGH PERFORMANCE

# People in organisations – discretionary behaviour, employee engagement and organisational performance

## LEARNING OBJECTIVES

- To examine perspectives on individual behaviour and concepts of perception, attitudes, values and emotions
- To evaluate the concept of discretionary behaviour and the link with employee attitudes and organisational performance
- To discuss the relevance of discretionary behaviour to organisational performance
- To identify the features of an organisational climate conducive to high performance

## INTRODUCTION

In 2001 the Chartered Institute of Personnel and Development (CIPD) published new standards of professional competence against which entrants into the HR profession would be assessed. Underpinning these professional standards was the CIPD's strategic vision of HR professionals as 'thinking performers'. The 'thinking performer' concept reflected a behavioural, work-based model of HR professionals as individuals who consciously and continuously seek to challenge existing practices with a view to improving these; to add value to organisational processes and activities in ways that support organisational goals; to proactively and creatively respond to 'customers' in a way that creates customer advantage.

As Ted Johns (2003), Chief External Examiner for the CIPD's professional qualification programme, puts it,

> **The thinking performer keeps in touch with the outside world, remains open-minded about change, understands the organisation's strategy, networks with customers, develops innovations that yield 'customer' advantage, prioritises strategically, focuses on the corporate contribution and maintains continuous professional development.**

## CIPD PROFESSIONAL STANDARDS

- *Personal drive and effectiveness* – a positive, 'can-do' mentality, anxious to find ways round obstacles, willing to exploit all available resources to achieve objectives
- *People management and leadership* – the motivation of others towards the achievement of shared goals, not only through formal authority but by personal example, a collaborative approach, professional credibility
- *Business understanding* – awareness of financial issues, of customer priorities, of the necessity for cost-benefit calculations in change initiatives
- *Professional and ethical behaviour* – professional skills, technical knowledge combined with integrity in decision-making
- *Added-value result achievement* – to achieve goals which deliver value-added outcomes for the organisation
- *Continuing learning* – commitment to continuous improvement and learning
- *Analytical and creative thinking* – the application of a systematic business-focused approach with innovation and creativity in problem-solving and seizing opportunities
- *Customer focus* – concern with perceptions of customers and willingness to act on customer feedback
- *Strategic thinking* – the ability to create an achievable vision for the future, to foresee longer-term developments, to envisage outcomes and their likely consequences, to select sound courses of action, to rise above the day-to-day detail, to challenge the status quo
- *Communication, persuasion and interpersonal skills* – the ability to transmit information to others convincingly and clearly, listening skills, sensitivity to the emotional, attitudinal and political aspects of organisational life

The concept of the 'thinking performer' can be broadened to include all employees whatever their role or level in the organisational hierarchy. The concept is based on the idea that people in organisations should be capable of delivering *operational results* in the areas for which they are accountable but that they should also *think about and reflect upon* what they are doing, how it adds value and whether it could be done differently. The underlying assumption is that all employees have the ability to engage in discretionary behaviour. Managers in particular have discretion in the way they apply specific HR practices and their behaviour towards employees.

The 'thinking performer' concept reflects wider changes in the world of work (see Chapter 1) and the implications of organisational restructuring, in the light of wider competitive pressures, for managers and employees. Adding value has become the new corporate mantra, especially in the service sector. In other words, the challenge for organisations is to stimulate employees at all levels to engage in discretionary effort or organisational citizenship behaviour, the type of positive, productive behaviour of employees motivated to 'go the extra mile'. The type of behaviour that cannot be enforced or commanded but relies on employee willingness to deliver.

## ILLUSTRATION

### The changed context of work

*A century ago, at the height of the scientific management revolution, companies broke complex manufacturing jobs into sequences of simpler tasks for which industrial engineers and managers set efficient work methods and performance standards. Companies could then hire uneducated, unskilled employees and train them to do a single task ... Today, this mode of work is virtually obsolete. Whatever the organisation – manufacturer or service provider, private or public, for-profit or not-for-profit – all of its employees need to understand and be able to implement its strategy. Much of the work done today is mental rather than physical. Automation has reduced the proportion of people in organisations who do manual work.*

*Employees are involved in more discretionary tasks, such as product development, marketing and customer relations. The challenge for organisations today is to how to enlist the hearts and minds of all their employees. Even those employees involved in direct production and service delivery must strive for continuous improvements in quality, reducing costs and process times to meet customers' expectations and keep up with the competition. Employees have to understand who their customers are, so they can find innovative ways to create value for them. Doing the job as it was done before is unlikely to be enough.*

Kaplan and Norton (2001) Marked impact, *People Management*, 25 October, p52

This chapter examines the concept of discretionary behaviour and the link with organisational performance. This is anchored in an initial review of perspectives of individual behaviour and concepts of perception, attitudes, values and emotions. The underlying assumption is that discretionary behaviour is closely linked to employee perceptions of fairness and equity at the workplace and that employee attitudes, views and perceptions of fairness can be influenced by a whole raft of HR and organisational practices which in turn shape workplace behaviour. Enlisting the hearts and minds of employees requires the sustained development of an organisational climate that is conducive to high performance and contribution. Chapter 5 develops this theme and is focused specifically on the process of motivation and engagement and its link to discretionary effort.

## PERSPECTIVES ON INDIVIDUAL BEHAVIOUR

At the workplace, an understanding of employee behaviour, and the attitudes, values and emotions that influence behaviour, can be valuable for a variety of reasons. As shown in

Chapter 6, it can be used to guide recruitment and selection strategies and form the basis for matching individuals to jobs, teams and the organisation. Understanding the components of individual behaviour can help make sounder predictions about future behaviour. As Chapter 11 illustrates, in situations of uncertainty and change, individual attitudes and values may harden and resist and inhibit change and contribute to conflict and under-performance.

In this chapter aspects of individual behaviour and difference are examined with a view to exploring and explaining the link between behaviour and human process advantage, or the way that people work, individually and collectively, to sustain high levels of organisational performance. As Chapter 2 has shown, HR practices in recruitment, selection, learning and development and reward can contribute to human capital advantage but such practices can be readily emulated. What is needed for superior organisational performance is a combination of human capital advantage and human process advantage.

As Boxall and Purcell (2003, p86) have suggested,

> **Human Resource Advantage, or exceptional value in human resources, can be traced to better people employed in organisations with better processes.**

However, organisational processes need to be applied fairly and equitably if they are to influence levels of satisfaction, commitment and loyalty to the organisation and lead to improved performance. Attitudes, values and emotions play a key role in employee perceptions of the fair application of organisational processes.

## Individual perception and attribution

The process of perception is a key factor in individual behaviour. Buchanan and Huczynski (2004: 215) define perception as 'the dynamic psychological process responsible for attending to, organising and interpreting sensory data'. Essentially, perception relates to the way in which we make sense of our environment and interpret and respond to events and people in the environment around us.

However, we do not receive information about what is happening around us passively and dispassionately or in the same way as others. We categorise and make sense of events and situations according to our own unique and personal frame of reference which reflects our personality, our past experiences, our knowledge, our expectations and current needs, our priorities and interests. Personality is a key influence on the process of perception. As Bowditch and Buono (2001: 46) suggest,

**Our personality acts as a kind of perceptual filter or frame of reference which influences our view of the world.**

It is thus our personal perception of our social and physical environment that shapes and directs our behaviour rather than some objective understanding of an external reality. The perceptual process is illustrated in Figure 9.

We are routinely subjected to a vast range of sensory data which requires sifting, sorting and interpreting and our perceptual process enables us to focus on certain stimuli that are significant to us and to ignore others. In other words, we use perceptual filters to identify or ignore sensory data. Perceptual filters can be external – for example, our attention is drawn more readily to stimuli that are large, colourful, loud, bright, and distinct, and affected by the context in which they are received. Internally, our perceptual process is influenced by our past learning and experiences, our current needs and priorities, by our personality, motivation and intelligence – all of which predisposes us to pay attention to certain stimuli over others.

This readiness to respond to certain stimuli in certain ways is referred to as the individual's *perceptual set* (Buchanan and Huczynski, 2004: 221) or our own, individual and unique version of our environment and our place in it, as illustrated in Figure 10 on page 96.

Our perceptual set relates to the meanings we attach to people, events and information from our environment and is influenced by a wide range of internal and situational factors. However, in making sense of our environment, we frequently make inferences or assumptions about what we perceive. We group shapes and patterns into meaningful

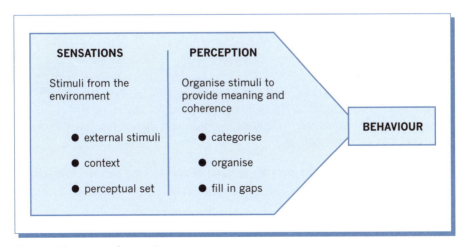

**Figure 9**  *The process of perception*

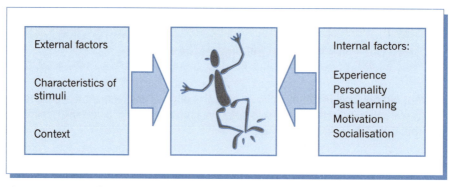

**Figure 10** *Factors influencing the perceptual set*

categories and tend to 'fill in gaps' where information is incomplete or ambiguous. Our perception of other people, in particular, can be distorted and we can make assumptions about the personalities, motivations and attitudes of others which can in turn influence our interaction with them. This so-called process of *perceptual distortion* can result in a range of organisational problems and conflicts. There are two related aspects of perceptual distortion that can impact on social interaction.

*Stereotyping* refers to the way in which we categorise people who we perceive to share similar characteristics – eg people with red hair have a quick temper, Scotsmen are mean, Americans are loud and brash. The *halo/horns effect* relates to the process of allowing a single characteristic to affect our overall perception of a person. The halo/horns effect has particular resonance for the process of selection where aspects of personal appearance can influence decisions of competence and suitability. Our perception of a person, once formed, can be enduring and we have a tendency to reinforce our perception by shaping what we see and hear so that this is consistent with our evaluation. The process of clinging to our perceptions is known as *perceptual defence* (Bowditch and Buono, 2001: 42).

## ACTIVITY . . .

*A man and his son were driving home from a football match when they were involved in a serious accident. The man was killed and his son seriously injured and rushed to hospital. In the operating theatre the surgeon recognised the boy and cried 'My God, it's my son!'*

Have you been able to understand this scenario, or did you have difficulty in making sense of it?

Could it be that we commonly perceive surgeons to be male?

Can you identify other common stereotypes at the workplace and what gives rise to them?

Closely linked to the process of perception is that of *attribution*, which relates to the process of attaching or attributing causes or reasons to events, actions and behaviours (Buchanan and Huczynski, 2004: 229). In attributing causes to situations we tend to look at people's abilities, skills and personalities (internal causality) or aspects of the situation or context in which the event has taken place (external causality). Our judgements about others are strongly influenced by whether we perceive a situation to arise from internal or external causes – eg a manager might attribute employee under-performance to laziness, lack of ability, or poor motivation rather than to a poorly designed job or work environment. As with perception, the process of attribution can be subject to individual bias.

## ACTIVITY . . .

*Val and Mary are senior university lecturers based in the Midlands. They have been working on a major research project and have had a paper accepted for an Industrial Relations conference in London. On the day of the conference they are waiting for the 6.30 am train to London when they meet the Dean of the business school waiting for the same train. 'Hello!' he says when he sees them. 'Are you off shopping?'*

How has the Dean perceived and interpreted the meeting with the two senior lecturers?

Can you provide similar practical examples to illustrate distortions or errors in personal perception?

What are the implications of perceptual distortion at the workplace?

## Attitudes, values and beliefs

In an organisational context, employee attitudes represent an important barometer of performance-related behaviours. Employee attitudes can affect levels of morale, commitment to the organisation, levels of absenteeism and, as we shall see later in this chapter, the nature and scope of discretionary behaviour which influences the level and quality of performance.

Attitudes refer to a predisposition to respond to events, situations and people in a positive or negative way. Thus employees may hold positive or negative views of their work and the organisation which can in turn influence their level of commitment and loyalty. Moreover, attitudes may be formed collectively within organisations and may become embedded into the culture of an organisation.

Attitudes are commonly regarded as having three component elements:

■ cognitive – the knowledge and beliefs held about an event, person, place

- affective – feelings/emotions about the event, person, place
- behavioural – the inclination to behave in a certain way as a means of responding to knowledge, feelings and emotions.

It is generally held that attitudes are shaped by beliefs and values. As Mullins (2005: 362) suggests, an attitude can be regarded as a state of readiness to respond in a certain way; beliefs are concerned with what is known/understood about the world, values are concerned with what is right and desirable. Mullins (2005: 362) quotes Gross that

> **to convert a belief into an attitude, a 'value' ingredient is needed which, by definition, is to do with an individual's sense of what is desirable, good, valuable, worthwhile and so on.**

O'Reilley and Pfeffer (2000) suggest that employees whose personal values are aligned with those of the organisation demonstrate higher levels of motivation and commitment, lower levels of turnover and better levels of performance and productivity. The implication is that organisational commitment is affected by individual attitudes, values, beliefs and emotions about organisational strategy and practice.

## ILLUSTRATION

### Help staff find meaning in their work

A third of employees think company values do not reflect their own, while a fifth feel no pride in working for their employer, new research has found.

The study *Meaning at Work*, by human capital management consultancy Penna, was based on interviews with 1,700 employees. It found a mismatch between employees' and directors' feelings, 90 per cent of directors believing their staff shared the same or similar values. But 6 per cent of people surveyed felt the organisation's values directly contradicted their own. The report concluded that this 6 per cent – so-called 'corporate terrorists' – couldn't be helped, and that employers should identify and 'exit' them. The report also said that companies should dedicate resources to creating meaning for others. If firms put effort into creating meaning, 55 per cent of employees said they would be more motivated, 42 per cent would be more loyal and 32 per cent would take more pride in their work.

Source: K. Hope (2005) *People Management*, 25 November, p10

Because of the importance of employee attitudes in organisational performance a number of methods have been devised to measure attitudes. Usually employee attitude surveys attempt to assess the cognitive element of attitudes or the knowledge and beliefs that employees hold about their work and the organisation.

However, the link between attitudes and behaviour is inconclusive. Although an attitude may indicate a predisposition to behave in a certain way this may not be realised for a variety of situational factors or because of social pressures on an individual to behave in a certain way. Attitudes may also differ in intensity and importance.

## ACTIVITY . . .

### Richer Sounds employee attitude survey results

*91% agreed that when they had a local problem the top management of the company were sympathetic and keen to help.*

*94% said they are kept well informed of what is going on in the company.*

*99% agree that Richer Sounds strongly believes in promoting from within.*

*97% said that Richer Sounds are considerate of family situations of employees.*

*91% said that they have the chance to contribute to the company's development.*

*92% agreed that it is fun working for Richer Sounds.*

*87% agreed that when the company makes a mistake, they had the opportunity to mention it.*

Taken from: J. Leary-Joyce (2004) *Becoming an Employer of Choice*, CIPD, p199

What do you consider to be the key factors in designing and implementing an employee attitude survey?

## Emotions

Studies of organisations often overlook the effects on behaviour of feelings and emotions. However, emotions are a natural feature of our psychological make-up and affect our behaviour at work just as they affect all aspects of our lives. As Wilson (2004: 99–100) puts it,

> **Feelings connect us with our realities and provide internal feedback on how we are doing, what we want and what we might do next ... Being in organisations involves us in worry, envy, hurt, sadness, boredom, excitement, and other emotions.**

Some jobs, particularly in service sector industries, contain a strong emotional content where employees may be required to demonstrate emotions such as caring for customers, being friendly, smiling and efficient. As Robbins (2003: 37) puts it, emotional labour requires employees to 'express organisationally desired emotions during interpersonal transactions'. This can create a dilemma for people when their job requires them to exhibit emotions that conflict with their actual feelings.

However, the creation of an organisational environment where positive emotions are encouraged (eg hope, pleasure, happiness, humour, excitement, joy, pride, involvement) can result in improved organisational performance, lower employee turnover and better health. As West (2005: 38) puts it,

> **When we feel positive emotions we think in a more flexible, open-minded way, and consider a much wider range of possibilities than if we feel anxious, depressed or angry ... Similarly, we are likely to feel greater self-control, cope more effectively and be less defensive in the workplace.**

The concept of emotional intelligence has emphasised the importance of emotions in organisational life. As Redman and Wilkinson (2002: 62) suggest, emotional intelligence relates to 'the ability to perceive, understand and express our feelings accurately and to control our emotions so that they work for us, not against us'. Emotional intelligence is seen as important in a range of social interactions and in individual adaptability and psychological well-being.

Research by Goleman (1998) has suggested that emotional intelligence is a crucial factor in leadership and that it accounts for over 85 per cent of the performance of effective leaders. Goleman identified 20 behavioural competencies associated with emotional intelligence which he grouped into the categories of self-awareness, self-management, social awareness and social skills.

## PAUSE FOR THOUGHT . . .

Read the following email sent by an undergraduate university student to his mother. Examine your perceptual process and emotional response while reading the letter. Did you find yourself making stereotypical assumptions? What does this tell you about your perceptual set, your attitudes, your values, your beliefs?

*Dear Mum*

*I know it's been a while since I was last in touch but I've been pretty busy. It's been an eventful few weeks so you might want to make sure you're sitting down while you read this.*

*Life at university is great and I'm settling in well but my room in halls wasn't ready for me when I arrived. Sleeping in the doorway of the newsagents was OK but it got a bit cold so I moved in with my friend Jake. He's great. Although he's only a couple of years older than me he's a real entrepreneur and has a chain of clubs where you can also get a massage. He makes shed-loads of money and says I can work for him too.*

*Jake's place is great but it's a bit untidy and I have developed a nasty little rash which I can't seem to get rid of.*

*Also Jake uses a lot of talcum powder in his clubs and one day the police came and took it away. They also took me away. But the policewoman was very nice to me and even came to visit me in prison. She's quite a bit older than me but when I get released I'm planning to move in with her and her three children. I know you'll like her. She used to live and work in Chicago and I'm sure you'll be interested in talking to her about that.*

*Well that's about it . . .*

*Now let me tell you that*

*I don't have a friend called Jake*

*I'm not in prison*

*I don't have a rash and I'm not romantically involved. But I did get a D for my Business Studies report and have spent my monthly allowance over one weekend and I wanted you to understand that things could be a lot worse.*

*Love you lots, Mum,*

*Rich*

## DISCRETIONARY BEHAVIOUR

In any work role or situation employees have a degree of choice and discretion over how they perform their tasks and responsibilities. The amount of discretion may be large or it

101

may be constrained by the nature of the production system and other situational factors. Nevertheless, as Appelbaum *et al* (2000: 25) put it,

**In any formal system of work controls, some effort remains that workers contribute at their discretion.**

Fox (1974: 16) distinguished between prescriptive and discretionary elements in work roles and suggested that 'task range' or the nature and scope and variety of tasks associated with a particular role could be highly specific or diffuse. In other words, the behaviours called for by the work role can be specifically defined and offer little choice in the way the work is done as in the case of an assembly line operative required to routinely and repetitively perform a simple set of tasks.

Alternatively, work role behaviours can require the use of a considerable amount of discretion in the way the job is performed as in the case of senior managers. Here what is required (Fox, 1974: 19) is not

**trained obedience to specific external controls, but the exercise of wisdom, judgement, expertise. The control comes from within – it is, in the literal sense, self-control. The occupant of the role must himself chose, judge, feel, sense, consider, conclude what would be the best thing to do in the circumstances, the best way of going about what he is doing.**

According to Fox (1974), Taylorism and scientific management focused on limiting discretion. Breaking down jobs into their most simple component elements, prescribing the way in which tasks were performed, providing close supervision and bureaucratic rules and regulations served to create a mutually reinforcing cycle of low trust relations. Nevertheless, Fox (1974: 19–20) argued that

**however elaborate the external controlling structure of mechanical, administrative, technical, or policy prescriptions ...no role can be totally diffuse or totally specific ... Even in tightly controlled jobs some residual element of discretion always remains.**

Increasingly, as organisations move into the so-called post-Fordist era and shift towards greater flexibility and responsiveness in a complex and turbulent environment, the challenge is to get employees to work 'beyond contract' and demonstrate a willingness to be flexible and use their imagination, creativity, initiative and enthusiasm in ways that might not be spelt out in their formal job descriptions.

Discretionary behaviour is thus about making choices about the quality, speed, attention and initiative involved in performing a particular job. It is an important concept because it relates to something that is crucial to job performance yet at the same time nebulous, elusive and difficult to define and not formally recognised or rewarded. Discretionary behaviour is fundamental to the employment relationship but the relationship is indeterminate and ill-defined.

As Purcell *et al* (2003: 5) suggest,

> **It is hard for the employer to define and then monitor and control the amount of effort, innovation and productive behaviour required … It [discretionary behaviour] may involve emotional labour (smiling down the phone), using knowledge to solve a problem or to suggest an alternative to the customer, or it may be internal to the work of the organisation, such as co-operating with team members, helping probationers learn shortcuts or sharing new ideas on work processes. One way or another, the employee chooses how conscientiously to undertake the job.**

Discretionary behaviour is closely linked with 'pro-social behaviour' (West, 2005: 38) or co-operation, altruism and a tendency to help others. It is likewise linked to *organisational ctizenship behaviour* (OCB) which has been characterised as comprising: 'civic duty' – constructive involvement in organisational processes beyond the minimum required to do the job; 'sportsmanship' – tolerating less than ideal working situations without excessive complaining; altruism – supporting others with organisationally relevant tasks; conscientiousness – going beyond the minimum role requirements expected by the organisation; courtesy – preventing the occurrence of work-related problems; cheerleading – encouraging others; and peacemaking – resolving disagreements and providing a stabilising force (Piercey *et al*, 2002: 376).

## ILLUSTRATION

### Look after your staff and they'll look after your customers

Customer service is crucial to the business strategies of most major organisations and employees are critical to their delivery. A number of studies have revealed powerful relationships between corporate performance and how staff behave and are managed. North American retailer Sears found a 10 per cent increase in employee satisfaction associated with a 2.5 per cent increase in customer satisfaction and a 1 per cent increase in sales. In the UK, Nationwide Building Society has found similar links between HR practices, employee commitment and mortgage sales.

The service sector makes up a whopping 70 per cent of European GDP growth, yet the UK's reputation in these industries is poor. Some, though, are getting it right; new CIPD research highlights how companies with high customer satisfaction scores are rewarding their front-line staff.

For the past year the CIPD and Aston University have been studying the practices of 22 UK-based organisations, covering a variety of service settings, and have found that a number of management and reward practices differentiate organisations.

All forms of performance-related pay and recognition were used more extensively by the high-performing organisations. Such schemes were centred on measures of customer satisfaction and service quality. Additionally, schemes aimed at the involvement of staff, the use of harmonised pay and single-status benefits were key in creating a sense of fairness and a positive psychological contract.

Source: D. Brown and M. West (2006) Pride and groom, *People Management*, 26 January, pp16–17

## THE RELEVANCE OF DISCRETIONARY BEHAVIOUR

The practice of discretionary behaviour is relevant to all organisational contexts. Increased pressure on organisations to deliver high-quality customised products and services places a premium on the value added by people whether this is in the form of knowledge and skill that improves product quality or in 'going the extra mile' that enhances customer service.

As the environment within which manufacturing organisations are required to compete has become more volatile and uncertain (see Chapter 1) there have been strong incentives for organisations to move towards flexible production systems based on employee involvement and participation (Piore and Sabel, 1984).

Technological developments have accelerated the nature and scope of products available and shortened product life cycles. Getting a new product to market can be a significant source of competitive advantage. Such changes have caused manufacturing organisations to move towards 'just-in-time', total quality management and continuous improvement initiatives to meet customer needs. They have also caused manufacturing organisations to re-evaluate the role of workers in the production process and the contribution that a skilled and motivated workforce can make to organisational performance.

Appelbaum *et al* (2000) researched the links between high-performance working practices (see Chapter 2) and organisational performance in 44 manufacturing sites between 1995 and 1997, and their study highlighted the importance of discretionary behaviour in the dynamic between HR practices and organisational performance. They identified three categories of generic people management practices that were critical to business performance. Recruitment, selection and training represented skill-enhancing practices which were important to ensure that employees had adequate skills and abilities to make a contribution; motivation practices which combined extrinsic and intrinsic rewards encouraged the use of discretionary effort; and practices designed to secure involvement and participation in decision-making provided an opportunity and incentive for employees to make a contribution. As Appelbaum *et al* (2000: 235) put it,

> **Plant managers who invest in the skills of front-line workers and include these workers in decision-making activities elicit discretionary effort by employees. This effort increases operational efficiency and competitive advantage.**

Understanding the link between employee perceptions of fairness and equity of treatment, commitment and organisational performance is also a critical aspect of the so-called 'black box' problem. HRM practices, in essence, comprise the work system that enables employees to use their skills, ability and motivation to demonstrate discretionary behaviour which results in higher levels of organisational performance.

Bowen *et al* (1999) argue that discretionary behaviour has particular resonance for service industries such as banks, the hotel industry and the retail sector because of the intangibility of service transactions and the consequences of employee behaviour for so-called 'moments of truth' where customers gather evidence to judge whether they have been treated fairly and well.

As Johnston (2004, p129) puts it,

Service excellence is both obtrusive and elusive. We know when we have received it and, rather more frequently, we know when we have not. Such service, both excellent and poor, has a strong emotional impact upon us as customers, creating intense feelings about the organisation, its staff and its services, and influencing our loyalty to it. Yet many organisations seem to find service excellence elusive, hard to grasp, and also difficult to deliver. Paradoxically, we, as individuals, instinctively know what it is and how simple it can be.

In a five-year study into the nature of service excellence and ways of putting it into operation, Johnson (2004) found that service excellence was not necessarily about exceeding customer expectations but rather more prosaically about being 'easy to do business with … There were no hassles or difficulties.' Conversely organisations with a poor service record were found to be those that were 'a pain, a nightmare to deal with'. Johnston (2004: 132) found that dimensions of excellent service fell into four categories and that characteristics of poor service were diametrically opposed to the 'excellent' characteristics. This is illustrated in Figure 11.

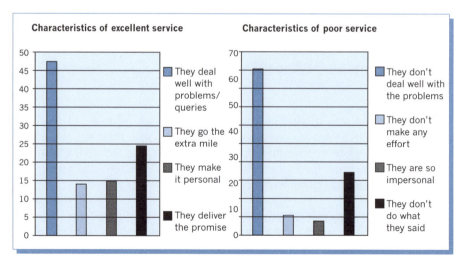

**Figure 11** *Characteristics of excellent and poor customer service*

Source: R. Johnston (2004) Towards a better understanding of service quality, *Managing Service Quality*, Vol.14, No.2/3, p132, reprinted with permission from Emerald Group Publishing Ltd

Johnston's (2004) study underscores the critical role of front-line employees in service delivery and meeting customer expectations. Many service businesses are labour-intensive and employees thus become the target of customer fairness perceptions.

Other studies have illustrated a link between employee attitudes, levels of commitment and satisfaction and organisational performance, and highlighted the importance of treating employees fairly (Bowen *et al*, 1999: 265). If employees trust the organisation and their managers to act fairly, this increases their loyalty and commitment to the organisation, which in turn promotes discretionary behaviour or the performance of activities that will help the organisation and its customers succeed.

Bowen *et al* (1999) argue that in service businesses there is a significant link between the treatment of employees and the treatment of customers and that levels of employee satisfaction correlate with levels of customer satisfaction. They term this dynamic the 'spillover effect'. As Bowen *et al* (1999, p277) put it,

> **The spillover effect suggests that if you treat employees fairly, they will treat their customers fairly. Fair HRM can be expected to lead directly to satisfied, committed employees willing to exert extra effort, which increases the likelihood that they will deliver the fair outcomes, procedures, and interpersonal treatment that customers expect, ie fair service.**

## ILLUSTRATION

### Singapore Airlines (SIA)

Singapore Airlines (SIA) is internationally recognised as one of the world's leading carriers. It has been consistently one of the most profitable airlines in the world. It routinely gets voted the 'best airline', 'best business class', 'best cabin crew service' … Presented below are a couple of extracts from interviews with senior SIA managers on what makes SIA a service champion.

*To be a winner, we have to continually strive to provide the very best service when compared with any industry. Whatever we do, we are in search of excellence and we are never willing to settle for what we have already achieved. Its good to be passionate, but you must be able to say 'I'm willing to kill it with a better program.'*

*The challenge in service is that there has to be consistency. Every time you board a SIA plane, you need to know that you will get the same consistent level of excellent service. While striving for consistency, we need people who can be flexible. I know this is a contradiction, but the worse thing about service delivery is when everybody just follows the book. I want staff to have a good relationship with the customer, without just following the rules. I want them to be flexible and creative. When we first started as a company, our former chairman drilled into us that regardless of whether you are a hangar assistant or a payroll clerk or an accountant, you are there because there's a customer willing to pay. This is our culture. We are focused on our customer. We also have very talented and good people. We have good industrial relations, good HR management, and we look after our staff well. Because when we look after our staff well, our staff will look after our customers well.*

Source: J. Wirtz and R. Johnston (2003) Interview with 'service champions', Singapore Airlines, What it takes to sustain service excellence – a senior management perspective, *Managing Service Quality*, pp10–19

Discretionary behaviour (or organisational citizenship behaviour) is thus strongly correlated with employee perceptions of fairness and trust at the workplace. Employee perceptions of fairness and equity of treatment permeate every aspect of HR practice from recruitment and selection, opportunities provided for training and development, systems of performance appraisal and reward and even the basis on which employees are released from the organisation. Bowen *et al* (1999: 269) highlight the consequences for employee perceptions of fairness and equity in the specific processes of recruitment, selection, performance appraisal and reward. These are summarised in Table 7.

Bowen *et al* (1999: 269) suggest that employee perceptions of how fairly they have been treated during the recruitment and selection process are related to the level of initial commitment to the organisation. During the selection process, applicants judge whether or not their skills and abilities have been accurately assessed and whether the selection decision was fair. They also judge whether the selection techniques used were relevant to the job; whether they were given sufficient opportunity to demonstrate their skills and abilities; whether the process was consistent between candidates; and whether selector bias was suppressed.

As suggested earlier, perceptions of fairness and equity apply to all aspects of the employment relationship. The concept of 'survivor syndrome' suggests that the manner in which redundancy situations are handled can have a significant impact on the psychological well-being, commitment and engagement of 'survivors'.

**Table 7** *Employees' sense of 'fair' HRM*

| Types of justice | Hiring | Performance appraisal | Compensation/ rewards |
|---|---|---|---|
| Distributive (evaluation of outcomes received) | Accuracy of evaluation Appropriateness of hiring decision | Rating meets expectations Outcomes based on ratings Outcomes meet expectations | External equity Internal equity Individual equity |
| Procedural (evaluation of procedures that determine outcomes) | Job-relatedness Opportunity to perform Consistency Bias suppression | Consistent standards Input from employees Rater is familiar Personal bias suppression Opportunity for reconsideration | Consistency Bias suppression Accuracy Correctability Representation |
| Interactional (judgement of how procedures implemented and how final outcomes explained) | Information on selection process Quality and timeliness of feedback Honesty Two-way communication Interpersonal treatment | Performance standards communicated Adequate notice Quality and timeliness of feedback Treating employees with respect | Explain inequity Explain changes Open communications |

Source: Bowen *et al* (1999) *HRM and Service Fairness*, p270

## PAUSE FOR THOUGHT . . .

Consider the following two examples of the handling of lay-off situations by two organisations. It doesn't take much to work out where levels of employee trust, engagement and commitment are likely to be higher.

Cisco Systems had for the first time to create a redundancy programme on a worldwide scale. Cisco described having to let people go as a 'trauma' for the company, but they handled it deftly, working on the one simple premise of preserving people's dignity. They also realised that the people who were leaving would get other jobs and would be potential customers for the company in their new roles. Equally they hoped that many would return as the good times rolled by again. The message this sent to survivors was clear: they worked for a company where people at the top not only cared, but communicated that and lived by it. That is a salutary example of how companies can keep people focused with clear, honest, timely communication and action.

Within a financial services firm job cuts affecting 3,000 people were announced at 12 noon on a Friday. At 1.00 in the afternoon the head of strategic planning's assistant was instructed to take the chauffeured black Mercedes across town and pick up £400 of sushi (on the company account) as she was having some friends over for dinner. This news travelled the corridors like wildfire and you can imagine the reaction of staff still grieving over 'lost' colleagues. The nice part of this story is that the strategic planner finally got fired too. Sadly, she got paid as well.

Source: M. Johnson (2004) *The New Rules of Engagement*, pp22 and 27

Bowen *et al* (1999) argue that organisational citizenship behaviours (OCBs) are a reflection of the positive attitudes of fairly-treated employees which spill over on to customers. This is illustrated in Figure 12.

## ILLUSTRATION

The following extracts, taken from Purcell *et al*'s (2003) study *Understanding the People and Performance Link*, illustrate how successful organisations are able to align their structure, HR policies and practices and relationships with employee values and expectations in a way that induces a high degree of discretionary behaviour on the part of managers and employees.

Nationwide Building Society launched a high-profile campaign around the principles of fairness and putting the customer first. The idea of mutuality is a key value which deeply influences the way it manages relations with customers and employees. This is reflected in a strategy based on PRIDE which has formalised organisational culture by asking employees to: Put members first, Rise to the challenge, Inspire confidence, Deliver best value, and Exceed expectations.

Tesco underwent considerable change in the mid-1990s to improve its competitive position, and a key aspect of its response has been to place greater emphasis on creating a customer-facing culture. Tesco have developed its own version of the balanced scorecard to help define the business more strongly and bring about culture change. The scorecard is translated into a 'steering wheel' with four quadrants – people, finance, customers and operations, and each store's performance is measured against specific targets in each area. The measures are updated each quarter and link to corporate measures which underpin the organisation's strategic objectives. The four quadrants of the scorecard are not weighted but as one retail director suggested, the people quadrant is the most important:'If we can recruit, maintain and deliver fantastic people, then operationally we can deliver.'

Selfridges embarked on an ambitious renewal and growth programme focused on improving the quality of the customer experience. The company introduced a range of initiatives including culture surveys, 360-degree appraisal, broadbanded pay, staff councils, greater care in recruitment and selection, and extensive training and development. Behind these innovations was an explicit effort to link organisational values to be aspirational, friendly and bold into dealings with customers, employees and the community.

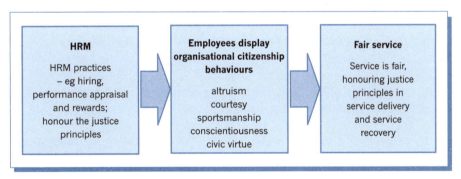

**Figure 12** *Organisational citizenship behaviours and HRM*
Source: Bowen *et al* (1999) *HRM and Service Fairness*, p277

## DISCRETIONARY BEHAVIOUR AND THE PSYCHOLOGICAL CONTRACT

The concept of the psychological contract has relevance to discretionary behaviour. The psychological contract is based on the reciprocal expectations and obligation of employers and employees. As Guest and Conway (2002: 1) suggest, the state of the psychological contract depends on the degree to which these obligations and expectations are met, the degree to which they are perceived to be fair and equitable, and whether there is trust that they will continue to be met in the future.

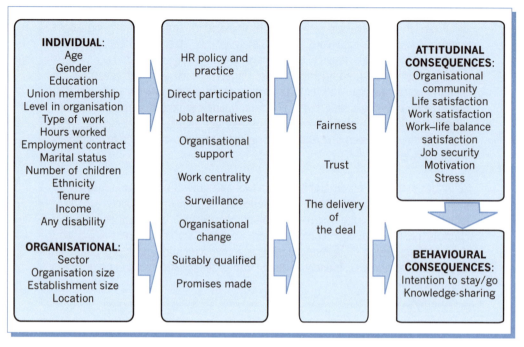

**Figure 13** *A model of the causes and consequences of the psychological contract*
Source: D. Guest and N. Conway (2002) *Pressure at Work and the Psychological Contract*, p2

Guest and Conway's (2002: 2) model of the psychological contract comprises four component elements, as illustrated in Figure 13.

The model assumes a causal link and suggests that the state of the psychological contract and consequent behavioural outcomes are influenced by a set of background individual and organisational features and a set of policy influences and work experiences including HR policies and practices, the degree of control and autonomy at work, the experience of organisational change as well as more individual issues such as the extent to which work is a central life value and the perceived ease of finding alternative employment.

Because psychological contracts are unwritten, employees may have unrealistic expectations of the organisation and feel unfairly treated as a result of organisational decisions and practices. Bowen *et al* (1999) suggest that HR practices should be designed to communicate the terms of the psychological contract clearly and consistently. As they put it (Bowen *et al*, 1999: 279),

> **Practices in hiring, performance appraisal, and rewards should send messages about what employee contributions the firm desires and what it will give employees in return. The practice of using realistic job previews in hiring is an example of how to shape accurate terms for the psychological contract.**

It is perhaps also relevant to note that HR policies exist to provide a framework for the exercise of employee discretion and autonomy. While discretionary behaviour has obvious benefits for the individual and the organisation, it needs to be exercised with responsibility.

In 1995, Barings Bank faced collapse after it emerged that rogue trader Nick Leeson had hidden losses amounting to £800 million in different house accounts. Leeson was found guilty of fraud, but the case highlighted serious reporting and management problems at the Bank which allowed him to handle vast amounts of money within a system that lacked appropriate checks and balances. More recently, the Hutton Report highlighted defective journalistic procedures and a serious lack of checks on the accuracy of reporting at the BBC which seriously damaged the corporation and resulted in the resignation of its chairman, Greg Dyke, a keen advocate of employee empowerment and freedom from restrictive management controls.

Philpott (2004) argues that what is needed is a balance in the workplace between discretion and constraint and a system of checks and balances to prevent discretionary behaviour becoming a vice rather than a virtue. In this context, performance management systems (see Chapter 8) have an important role to play in encouraging responsibility and autonomy so that employees are given the ability, motivation and opportunity to exercise discretion but are likewise aware of the consequences and implications of their actions.

Change in the psychological contract can affect employee perceptions of equity and fairness. As outlined in Chapter 1, the last decade has resulted in massive change for organisations, managers and employees, and the way in which changes have been implemented can have a dramatic influence on employee attitudes and, as a result, levels of morale and motivation.

## ILLUSTRATION

### Love me or lose me

I recently conducted a study in a large telecommunications company that was experiencing high levels of absenteeism. In the face of widespread competition in the

1990s, the company had signalled its intention to become more customer-focused. It committed itself to devolved decision-making and joint problem-solving with customer service staff, and to a programme of training and development, skill enhancement and performance-based pay.

The company made some – largely ineffectual – attempts to fulfil those commitments, but by the time I was brought in it was clear that many employees were disenchanted. They felt that the firm had failed to do what it said it would – in other words, that their psychological contract had been violated.

Individuals in a work unit tend to have a shared understanding of the terms of their psychological contract and to agree on an interpretation of the organisation's behaviour. A belief that the company has broken its promises to employees can result in lower discretionary effort. That was certainly the case in the company I studied. Employees had a strong perception that their psychological contract had been breached. There was a widespread belief that the organisation did not do what it said it was going to do. This had behavioural consequences. In particular, staff who believed the firm had not fulfilled its obligations were significantly more likely to be absent from work.

These findings have important implications for management practice. Where firms declare an intention to be customer-focused and committed to a complementary set of HR practices, they help to define their obligations to staff. These obligations come to form part of the psychological contract. If the company then fails to live up to those expectations, employees may feel resentful and betrayed. This may generate a loss of trust and lead to a reduction in employees' contributions. Such behaviour can have serious implications for the quality of service provided by customer-contact employees. Disaffection can spill over into negative interactions with customers and weaken performance.

Source: S. Deery (2005) Love me or lose me, *People Management*, 25 November, pp36–7

## KEY LEARNING POINTS

- Our behaviour is a function of how we perceive events, situations and people, and attribute causes and reasons to these events. The processes of perception and attribution can have a strong impact on organisational decision-making and problem-solving and employee responses to organisational decisions and practices.
- Discretionary behaviour refers to the degree of choice employees have in performing their jobs. It is about making choices about the quality, speed, attention and initiative involved in job performance.

■ Discretionary behaviour is closely linked to employee perceptions of fairness and equity at the workplace and employee attitudes, views and perceptions of fairness are in turn influenced by a wide range of HR and organisational practices which in turn shape employee behaviour.

■ Perceptions of fairness affect employee reactions to organisational policy and decision-making and HR practice, and can affect commitment and emotional attachment to the organisation.

■ Discretionary behaviour has relevance in all work situations but has particular relevance within service industries where the satisfaction of employees and their willingness to demonstrate discretionary behaviour spills over into the treatment of customers.

## Additional reading

Heracleus L., Wirtz J. and Johnston R. (2004) Cost-effective service excellence – lessons from Singapore Airlines, *Business Strategy Review*, Vol.15, No.1, pp33–8

Hutchinson S., Kinnie N. and Purcell J. (2003) *Bringing Policies to Life: Discretionary behaviour and the impact on business performance*, Work and Employment Research Centre working paper series 2003:12, University of Bath

Johnston R. (2003) *Delivering service excellence: the view from the front line*, Institute of Customer Service

## Web-based sources of information

http://gmj.gallup.com

www.greatplacetowork.co.uk

www.ukwon.ntu.ac.uk

www.workingbalance.co.uk

## REFERENCES

Appelbaum E., Bailey T., Berg P. and Kalleberg A. (2000) *Manufacturing Advantage. Why High Performance Work Systems Pay Off*, Ithaca and London, ILR Press

Bowditch J. and Buono A. (2001) *A Primer on Organizational Behaviour*, 5th edition, New York, John Wiley

Bowen D., Gilliland S. and Folger R. (1999) HRM and service fairness: how being fair with employees spills over to customers, in R. Schuler and S. Jackson (eds) *Strategic Human Resource Management*, Oxford, Blackwell

Boxall P. and Purcell J. (2003) *Strategy and Human Resource Management*, Basingstoke, Palgrave

Brown D. and West M. (2006) Pride and groom, *People Management*, 26 January, pp16–17

Buchanan D. and Huczynski A. (2004) *Organizational Behaviour. An Introductory Text*, 5th edition, Harlow, FT/Prentice Hall

CIPD (2003) The concept of the thinking performer, **www.cipd.co.uk**

Deery S. (2005) Love me or lose me, *People Management*, 25 November, pp36–7

Fox A, (1974) *Beyond Contract: Work, power and trust relations*, London, Faber & Faber

Goleman D. (1998) *Working with Emotional Intelligence*, London, Bloomsbury

Guest D. and Conway N. (2002) *Pressure at Work and the Psychological Contract*, Research Report, London, CIPD

Hope K. (2005) Help staff find meaning in their work, *People Management*, 25 November, p10

Johnson M. (2004) *The New Rules of Engagement, Life-Work Balance and Employee Commitment*, London, CIPD

Johnston R. (2004) Service productivity: towards understanding the relationship between operational and customer productivity, *Managing Service Quality*, Vol.14, No.2/3, pp129–33

Kaplan R. and Norton D. (2001) Marked impact, *People Management*, 25 October, pp52–7

Leary-Joyce J. (2004) *Becoming an employer of choice*, London. CIPD

Mullins L. (2005) *Management and Organisational Behaviour*, 7th edition, Harlow, FT/Prentice Hall

O'Reilly C. and Pfeffer J. (2000) *Hidden Value: How great companies achieve extraordinary results with ordinary people*, Boston, Harvard Business School Press

Philpott J. (2004) By the book, *People Management*, 28 October

Piercy N., Lane N. and Cravens D. (2002) A gender perspective on salesperson organisational citizenship behaviour, sales manager control strategy and sales unit effectiveness, *Women in Management Review*, 17, pp373–91

Poire M. and Sabel M. (1984) *The Second Industrial Divide*, New York, Basic Books

Purcell J., Kinnie N., Hutchinson S., Rayton B. and Swart J. (2003) *Understanding the People and Performance Link: Unlocking the Black Box*, CIPD Research Report, London, CIPD

Redman T. and Wilkinson A. (2002) *The Informed Student Guide to Human Resource Management*, London Thomson Learning

Robbins S. (2003) *Essentials of Organizational Behaviour*, International edition, New Jersey, Prentice Hall

West M. (2005) Hope springs, *People Management*, 13 October, pp38–9

Wilson F. (2004) *Organizational Behaviour and Work. A Critical Introduction*, 2nd edition, Oxford, Oxford University Press

Wirtz J. and Johnston R. (2003) Interview with 'service champions' Singapore Airlines: what it takes to sustain service excellence – a senior management perspective, *Managing Service Quality*, Vol.13, No.1, pp10–19

# Motivation, empowerment and discretionary effort

## INTRODUCTION

The previous chapter examined the concept of discretionary behaviour and the importance of employee attitudes and perceptions of fairness in demonstrating the type of positive, customer-focused behaviours that result in superior organisational performance. The point was made that discretionary behaviour may be highly valued and sought after but cannot be commanded or forced – it relies on the willingness of employees to deliver it.

Discretionary behaviour stems from discretionary effort – the willing contribution of people who are committed to the purpose and values they are working towards and are motivated to 'go the extra mile'. By the same token, discretionary behaviour can be withdrawn where employees perceive they have been unfairly treated. Discretionary behaviour is thus closely linked to concepts of motivation, engagement and work ownership.

Motivated employees generate high levels of performance, are enthusiastic and energetic and are committed and loyal to the organisation. They are likely to demonstrate a range of discretionary behaviours in overcoming organisational problems, be prepared to use their job knowledge for the benefit of the organisation, and accept change.

By contrast, de-motivated employees are likely to be apathetic, complacent and even subversive. They are more likely to have higher levels of absence. It is self-evident that organisational performance is likely to be greater with motivated and engaged employees. However, there is considerable evidence that many employees are greatly under-utilised at the workplace.

A study by the Gallup organisation based on a large sample of the UK workforce (Buckingham, 2001) identified three discrete groups of employees, which were categorised as follows;

- engaged employees – 17 per cent of the sample fell into this category of loyal, committed, productive and task-effective employees
- non-engaged employees – 63 per cent of the sample fell into this category and were characterised as being productive in the sense of doing what was asked of them but not psychologically bonded to the organisation. This category of employees were instrumentally motivated; they could be tempted by job vacancies elsewhere and were responsive to financial incentives but cynical about higher-order appeals to loyalty
- Actively disengaged employees formed the remaining 20 per cent of the sample and comprised employees who were physically present but psychologically absent. They demonstrated behaviours and attitudes that were negative, uncooperative and even hostile. According to Buckingham (2001: 37) such employees were 'intent on sharing with colleagues the many reasons for which they believe their organisation is such a rotten place to work'.

Gallup estimated that actively disengaged employees cost the British economy between £37.2 billion and £38.9 billion due to their low retention, high absenteeism and low productivity (**www.gmj.gallup.com**). Moreover, the research found that the longer employees remained with an organisation, the more disengaged they became. The study concluded that over time, organisations systematically depreciate their human capital. Guest and Conway's (2002) research into employee well-being and the psychological contract found that more than half of line managers were failing to motivate and improve the performance of staff.

In 2003, a research report into comparative levels of UK competitiveness lead by Michael Porter and funded jointly by the ESRC and DTI, highlighted low levels of innovation and an enduring performance and productivity gap in the UK when compared with the USA and European rivals France and Germany. Despite working longer hours than other European countries, the UK's level of productivity lags behind that of its principal competitors.

Research by the Policy Studies Institute (2000) found that the proportion of people who felt completely satisfied with their work fell from 52 to 45 per cent between 1992 and 2000. The ESRC 2000 Employment Survey found that work intensification, greater control and surveillance and long hours were key factors contributing to lower levels of job satisfaction and personal commitment to the organisation, especially among those with higher levels of education. The CIPD annual absence survey (2005) reported a rise in absence levels among participants to 4 per cent or 9.1 working days at an average cost of £588 per employee. The principal causes for the increase were identified as workload, management style and organisational change and restructuring.

Such evidence flies in the face of corporate rhetoric about people as an organisational asset. As Johnson (2004: 14–15) puts it,

> **We've been really good at disengaging our employees these last years. We've spent millions in consulting fees to find ways to cut our employees' pensions and health benefits and then we say we want you to be part of our brand. We've fired thousands of people after mergers and sell-offs and our websites proclaim that one of our goals is to be an employer of choice. We've cut personal and professional development programmes to the bone and then we expect our employees to be up-to-speed and enthusiastic.**

Work remains a fundamental aspect of people's lives and although many are satisfied with the work they do, many are not. Evidence as to the quality of working life is mixed and generalisations are difficult as patterns of workplace change affect different people in different ways. This chapter evaluates the concept of motivation and discretionary effort as a critical factor in individual, group and organisational success. It reviews traditional classical approaches to motivation at work and highlights renewed interest in the topic in the light of the link between the management of people and organisational performance.

## ILLUSTRATION

### Charlie

For 20 years, Charlie, a baggage handler, was an asset to his airline. Callous rule changes and harsh supervisory treatment, however, led him to covertly retaliate. For months he carefully evened the score by tearing off a few baggage tags each shift. Each missing tag caused the airline both service headaches and lost dollars.

Source: D. Bowen *et al* (1999) HRM and service fairness: how being fair with employees spills over to customers, in S. Schuler and S. Jackson (eds) *Strategic Human Resource Management*, p264

Theories of motivation and techniques for securing discretionary effort and channelling this into superior organisational performance have evolved over a period of time and reflect different environments and different attitudes to work and workers.

Traditional approaches were based on assumptions that people acted rationally to maximise the economic return on their labour. Scientific management saw people as motivated solely by financial gain. The human relations approach recognised the motivating potential of social groups and the nature of the work undertaken in giving employees the opportunity to use creativity and initiative at work. More recently, in the context of large-scale and discontinuous change the issue has become how employees exercise discretionary effort and the choices made about how they work. Central to such debates are concepts of empowerment, engagement, the psychological contract and the role of HPWS in creating an environment in which employees become stakeholders in the success of the organisation.

## CONTENT AND PROCESS THEORIES OF MOTIVATION

People differ in a large variety of ways and individual differences can have a significant impact on behaviour at work. Motivation is a broad concept relating to individual preferences and the strength of those preferences to behave in certain ways. It is used to consider why people work and what can make some people put in a greater degree of effort.

The study of motivation and establishing ways of motivating employees to greater levels of productivity and performance has been an enduring and major theme of research into the management of people at work. It is a subject that is characterised by an extensive body of theory, distinct traditions, debates and controversies but no definitive consensus about what motivates people at work and what might be done to improve worker motivation.

Approaches to the study of motivation can be broadly categorised under the generic headings of 'content' or 'process' theories. Content theories are 'needs'-based and start from the basic assumption that human beings have certain needs – eg money, friendship, power – which they seek to satisfy. In relation to motivation at work, the challenge becomes the creation of an organisational climate for the satisfaction of needs. Thus content theories focus on specific factors that motivate people – ie the *what* of motivation.

Process theories of motivation start from a different set of assumptions namely, that we are not motivated to satisfy pre-determined needs but rather respond to challenges and opportunities that we are presented with. Process theories see motivation as a complex and individual process and are more concerned with identifying the interaction of factors that influence behaviour and the exercise of discretionary effort. In other words, process theories focus on the *how* of motivation.

Although reflecting different starting assumptions, content and process theories of motivation can nevertheless be regarded as compatible rather than mutually exclusive because both provide insights into human behaviour and effort at the workplace.

This section thus reviews both content and process theories of motivation and considers their practical application in job and work design.

**Content theories**
- Maslow and Alderfer and the Hierarchy of Needs
- Herzberg's Two-Factor Theory of Motivation
- McClelland and Achievement Needs

**Process theories**
- Vroom, Porter and Lawler and Expectancy Theory
- Adams and Equity Theory
- Locke and Goal Theory

## The hierarchy of needs

One of the best known models of motivation is that of Maslow (1943) who argued that people have specific needs which can be conceptualised as a hierarchy incorporating basic needs and higher-order needs. Maslow's hierarchy is often represented as a pyramid (see Figure 14) because once lower-order needs have been satisfied they no longer act as a strong motivator and higher-order needs become more influential. The final stage in the hierarchy is that of self-actualisation or the fulfilment of individual personal potential.

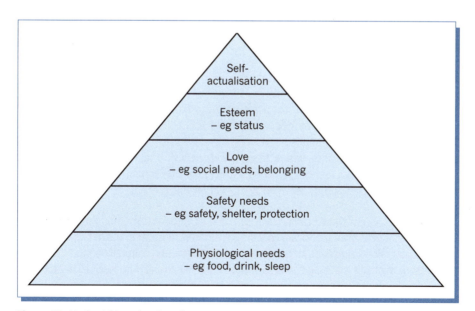

**Figure 14** *Maslow's hierarchy of needs*

Maslow's hierarchy was modified by Alderfer (1972), who reduced it to three categories – those of Existence or survival needs, Relatedness or social interaction needs, and Growth or the desire to achieve and develop individual potential (thus the ERG model). Alderfer argued that these needs represented more of a continuum than a hierarchy because more than one need might be activated at the same time.

## Herzberg's (1968) two-factor theory of motivation

Herzberg's two-factor theory of motivation identifies two sets of factors, which influence motivation. Both sets of factors are important but perform different functions. *Hygiene* factors are concerned with pay, company policy, supervisory style, status, security and working conditions and serve to prevent job dissatisfaction.

However the function of hygiene factors is to prevent job dissatisfaction and perceptions of unfairness and inequality, they do not create satisfaction or positive attitudes and discretionary effort. This is the task of the *motivating* factors, which include achievement, advancement, growth, recognition, responsibility and work itself. According to Herzberg, there is a limit to the benefits to be gained by simply improving hygiene factors. Doing so would remove dissatisfaction but would not result in higher motivation or increased performance. For employees to be satisfied, committed and motivated to discretionary effort, motivating factors have to be built into the design of jobs and the nature of rewards available as discussed later in this chapter.

McClelland's (1961) Achievement Needs Theory argues that an individual's motivation is influenced by three basic needs – the need for affiliation, achievement and power – and that people develop a bias towards one of these needs. People with high affiliation needs seek social relationships at work whereas those with a high power need strive for organisational leadership or influence. A high need to achieve is perhaps the most desirable organisational attribute in employees.

According to McClelland, need to achieve comprises both intrinsic and extrinsic motivation and is influenced by education, social and cultural background and values. People with a high achievement need seek out situations where they have personal responsibility for performance, where they receive clear and unambiguous feedback on performance, where the tasks and goals are moderately challenging and where they have the opportunity to consistently move on to more challenging tasks.

Content theories of motivation can be criticised on conceptual and methodological grounds. Maslow's hierarchy was not specifically concerned with work motivation and has been criticised as vague, generalised, simplistic, lacking in a predictive basis and culturally bound (reflecting white American middle-class values and aspirations) (Buchanan and Huczynski, 2004:246).

Herzberg's two-factor theory has likewise been criticised, principally on the grounds that the methodology used determined the results. Herzberg's findings were based on asking accountants and engineers to identify what they liked and disliked about their jobs and this form of self-reporting, critical incident research reflects an attributional bias. In other words we tend to attribute satisfactory work incidents to our own performance whereas we attribute dissatisfying aspects to external factors. The suggestion that hygiene factors don't cause satisfaction at work undermines the philosophy and practice of incentivised pay. Herzberg's work has also been challenged on the grounds that it has limited applicability to people employed in largely routine, prescribed, repetitive and monotonous jobs and yet these are precisely the occupations where motivation is a challenge for managers.

Nevertheless, despite their limitations, content theories remain influential and relevant. They emphasise that behaviour at work is influenced by a range of motives and situational factors and have highlighted the specific importance of certain factors such as job and work design on levels of motivation and discretionary effort.

## Process theories of motivation

In contrast to content theories, process theories of motivation highlight the complex, individual and idiosyncratic nature of motivation. Process theories emphasise the influence of the exercise of individual choice in motives and how these are achieved. They underscore the discretionary nature of motivation – ie that we act in a rational way informed by our perceptions and expectations of a range of external and internal influences.

The basic process theory of motivation is based on the concept of *expectancy*, which provides a framework for explaining how individual choice in motivation operates. In essence, Expectancy Theory suggests that individuals will respond to their expectations that particular behaviours will result in particular outcomes.

In other words, if I expect that working hard and consistently over a period of time and taking on additional responsibilities will result in promotion and promotion is something I value, then I will be motivated to work hard and consistently to achieve that outcome. If, on the other hand, I expect that working hard and volunteering to take on additional responsibilities will result in my being overburdened with work and taken advantage of, then my willingness to do so may be very different.

Vroom's (1964) model of expectancy was based on three variables:

- *Valence* relates to the preference for certain outcomes over others and can be positive, negative or neutral
- *Instrumentality* refers to the extent to which performance will produce a valued outcome
- *Expectancy* refers to the perception of the probability that a particular action will result in the desired outcome.

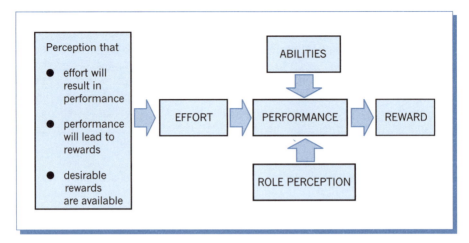

**Figure 15** *Porter and Lawler's model of work motivation and performance*

When an individual chooses between alternative courses of action which involve uncertain outcomes, his or her behaviour will be affected by preferences for certain outcomes but also the degree to which he or she believes that these outcomes are possible. The strength of expectations is influenced by past experiences. Motivation thus exists where there is a clearly perceived relationship between performance and outcome and where the outcome is seen as satisfying a particular need.

Vroom's typology was developed by Porter and Lawler (1968) into a more comprehensive model of work motivation and performance, as illustrated in Figure 15. The model shows that effort is mediated by an individual's abilities, traits and perceptions of his or her role.

Other aspects of process theories of motivation focus on the use of external and internal comparisons to explain discretionary effort and behaviour. Adams' (1963) Equity Theory suggests that individual perceptions of fairness of treatment result from comparisons with the treatment of others. We are motivated to act where we perceive that we have been treated unfairly or unjustly. Equity Theory suggests that we compare our rewards (pay, recognition) and contributions (time, effort, ideas) with the rewards and contributions of others. Where we perceive inequity to exist, this creates tension and motivates us to act to reduce or remove that tension.

Locke's (1968) Goal Theory is also useful in informing the process of motivation. Goal theory suggests that our goals are an important influence on our behaviour and that the combination of goal difficulty and our individual commitment to the achievement of a specific goal influences the amount of effort we are prepared to exert. Goal theory underlies the development of SMART objectives in performance management (see Chapter 8).

## ACTIVITY . . .

Hollyforde and Whiddett (2002) argue that because motivation is personal, organisations cannot impose it. A manager's job, they say, is to understand each person's expectations of, and contribution to, the company, regardless of where he or she is in the workplace hierarchy. A good manager will be able to use that understanding in order to motivate. They identify key motivational practices, as follows:

- Design jobs in a way that gives people responsibility for the outcomes of their work.
- Provide clear and realistic goals and standards.
- Ensure that people have the resources to do their job.
- Give credit where credit is due and make sure it is known within the team.
- Provide unambiguous and honest feedback.
- Provide learning and development opportunities.
- Implement reward packages that reflect the job and the external market rate.
- Create an environment governed by fairness and respect.

Evaluate your own work environment and organisation against these motivational practices.

What changes would be desirable?

## THE RELATIONSHIP BETWEEN MOTIVATION AND JOB DESIGN

Job design is a key feature of the relationship between an individual and his or her work and a key practical aspect of motivation theory is closely linked to the design of jobs and work systems in a way that facilitates and encourages discretionary effort. As with the study of motivation, links between work design and motivation reflect different conceptualisations and assumptions about employee behaviour which are themselves a product of different historical contexts.

### Scientific management

Frederick Taylor's studies into ways of increasing productivity at the Bethlehem Steel Corporation in the 1920s culminated in scientific management as a means of increasing productivity through restructuring work and the work process and the provision of monetary incentives for higher levels of output. The underpinning rationale of scientific management was based on a number of assumptions about people, work and motivation.

Scientific management argued that there was one best way in which work could be organised and undertaken and that workers were motivated by undertaking work in the most efficient way and receiving financial reward. The key features of scientific management include:

- task fragmentation or breaking down jobs into their most simple component elements
- deciding on the best way to perform a job including the work layout
- training employees to carry out the job in the prescribed manner
- closely supervising and controlling the process
- rewarding employees financially for meeting output targets.

Scientific management underpinned Fordist mass production line technology. The key characteristics of mass production are identified by Buchanan and Huczynski (2004: 85) as mechanical pacing of work, no choice of tools or methods, repetitiveness, minute subdivision of product, minimum skill requirements and surface mental attention. Task fragmentation meant that jobs could be done by unskilled workers with limited training and that workers were more interchangeable and dispensable. Work standardisation also meant that production could become predictable and more easily controlled by management.

However, there were considerable shortcomings associated with scientific management. Task fragmentation and standardisation results in alienation and is associated with fatigue, boredom and distraction leading to high levels of turnover, absenteeism, accidents, stress and poor labour relations.

Scientific management and Fordist production systems have been replaced by so-called post-Fordist high-performance work design as levels of competition and customer demand have prompted more flexible approaches to production as a critical component of organisational performance. Nevertheless it would be inaccurate to dismiss scientific management as outdated and obsolete. The routinised repetitive, standardised and controlled forms of working within call centres continue to reflect the principles and drawbacks of scientific management. Call centre work illustrates that scientific management represents a plausible, cheap and easy to operate form of work organisation within specific organisational settings.

## The human relations approach

The human relations approach highlighted the shortcomings of scientific management and emphasised the need for a more humane and satisfying approach to job and work design. A significant step in understanding worker motivation took place in the USA in a series of studies that have come to be known as the Hawthorne experiments. The management of the company in which these experiments were conducted was concerned with the physical conditions of work and how these affected work performance.

Between 1924 and 1932 five sets of detailed experiments were conducted. The initial experiments with lighting and humidity levels had limited results and led to a broadening of the research to incorporate pay rates, hours of work, rest breaks, supervision and employee attitudes. The most significant findings highlighted the motivating potential of social groups at work, the role of leadership in motivation and the effects on levels of motivation of employee participation in decision-making at work. The Hawthorne studies demonstrated that a balance was needed between job and task needs and human psychological needs; between organisational demands for productivity and employee needs for challenge, achievement and recognition.

The importance of social needs and organisation within work groups was reinforced by the so-called Tavistock studies which developed the concept of the organisation as a system in which component elements interacted in mutual co-dependence. Trist and Bamforth's (1951) studies of the Durham coalmining industry showed that the social aspects of technical work systems were crucial in achieving efficiency and productivity. The study found that the introduction of mechanised technology into mines reduced the amount of social interaction, team work, levels of discretion and 'responsible autonomy', with a consequent deterioration in productivity levels. Prior to mechanisation miners worked in multi-skilled groups with collective responsibility for a range of tasks. Mechanisation required a specialised division of labour and segmentation of miners into specific roles. The mechanised system undermined the cohesion of groups.

Other significant contributions to the study of motivation and job design include that of Goldthorpe *et al* (1968) and Burawoy (1979). Goldthorpe *et al* in their study of workers at the Vauxhall car production plant identified what they termed an 'instrumental orientation' to work whereby workers were prepared to work on a monotonous production line in exchange for high pay which provided them with the means to pay for cars and holidays. Workers with an instrumental orientation to work see work not as a central issue but rather as a means to an end. Burawoy (1979) presented contrary evidence of workers resisting attempts to apply Taylorist forms of work control.

## ACTIVITY . . .

It has been suggested that temporary staff demonstrate instrumental attitudes towards work. The basis of temporary work contributes to an instrumental orientation in that, until recently, many temporary staff received less favourable treatment and had no rights to join occupational pension schemes or access to benefits available to permanent staff. The very nature of their employment status makes their employment insecure. Such factors influence the levels of trust, loyalty and commitment of temporary staff to the organisation.

Temporary workers may be less reliable, have higher levels of turnover, be unwilling to work beyond contract or the specific requirements of their job role and be motivated solely by financial concerns. Such aspects of behaviour are not surprising given that reliability, stability and discretionary behaviour are linked to employee commitment and with temporary staff the nature of that commitment is transient.

The challenge for the organisation is therefore to encourage discretionary behaviour while retaining the flexibility that temporary workers allow.

How might this be achieved in practice?

## TECHNIQUES OF JOB DESIGN

Early job design techniques were focused on improving motivation through eliminating boredom and monotony at work and increasing variety. Specific job design techniques included job rotation, job enlargement and job enrichment.

*Job rotation* involves switching employees from task to task at regular intervals. It may lead to the acquisition of additional skills but does not necessarily result in the development of skill level.

*Job enlargement* involves the re-configuration and combination of a variety of tasks. It can provide variety but can be resisted if perceived as simply increasing the number of tasks to be performed.

*Job enrichment* is a 'technique for broadening the experience of work to enhance employee need satisfaction and to improve work motivation and performance' (Buchanan and Huczynski, 2004: 260). Job enrichment is closely linked to Herzberg's two-factor theory of motivation and is focused on designing jobs in a way that provides greater opportunity for advancement, achievement and recognition. To achieve this Herzberg advocated the use of *vertical loading* or methods for enriching work and providing motivation by removing controls, increasing accountability, providing feedback, using natural work groups, providing special assignments and giving additional authority (Buchanan and Huczynski, 2004: 261).

The principle of job enrichment underpins Hackman and Oldham's (1980) job characteristics model which suggests a causal chain between job features or characteristics, critical psychological states and outcomes of motivation, satisfaction and work effectiveness. Hackman and Oldham suggest that higher levels of motivation and effectiveness are achieved when individuals experience psychological states of meaningfulness of work, responsibility and knowledge of results which stem from five core job characteristics. These five core job characteristics can be summarised as follows:

- skill variety or the extent to which a job involves a range of activities requiring a range of skills
- task identity or the extent to which a job allows for completion of a complete piece of work
- task significance or the extent to which a job has a significant impact on others either within the organisation or outside
- autonomy or the extent to which a job allows for discretion and initiative in how it is carried out
- feedback or the extent to which a job provides clear feedback on performance.

Skill variety, task identity and task significance affect the experienced meaningfulness of work; autonomy influences the experienced responsibility for work; and feedback relates to the knowledge of results and standard of performance. Hackman and Oldham also developed the Job Diagnostic Survey (JDS) questionnaire whereby scores are allocated according to the extent to which job characteristics are present in any given job. The questionnaire provides a score for the Motivating Potential Score (MPS) or level of job enrichment of a job.

## THE RELATIONSHIP BETWEEN MOTIVATION AND REWARD

A central theme of the study of motivation is what motivates people and how people can be motivated to higher levels of discretionary effort. If motivation is a dynamic process and we continually seek to satisfy our needs through work, then motivation will always involve a balancing act between employee needs for rewards and other satisfaction at work with the needs of the organisation and the use of other resources. Nevertheless, this is not to suggest that the needs of the organisation are incompatible with those of the individual.

The way in which the work process is designed will determine the nature of the rewards available. Taylor and advocates of scientific management argued that efficiently organised work and financial reward motivated employees. Money is clearly a powerful motivator but the extent to which people are motivated solely by financial gain is dependent on their individual circumstances and other psychological needs to which they seek satisfaction through work.

The relationship between motivation and reward is frequently categorised under the broad headings of *extrinsic* and *intrinsic motivation*. Extrinsic motivation relates to valued outcomes, which are external and provided by others such as pay, promotion, praise and recognition. Intrinsic motivation is related to valued outcomes or benefits that come from the individual such as feelings of satisfaction, competence, self-esteem and accomplishment (Buchanan and Huczynski, 2004: 261).

Individual motivation, levels of satisfaction and work performance are determined by the comparative strength of needs and expectations and the extent to which they are

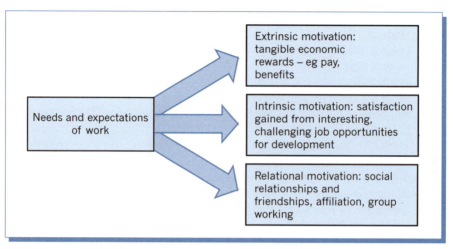

**Figure 16** *Needs and expectations of work*

met. Individual needs and expectations can thus vary between individuals and can change over time. The link between performance and reward is explored more fully in Chapter 8.

## ILLUSTRATION

### Extrinsic and intrinsic motivation

People management

Employees should share in the rewards when their organisation has been successful; conversely, when it has been unsuccessful, they should feel some of the pain. When Brian Baker, Mobil's chief operations officer, first linked incentive compensation to Mobil's balanced scorecard, his peers at the company chided him about how much time his people spent studying the scorecard results each month. 'I think it's fabulous,' Baker responded. 'For one hour each month, every employee takes out the scorecard and looks at the most important thing in their business – whether we are winning or losing against the targets. They're doing this to see how much money they are going to get. We would not have had that same focus on the scorecard and the individual business objectives if we hadn't made the link to pay.'

Kaplan and Norton (2001) Marked impact, *People Management*, 25 October, p53

## ILLUSTRATION
### Bromford Housing Association

Bromford Housing Association is dedicated to the provision of affordable housing and associated care and support services. It came in at number three in the *Sunday Times* 100 Best Companies To Work For and number six in the *Financial Times* Great Workplaces, UK list. This is not a grand place with gyms, crèche or concierge services. As the Housing Director says, 'We are not into flash offices and we have strains on accommodation in our area offices. We hadn't appreciated the importance of teamwork, sense of purpose, standing for the principles, supporting each other and personal development opportunities. They clearly matter far more than we had realised. The *Sunday Times* endorses that we have been doing the right things.'

Source: J. Leary-Joyce (2004) *Becoming an Employer of Choice*, CIPD, p106

## THE RELATIONSHIP BETWEEN MOTIVATION, JOB SATISFACTION AND JOB PERFORMANCE

Theories of motivation can be used to explain employee behaviour and performance when motivation is blocked and employees are unable to satisfy their needs and expectations. Mullins (2005: 475–6) argues that where an individual's motivational drive is blocked, two outcomes are possible: the individual may engage in constructive, problem-solving behaviour to remove the barrier or blockage or he or she may engage in defensive, negative behaviour.

Negative behaviour may be overt and aggressive and may take the form of a physical or verbal attack, rage, abusive language, or may be covert and displaced and result in withdrawal, apathy, refusal to accept responsibility, poor timekeeping, absenteeism or even resignation.

Withdrawal or job avoidance behaviour can be viewed within a wider context of employee satisfaction and commitment. Although commitment is a complex subject and there are many different facets of commitment, research (Meyer and Allen, 1991: 12) has suggested three key components:

- affective commitment – the extent to which an employee feels emotionally attached to the organisation
- continuance commitment – the extent to which an employee feels that the costs and risks associated with leaving the organisation would outweigh the benefits
- normative commitment – the extent to which an employee feels a sense of obligation and duty to the organisation.

It is self-evident that people who are more committed to the organisation are less likely to leave. In the case of affective commitment and to a lesser degree, normative commitment, their continued presence is enthusiastic and engaged. However, continuance commitment can reflect the fact that employees remain with an organisation because they have no alternative. In such circumstances their degree of engagement may be reduced and the potential for the development of job avoidance behaviour increased.

Studies of labour turnover have identified the psychological reasoning behind resignation and have suggested a number of distinct stages whereby job dissatisfaction can progress into resignation. Mobley (1977) suggests that an employee will evaluate his or her current job, evaluate the expected utility of a job search and the cost of leaving, look for alternative employment, and compare this to their present job. If the comparison is favourable, he or she will leave.

At any stage in the process, however, the employee may re-evaluate the present position and decide to remain – if, for example, labour market conditions are unfavourable or as a result of the perceived ease of movement. The dissatisfaction felt may be expressed in other forms of 'withdrawal' such as absence, low productivity, lateness, and poor customer service. Such 'job avoidance' behaviour thus represents an indirect symptom of the employee's desire to leave.

## ACTIVITY . . .

Joe works as a customer account administrator for a major international car manufacturer. The market for cars is highly competitive and suffers from a high level of over-capacity. Recently the organisation scaled down the size of the department as part of a wider cost-cutting strategy. This is how Joe describes his level of motivation:

*Morale in the department has hit rock bottom. They let all those people go, and now there's no one to do the work. Over the years managers have asked us to use our initiative and make decisions in our work. So we've done that, we've become more efficient, but now they just want us to take on more work. And for what? Nothing! We're just expected to do more work – and meanwhile we get told in the newsletter that a director in the States has been awarded a $22 million bonus.*

*Well, I'm not doing it. I've already started to refer customer queries to my supervisor and manager that I used to deal with, and I'm going to do more of that. Appraisals are voluntary and they want us to discuss our roles and responsibilities and agree objectives, but I'm refusing. I'm going to take time off sick. Other people abuse the system, so why shouldn't I? We all know that there are people in the department on long-term sick who are swinging the lead. Last Christmas they all got a hamper but those who hadn't had a day's sickness all year got an umbrella. It was an insult.*

What can be done to eliminate job avoidance behaviours and increase job satisfaction?

Although motivation theory can be helpful in explaining the causes and consequences of dissatisfaction at work there is no compelling evidence that job satisfaction leads to improved performance and the precise nature of the link between job satisfaction and performance remains contested. Job satisfaction is a complex concept and difficult to measure objectively. As Mullins (2005: 701) suggests, job satisfaction can be influenced by a wide range of diverse variables including individual factors (personality, education, ability, orientation to work); social factors (work relationships); cultural factors (underlying attitudes, beliefs and values); organisational factors (organisation size and structure, HR policies and practices, leadership style); and environmental factors (economic, social, political influences).

Contemporary approaches recognise that job satisfaction, employee commitment and work performance need to be considered within a wider context of work and organisational design, work–life balance, psychological well-being and the creation of a work environment conducive to high performance.

## PAUSE FOR THOUGHT . . .

Both process and content theories of motivation provide a framework within which to consider how best to motivate staff to demonstrate discretionary effort. Motivation theory emphasises the following:

- the significance of needs and wants – people will be better motivated if their work experience satisfies their social and psychological needs and wants as well as their economic needs
- extrinsic and intrinsic motivating factors – extrinsic rewards are important in attracting and retaining employees and preventing dissatisfaction, but intrinsic rewards may have longer-term and deeper impact on motivation
- the importance of expectations – the degree to which people are motivated will depend not only on the perceived value of the outcome of their actions (goal or reward) but also on their perceptions of the likelihood of obtaining a worthwhile reward (their expectations)
- the influence of goals – individuals are motivated by having specific goals and will perform better when they are aiming for difficult goals which they have accepted and when they receive feedback on their performance
- the influence of orientation – organisations may have expectations about how their motivating strategies will improve performance as well as helping to attract and retain employees, but this may not be entirely under the control of managers because of people's orientations (preferences for what they want from work) and reactions (their attempt to control their environment regardless of what the organisation wants them to do)

- the importance of equity – perceptions of fairness of treatment are an important influence on discretionary effort; perceptions of unfairness may result in withdrawal and job avoidance behaviours
- the importance of context – concepts of motivation, discretionary effort and empowerment need to be considered within a wider organisational context. The leadership and management role is crucial in creating and sustaining an environment conducive to employee engagement, empowerment and high performance.

## ACTIVITY . . .

A number of indicators point to lower levels of job satisfaction by public sector employees. For example, despite the existence of strong absence management policies, absence levels are rising and are considerably higher than in the private sector. Stress levels in the public sector are also higher with the highest levels reported in the NHS and local government (CIPD, 2005).

Lower levels of job satisfaction by public sector employees can be attributed to a variety of causes. Public sector organisations have experienced considerable change. Most state-run corporations have been privatised (telecommunications, utilities) and state-run services (eg the NHS, the educational system) have been required to operate along more commercial lines. Restructuring and the introduction of market-driven reforms has prompted far-reaching reforms of employment and management practice and public sector work is increasingly carried out under some form of sub-contracting or franchising arrangement.

Despite market-driven reforms, however, public sector decision-making remains inherently political. Government influence, the legal framework of public policy and public scrutiny of the quality of public sector service delivery has increased in intensity as a result of the introduction of league tables publicising poorly performing school, hospitals and local authorities. Managerial decision-making and employment practice is thus subject to a wide variety of legal, political and economic constraints and influenced by a multiplicity of stakeholders. Customer expectations of public sector services have also been transformed with customers expecting high-quality services and standards which are 'joined up' across different agencies and public bodies. There are additional expectations that public sector services should be responsive and utilise appropriate forms of electronic delivery. Contextual and structural change has contributed to initiative overload and 'change fatigue'.

What could be done to improve levels of job satisfaction within public sector organisations?

## AUTONOMOUS TEAMWORKING

The concept of autonomous, self-managed teams is also central to job and work design. The Hawthorne experiments and other research studies have underscored the powerful influence of groups and social processes on individual behaviour, motivation and performance. Work is a group activity and informal groups within the organisation can exert significant controls over the attitudes and behaviours of individual employees.

Autonomous self-managed teams are seen as a central feature of high-performance work systems and a key contributor to organisational performance (Appelbaum *et al*, 2000; Purcell *et al*, 2003). Teamworking is seen as leading to improved decision-making, greater innovation and more effective problem-solving.

Within high-performance work systems autonomous teamworking refers to the process of allowing work teams a degree of autonomy, discretion and self-regulation in how the work is performed. Teams are required to achieve specific gaols but have discretion how goals are achieved and a degree of freedom over the planning and execution of their work. Feedback mechanisms relate to the performance of the team as a whole rather than individual members.

### ILLUSTRATION

#### BMW Group Plant

In November 2003 BMW Group Plant Oxford achieved the CIPD *People Management* award for transforming their notorious Cowley manufacturing plant through self-managed teamworking. Monika Lampe, change manager at BMW Group Plant Oxford, says that a revamp of working practices was essential. 'We were in a competitive market and to compete as a business we had to create a culture of success. We had to change the processes, attitudes and behaviour and to empower staff and involve them in the process.'

In 2000 the firm invested £230 million in refitting the Oxford plant and launched a major change programme called the New Oxford Way (NOW). This focused on key challenges of upgrading the site and processes to world-class standards and integrating the different BMW and Rover cultures, experiences and expectations. The central elements in the implementation of changes was Working in Groups (WINGS) which involved the creation of hundreds of 'self-steered' teams of between eight and 15 people across the plant's manufacturing areas. WINGS teams have been given the power to tackle production problems themselves, when previously they would have called on other departments. In addition, rather than being management-led, the focus is now on initiative and self-management, and employees have received training in coaching and working as part of a team. The day-to-day duties of one person from each WINGS team have been halved so that they can concentrate on developing their team members and the way the team operates.

Since it began encouraging the involvement of employees, BMW Group Plant Oxford has implemented over 8,000 ideas from employees and exceeded production targets by 60 per cent, which has contributed to savings of £6.3 million.

Source: A mini adventure, *People Management*, 6 November 2003, pp30–2

## EMPLOYEE ENGAGEMENT AND EMPOWERMENT

Alongside autonomous teamworking, high-performance working systems have emphasised specific approaches to securing employee engagement through empowerment. Increasingly, to address the challenges and demands of a competitive and turbulent environment, broad-based organisational strategies are needed to develop and sustain high levels of competence, commitment and contribution. Employee engagement is seen as the key to organisational performance and competitive advantage.

The previous chapter explored the links between discretionary behaviour and concepts of employee engagement and commitment. Engaged employees are more likely to be motivated, enthusiastic, committed and to demonstrate the discretionary behaviour and effort that results in improved organisational performance.

An IES report (2004) defined engagement as 'one step up from commitment' and characterised by

**a positive attitude held by the employee towards the organisation and its values. An engaged employee is aware of business context, and works with colleagues to improve performance within the job for the benefit of the organisation. The organisation must work to develop and nurture engagement, which requires a two-way relationship between employer and employee.**

The behaviours identified as associated with employee engagement included belief in the organisation, desire to work to make things better, understanding of the business context and the 'bigger picture', being respectful of and helpful to colleagues, willingness to 'go the extra mile', and keeping up to date with developments in the field (IES, 2004). The IES research found that employee engagement was closely linked to feelings and perceptions around being valued and involved, and that the key drivers of engagement included effective leadership, two-way communication, high levels of internal co-operation, a focus on employee development, a commitment to employee well-being and clear, accessible HR policies and practices to which managers at all levels were committed.

## ACTIVITY . . .

The Gallup Organisation has produced an Employee Engagement Index survey which examines employee engagement levels in a variety of contexts. The 12-question survey measures employee engagement and the links with business outcomes, including retention, productivity, profitability, customer engagement and safety.

Visit the Gallup website (**www.gmj.gallup.com**) to review the measures used to assess employee engagement and profiles of organisations with high levels of employee engagement.

Empowerment relates to organisational arrangements that give employees more autonomy, discretion and unsupervised decision-making responsibility (Buchanan and Huczynski, 2004: 267). Empowerment can take different forms and can include a range of initiatives such as information-sharing, problem-solving and task autonomy (Wilkinson, 2001: 350).

The concept of empowerment suggests that employees at all levels in the organisation are responsible and accountable for their actions and should be given the responsibility and authority to make decisions about their work. Empowerment implies the ability to communicate, to learn, to exercise initiative, to solve problems, to work independently or in teams. Argyris (1998: 100) suggests that employee empowerment is closely linked to the concept of commitment and, in particular, to what he describes as 'internal commitment' where individual employees define tasks and the behaviour required to perform tasks and management and individual employees jointly define challenging performance goals.

## ILLUSTRATION

### Madame Tussaud's

Madame Tussaud's has been transformed in recent years, but it's not only visitors who can see the difference – there have been equally big changes taking place behind the scenes. 'The team was keen to launch a new vision and set of values in support of our culture, and was very clear about what that culture should look like,' says Nick Allsop, group training and development manager. Emphasising customer service and employee empowerment, the values include one called 'edge', which is about having the confidence to take difficult decisions. 'It says to our front-line people that it's okay for you to make decisions that are in the best interests of our customers because you see things at first hand, so you have our full support to make difficult decisions,' Allsop explains. An incentive scheme that supports the vision of creating 'magic moments' for visitors has also proved a bit hit with staff. The scheme rewards employees who go the extra mile with 'magic miles' that they can collect and exchange for gifts – from DVD players to cars. Like the social events laid on for staff, the scheme plays a part in the group's evolving retention strategy, which is part of a wider talent management agenda that also takes in training and development.

Source: *People Management*, 25 November 2004, pp34–6

Empowerment thus needs to be analysed within a broader context of organisational practice. Research shows that empowerment can be effective in raising both productivity and profitability. Wall and Wood's (2002) study of UK manufacturing companies found that from a range of management practices, empowerment was more effective than the introduction of new technology or spending on research and development.

The study found that the success of empowerment initiatives was dependent upon the specific features of the manufacturing production system, but that empowerment techniques were beneficial where employees were required to deal with 'ambiguity, changing demands and innovation' in the production process. As Wall and Wood (2003: 37) put it,

**With empowerment, an individual's knowledge develops more rapidly and to a deeper level, he or she takes a broader and more proactive orientation towards the job and is more willing to suggest new ways of doing things and engage in meaningful team work.**

However, few organisations have created conditions that are conducive to empowerment and much of the evidence suggests that organisations have adopted a piecemeal ad hoc approach to empowerment rather than taking an integrated and holistic approach (Wilkinson, 2001). Despite the benefits, Wall and Wood (2002) found that empowerment was not widely practised and was less popular than quality improvement initiatives such as TQM and JiT manufacturing. They found that less than a quarter of UK manufacturing companies practised employee empowerment to any great extent.

The reality for many employees has been a widening gap between the rhetoric of empowerment and the reality of work intensification, increased organisational stress and insecurity at work. The effects of change, organisational restructuring and increased insecurity invariably generate a tendency to 'play it safe', to 'keep your head down' – hardly empowered behaviours.

Moreover, as Wilkinson (2001) suggests, employees empowered to take decisions are sceptical and unwilling to use their discretion if they feel constantly under the scrutiny of managers. As Argyris (1998: 98–100) puts it,

> **Managers love empowerment in theory but the command-and-control mode is what they trust and know best ... Employees resent executives preaching internal commitment while continuing to demand external commitment.**

## EMPLOYEE ENGAGEMENT, EMPOWERMENT AND THE PSYCHOLOGICAL CONTRACT

Motivation and discretionary effort is strongly influenced by the dynamic, ongoing interactions between employees and their organisation. Organisational norms and values, authority structures and organisational processes and practices can all impact on levels of employee satisfaction, enthusiasm, motivation and engagement.

Bowditch and Buono (2001: 86) suggest that levels of motivation depend upon

> **the extent to which people's expectations of what the organisation will provide them and what they owe the organisation in return matches the organisation's expectations of what it will give and receive [and] the nature of what is actually exchanged.**

This reciprocal relationship is often referred to as the psychological contract. As Bowditch and Buono (2001: 86) suggest, certain material benefits and rewards may be explicitly stated and agreed but the 'psychological income' of satisfaction and expectations of challenging and rewarding work may be less explicitly defined.

In the context of large-scale change the critical issue becomes how change affects discretionary behaviour and the choices individuals make about how they work. Herriot and Pemberton (1995) have argued that the psychological contract for many employees has changed fundamentally. Whereas the traditional psychological contract was based on long-term commitment, security, steady progression through the organisational hierarchy, the 'new' psychological contract is more transactional and based on short-term, flexible arrangements and the offer of employability.

Research (eg Coyle-Shapiro and Kessler, 2000; Briner and Conway, 2004) has shown that when employees perceive that the organisation has breached their psychological contract, or their expectations about work and progression, they feel less committed to the organisation. In such circumstances job satisfaction and commitment also dips.

Purcell *et al*'s (2003) study of the impact of HR practices on organisational performance, especially in organisations undergoing change, showed why a breach in the psychological contract can lead not just to a reduction in commitment to the organisation but also to a decline in work performance. Purcell *et al*'s (2003) people and performance model identifies a direct link between employee ability, motivation and opportunity to participate, and HR policies for recruitment, training, performance management and reward. In addition, management behaviour (their respect for employees, the degree of support and encouragement they provide, their trust in people and the effectiveness of their leadership) will influence the degree to which employees feel committed to the organisation and are motivated to perform.

Purcell *et al*'s (2003) study found the following factors to be strongly associated with high levels of employee engagement:

- effectiveness of communications – the amount of information employees received about how well the company was performing and how they contributed to the company achieving its business objectives
- satisfaction with performance appraisal methods, pay and benefits
- sense of job security
- the provision of good opportunities to express grievances and issues of concern
- involvement in decisions affecting the job or work
- positive and supportive relationships with managers
- high levels of job satisfaction stemming from degree of influence felt over the job, the amount of respect gained and a sense of achievement in doing the job.

## KEY LEARNING POINTS

- Theories of motivation and techniques for promoting employee engagement and discretionary effort have evolved over time and reflect different attitudes to work and workers.
- Content theories of motivation assume that people have certain needs which they seek to satisfy.

- Process theories suggest that people respond to challenges and opportunities they are presented with.
- Empowerment relates to organisational arrangements that give employees more autonomy, discretion and unsupervised decision-making responsibilities.
- Motivated and engaged employees are likely to be more committed to the organisation, more loyal, more likely to demonstrate discretionary behaviour and accept change. However, evidence suggests that many employees remain vastly under-utilised within organisations.

## Additional reading

Holbeche L. and Springett N. (2003) *In Search of Meaning in the Workplace*, Roffey Park, **www.roffeypark.com/reports**

Towers Perrin. (2003) Understanding what drives employee engagement, *Working Today*

Sappal P. (2004) Long engagement, *People Management*, 9 December, pp31–3

### Web-based sources of information

http://gmj.gallup.com/

www.dti.gov.uk/work-lifebalance/

## REFERENCES

Adams J. (1963) Towards an understanding of inequity, *Journal of Abnormal and Social Psychology*, Vol.67, No.4, pp422–36

Alderfer C. (1972) *Human Needs in Organizational Settings*, New York, Free Press

Appelbaum E. Bailey T., Berg P. and Kalleberg A. (2000) *Manufacturing Advantage. Why High Performance Work Systems Pay Off*, Ithaca and London, ILR Press

Argyris C. (1998) Empowerment: the emperor's new clothes, *Harvard Business Review*, May-June, pp98–105

Bowditch J. and Buono A. (2001) *A Primer on Organizational Behaviour*, 5th edition, New York, John Wiley

Bowen D., Gilliland S. and Folger R. (1999) HRM and service fairness: how being fair with employees spills over to customers, in R. Schuler and S. Jackson (eds) *Strategic Human Resource Management*, Oxford, Blackwell

Briner R. and Conway N. (2004) Promises, promises, *People Management*, 25 November, pp42–3

Buchanan D. and Huczynski A. (2004) *Organizational Behaviour. An introductory text*, 5th edition, Harlow, FT/Prentice Hall

Buckingham M. (2001) What a waste, *People Management*, 11 October, pp36–9

Burawoy M. (1979) *Manufacturing Consent*, Chicago, University of Chicago Press

CIPD (2005) *Absence Management Survey of Policy and Practice*, July

Coyle-Shapiro J. and Kessler I. (2000) Consequences of the psychological contract for the employment relationship, *Journal of Management Studies*, Vol.37, No.7, pp903–30

ESRC (2000) *Working in Britain Survey*, available at **www.esrc.ac.uk**

Flade P. (2003) Great Britain's workforce lacks inspiration, *Gallup Management Journal*, 11 December, available at **http://gmj.gallup.com**

Goldthorpe J., Lockwood D., Bechhofer E. and Platt J. (1968) *The Affluent Worker: Industrial attitudes and behaviour*, Cambridge, Cambridge University Press

Guest D. and Conway N. (2002) *Pressure at Work and the Psychological Contract*, Research report, London, CIPD

Hackman J. and Oldham G. (1980) *Work Redesign*, Addison Wesley

Herriot P. and Pemberton C. (1995) *New Deals*, Chichester, Wiley

Herzberg F. (1968) One more time: how do you motivate employees? *Harvard Business Review*, Vol.46, No.1, pp53–6

Hollyforde S. and Whiddett S. (2002) *The Motivation Handbook*, London, CIPD

Johnson M. (2004) *The New Rules of Engagement, Life–Work Balance and Employee Commitment*, London, CIPD

Kaplan R. and Norton D. (2001) Marked impact, *People Management*, 25 October, pp52–7

Leary-Joyce J. (2004) *Becoming an employer of choice*, London, CIPD

Locke E. (1968) Towards a theory of task performance and incentives, *Organizational Behaviour and Human Performance*, Vol.3, No.2, pp157–89

Maslow A. (1943) A theory of human motivation, *Psychological Review*, Vol.50, No.4, pp370–96

McClelland D. (1961) *The Achieving Society*, Princeton, New Jersey, Van Nostrand

Meyer J. and Allen M. (1991) A three-component conceptualisation of organisational commitment, *Human Resource Management Review*, 1, pp61–89

Mobley W. (1997) Intermediate linkages in the relationship between job satisfaction and employee turnover, *Journal of Applied Psychology*, Vol.62, No.2, pp237–40

Mullins L. (2005) *Management and Organisational Behaviour*, 7th edition, Harlow, FT/Prentice Hall

*People Management*, 6 Novemeber 2003, pp30–2

*People Management*, 25 November 2004, pp34–6

Porter L. and Lawler E. (1968) *Managerial Attitudes and Performance*, Homewood, IL, Irwin

Porter M. and Ketels H. (2003) UK competitiveness: moving to the next stage, DTI Economic Paper No. 3, ESRC

Purcell J., Kinnie N., Hutchinson S., Rayton B. and Swart J. (2003) *Understanding the People and Performance Link: Unlocking the Black Box*, CIPD Research report, London, CIPD

Robinson D., Perryman S. and Hayday S. (2004) *IES Report 408*, April

Rousseau D. (1995) *Psychological Contracts in Organisations*, London, Sage

Trist E. and Bamforth K. (1951) Some social and psychological consequences of the longwall method of coal-getting, *Human Relations*, Vol.4, No.1, pp3–38

Vroom V. (1964) *Work and Motivation*, New York, John Wiley

Wall T. and Wood S. (2000) Delegation's a powerful tool, *Professional Manager*, Vol.11, No.6, p37

White M. (2000) *Working in Britain in the Year 2000*, Policy Studies Institute

Wilkinson A. (2001) Empowerment, in Redman T. and Wilkinson A. (eds) *Contemporary Human Resource Management*, Harlow, FT/Prentice Hall

# Investing in human capital – attracting, securing and retaining talent and ability

## CHAPTER 6

## LEARNING OBJECTIVES

- To discuss the nature of individual difference at work, and the significance of psychological fit in recruitment and selection
- To evaluate the nature and scope of human resource planning and its role in integrating HR and business strategy
- To outline the key elements and stages of a systematic approach to recruitment and selection
- To critically evaluate recruitment and selection methods and techniques
- To discuss key features of retention strategy

## INTRODUCTION

The world of work has changed and continues to change at a rapid pace. In an increasingly competitive and turbulent environment human capital represents a source of competitive organisational advantage. Couched in these terms, the interrelated processes of human resource planning, recruitment, selection and retention are critically important for organisational survival and success and central to HR and business strategy.

The organisation needs to ensure that it has sufficient people with appropriate skills and abilities to meet current strategic requirements but also to contribute to growth, development and innovation in the future. Effective planning, resourcing and retention represents the cornerstone of the organisation's ability to employ not just skills and experience but the talent to adapt to change and meet the demands placed on organisations by wider environmental pressures. As Michaels *et al* (2001) put it,

> **Talent is now a critical driver of corporate performance ... a company's ability to attract, develop and retain talent will be a major competitive advantage far into the future.**

Value-adding resourcing strategies create sustained competitive advantage by attracting employees capable of enhancing the differentiation of the organisation's products, services and systems and by improving the quality of the applicant pool while simultaneously reducing staffing costs through more thoughtful design of assessment (Taylor and Collins, 2000: 318).

Over time, the synergy created by value-adding resourcing strategies contributes to employer branding and the development of a reputation as an employer of choice thus easing future resourcing challenges. In keeping with the resource-based view of the firm, value-adding resourcing contributes to the inimitability and non-substitutability of human resources. As Taylor and Collins (2000: 320) put it,

> **The ability of a firm to develop an effective recruitment strategy for its context is, of itself, a unique competency requiring considerable effort and innovation.**

However, the supply and demand for human resources are affected by a wide range of diverse influences and situational factors. Persistent skill gaps and deficiencies (Chapter 7) are creating recruitment problems and affecting the ability of organisations to improve levels of performance. The CIPD Recruitment, Retention and Turnover Report (2005), which tracks a matched sample of organisations over time, found that 85 per cent of organisations were experiencing recruitment difficulties due to a lack of specialist skills and experience in potential recruits. The same report found an increase in the number of organisations experiencing difficulties in retaining people.

Resourcing strategies that match the needs of the individual with those of the organisation are likely to result in higher levels of satisfaction, commitment and performance. However, evidence suggests that established resourcing methods are insufficient and that organisations need to look for new methods and sources of recruitment and selection that reflect their specific context if they are to compete for talented employees in increasingly sophisticated and competitive labour markets.

## ILLUSTRATION

### Council taps new talent pools to ease shortages

Nottingham City Council has solved problems in recruiting support workers – at almost no cost – by tapping into new talent pools and accessing funding to help unemployed people back to work. The council had spent £4,500 on recruitment advertising in 12 months for residential social workers but the adverts had failed to attract people and agency staff had to be employed at huge costs.

To combat the problem, the council identified the skills needed by residential social workers and found a local college to run a 12-week, pre-employment scheme of 16 hours per week so that unemployment benefits were not affected. Then it targeted areas of high unemployment. To date, 13 people have completed the course, nine have been recruited to permanent posts and four held on a relief register which acts as an internal agency. The initiative has been rolled out to recruit other support workers such as catering and administrative assistants. The initiative was resourced by accessing national and regional funding for reducing unemployment.

Source: *People Management*, 16 September 2004, p13

Demographic patterns point to an increasingly heterogeneous labour force with different backgrounds, customs, traditions, characteristics and identities. Stepping into any high street store demonstrates the diversity of the British labour force. Legislation exists to protect individuals at the workplace from discrimination on the grounds of race, sex and disability. However, the 'business case' suggests that those organisations who genuinely embrace individual difference and diversity, as opposed to merely complying with legislation, stand to succeed in increasingly tight and competitive labour markets. Such organisations are able to draw on a wider talent pool and tune into the tastes and preferences of customers.

This chapter reviews and evaluates the resourcing process. It begins with a consideration of individual difference as a key factor in the process of psychologically matching the individual to the organisation. It continues with a review of the component elements of a systematic approach to resourcing on the basis that resourcing needs to be a planned, structured, integrated and systematic process regardless of organisation size, sector or characteristics. Even in smaller organisations a systematic approach to human resourcing will ensure that the organisation has the human resources it needs now and for its future development. The effectiveness of strategic, value-adding human resourcing can be undermined if the quality of the process is deficient and inadequate. The analysis ends with a consideration of retention strategy.

## INDIVIDUAL DIFFERENCE

An understanding and awareness of individual differences at work is an essential aspect of management generally and human resource management specifically. Chapters 4 and 5 have shown how individual perceptions of fairness and equity at the workplace and employee attitudes, values and beliefs can influence discretionary behaviour and effort. Chapter 7 discusses the importance of individual differences in learning for the design of appropriate learning and development activities.

The aim of recruitment and selection is to ensure the effective integration and socialisation of the individual into the organisation. In other words, finding an individual who generally 'fits in' with the culture of an organisation and is able to undertake a range of possible tasks (Taylor, 2005: 143). As the Britannia example illustrates (see box below), some organisations adopt the philosophy of 'select for attitude, train for skill'. The underpinning rationale here is that if the organisation requires employees to behave in certain ways – ie be adaptable, be prepared to work flexibly, work as part of a team, be enthusiastic towards customers – then it is easier to recruit people with such attitudes in the first place. It is certainly very difficult to change attitudes. Taking on people with the 'right' attitudes ensures a greater fit with organisational values and culture. Employees can subsequently be trained to acquire the necessary knowledge and skills for effective job performance. Evidence suggests that the person–organisation fit is likely to grow in importance (Kwiatkowski, 2003: 387).

## ILLUSTRATION

### Britannia Building Society

Britannia Building Society is to launch a new recruitment scheme focusing on candidates' attitudes and behaviours rather than on their job skills. 'We want to bring individuals into the organisation that are aligned with the basic values we're looking for,' said Mark Farmer, change manager at Britannia.

Traditionally recruitment has focused on candidates' skills and abilities rather than their personal values. Farmer believes that the new focus will improve retention and help the business develop better customer relationships. Job vacancies at Britannia will be advertised to highlight the importance of corporate strategy and values, and first-round interviews will focus exclusively on values and behaviours. It is only in the second round of interviewing that candidates will be assessed on the technical skills appropriate to the job.

*People Management*, 3 June 2004, p12

## Personality

The concept of personality lies at the heart of individual difference.

Personality refers to a set of specific characteristics which predispose us to behave in certain ways. Buchanan and Huczynski (2004: 143) define personality as

**the psychological qualities that influence an individual's characteristic behaviour patterns, in a stable and distinctive manner.**

Attempts to identify and categorise the component elements of personality have focused on personality traits, or relatively stable qualities or attributes that influence behaviour in a specific direction – eg shyness, reliability, moodiness (Buchanan and Huczynski, 2004: 144). There is now some consensus from research that there are five distinct traits that capture distinct differences between people, the so-called Big Five, which form the basis for most psychometric measures of personality.

- extroversion/introversion
- agreeableness/hostility
- conscientiousness/heedlessness
- emotional stability/instability
- openness of intellect/closed-mindedness.

There are two broad approaches to the study of personality which reflect the relative influence of innate, inherited characteristics and that of the environment – the so-called nature/nurture debate.

*Nomothetic approaches* view personality as largely inherited, genetically determined and enduring, and claim that it is possible, therefore, to measure and predict ways in which certain personality types will behave in certain circumstances (Mullins, 2005: 342). *Idiographic approaches* view individual personality as shaped by the environment and thus claim that personality can change and may not be readily or accurately measured. Although these represent distinct approaches, they are also complementary, and it is generally recognised that both inherited genetic and situational factors influence behaviour.

Nevertheless, the distinction remains relevant for organisational decision-making in recruitment and selection. As discussed later in this chapter, psychometric measures of personality are growing in use as a means of securing a match between the individual and the job, team and organisation, particularly in customer-facing roles where specific aspects of personality are regarded as crucial. Viewing personality as shaped by the interaction between innate and environmental factors underscores the importance of organisational influences and practices that shape behaviour, such as the creation of a clear vision and set of values, an appropriate culture and job design initiatives to improve motivation and performance.

## Equality of opportunity and diversity

The selection process is focused on discriminating between candidates for employment and making judgements as to which candidates may be most suitable. Where discrimination becomes unfair is when it is based on prejudice, and there exists within the UK context, legislation which defines and protects the rights of employees. This is summarised in Table 8 on page 152. The implication of legislation for resourcing is that employers must demonstrate objectivity and fairness in recruitment and selection and the basis on which employment decisions are made.

Table 8  *Anti-discrimination legislation*

| Legislation | Areas covered |
| --- | --- |
| Race Relations Act 1976<br>Race Relations (Amendment) Act 2000 | Discrimination unlawful on grounds of race, colour, nationality, ethnic or national origin<br>Public authorities have duty to promote race equality |
| Sex Discrimination Act 1975<br>Gender Recognition Act 2004 | Discrimination unlawful on grounds of sex, marriage or reassigned gender |
| Equal Pay Act 1970 (as amended) | Equal pay and benefits where men and women engaged in like work, work rated as equivalent under a job evaluation study or work that is of equal value |
| Disability Discrimination Act 1995 | Discrimination unlawful on grounds of disability |
| Human Rights Act 1998 | Rights not to be discriminated against |
| Rehabilitation of Offenders Act 1974 | Protection from discrimination for certain categories of offenders |
| Asylum and Immigration Act 1996 | Ensuring right to work |
| Age discrimination | Discrimination on the grounds of age will become unlawful in October 2006 |

A feature of many high-performance organisations is a move beyond compliance with non-discrimination legislation to the creation of an organisational culture that embraces diversity.

## Diversity

Kandola and Fullerton (1998: 8) define diversity as follows.

**The basic concept of managing diversity accepts that the workforce consists of a diverse population of people. The diversity consists of visible and non-visible differences which will include factors such as**

> **sex, age, background, race, disability, personality and work-style. It is founded on the premise that harnessing these differences will create a productive environment in which everybody feels valued, where their talents are being fully utilised and in which organisational goals are met.**

The concept of diversity is focused on the business benefits of making the most effective use of the skills, abilities and potential of all employees. Whereas equality of opportunity initiatives are often focused on compliance with legislation and the needs of minority groups, diversity is a much broader, more inclusive concept focused on the challenge of meeting the needs of a culturally diverse workforce and of sensitising workers and managers to differences associated with gender, race, age, nationality as a way of maximising the potential productivity of all employees (Ellis and Sonnenfeld, 1994: 82). The business case for diversity has been reinforced by demographic trends and skill shortages.

Diversity is thus another key component of high performance. This is reflected in the so-called MOSAIC framework which Kandola and Fullerton (1998) use as an acronym for **M**ission and values, **O**bjective and fair process, **S**killed workforce, **A**chieve flexibility, **I**ndividual focus, and **C**ulture that empowers.

## HUMAN RESOURCE PLANNING

Organisational recruitment and selection is also informed by the organisation's approach to human resource planning (HRP). An organisation needs to know that it has people with the right skills and competencies to achieve its existing goals and strategies but also that it has resources for future growth and development. This is where human resource planning comes in.

HRP represents a tool for translating strategic intent into practical action. HRP can be 'hard' or 'soft' in orientation. It can focus on planning as a statistical, modelling activity where employees are managed as tightly and efficiently as any other organisational resource. This is a narrow, mechanistic approach which aims to identify numerical gaps and to take corrective action. A softer approach to HRP takes a broader, more holistic approach and emphasises the integration of planning with a range of HR policies to gain employee commitment to organisational goals and strategies as reflected in the IPM (1992) *Statement on Human Resource Planning*.

> **Human Resource Planning is the systematic and continuing process of analysing an organisation's human resource needs under changing conditions and integrating this analysis with the development of personnel policies appropriate to meet those needs. It goes beyond the development of policies on an individual basis by embracing as many aspects of managing people as possible with a key emphasis on planning to meet the skill and development needs of the future.**

Although there is ongoing debate as to the relevance of HRP within volatile and discontinuous environments, Marchington and Wilkinson (2005: 158) suggest that HRP is just as, if not more, important during turbulent times to ensure that employers have the right staff of the right quality and quantity available at the right time. Marchington and Wilkinson (2005: 159) go on to suggest that HRP is important for the following reasons:

- It facilitates the effective integration of HR and business plans.
- It allows for more effective control of employment costs.
- It allows employers to make informed judgements about the skills/attitudes mix required by the organisation and to feed this into HR strategy development.
- It provides a profile of the current workforce which informs the management of diversity and equality of opportunity.

HRP is concerned with forecasting the organisation's demand for labour in the future, forecasting the supply of labour, both internally and externally, and reconciling these forecasts. Any gaps identified – eg an identified shortfall or surplus in labour requirements – in turn informs subsequent HR policies and plans. Each of these stages is considered below.

## Forecasting demand for labour

Forecasting an organisation's demand for labour is focused on identifying anticipated demand for the organisation's products/services (as articulated by marketing plans, proposals for technological change, etc) and identifying the implication of strategic direction for the number and type of employees required. Specific techniques associated with labour demand forecasting include:

- projections – where the ratio of product/service levels to labour employed has been accurate in the past, projections based on such ratios can be used to indicate the amount of labour required in the future to meet business goals

- current base plus – the organisation starts from existing levels of labour and any increases need to be justified in terms of increased contribution (For example, a building materials supply company required branch managers to demonstrate an increase in business of £110,000 before being allowed to recruit an additional employee)
- managers being required to make judgements about future labour requirements based on their knowledge and experience.

## Forecasting internal supply

Forecasting the internal supply of labour starts with an audit of the current workforce in terms of characteristics such as age, skills, length of service, and gender, and predicts likely internal movements through turnover, wastage, promotions, and retirements.

Information about internal movements can highlight problems areas such as high levels of labour turnover in specific areas and thus provide the basis for specific interventions focused on staff retention which can in turn reduce costs, improve productivity and contribute to organisational performance. Ratios based on current workforce profiles can also be used in benchmarking (Chapter 3) and in formulating the consequences of different scenarios (Chapter 11).

## Forecasting external supply

Forecasting the external supply of labour takes account of the characteristics of local and national labour markets in order to identify the levels of suitably qualified employees available to the organisation.

A number of factors affect the external supply of labour on which an organisation might draw. Locally, labour markets may be influenced by levels of unemployment in the area, by the number of employers competing for similar sources of labour, by the number and qualifications of local school-/college-leavers, by the reputation of the employer in the locality and by the cost of housing and availability of local transport networks.

Nationally, labour markets can be influenced by general levels of unemployment and shortages in specific occupations, the number of graduates from specific subject disciplines, by government and industry training schemes and by UK and EU legislation governing employment issues such as working time (Marchington and Wilkinson, 2005: 164–5).

## Reconciling demand and supply

A comparison of the demand for labour in order to meet organisational goals and strategies and sources of supply is likely to result in different scenarios and different HR policies. Equality between demand and supply is likely only in very stable conditions.

Where demand for labour exceeds supply, the organisation is likely to be involved in recruitment and selection activities in order to acquire the necessary skills and competencies. Where internal supply exceeds demand, HR plans will need to be focused on eliminating the surplus through redeployment, freezing recruitment and redundancy. Either way getting it wrong can have serious repercussions for the business as the BA example below illustrates.

## ILLUSTRATION

### BA chaos blamed on lack of staff

BA has come under fire for poor workforce planning following a series of chaotic days last week that included flight delays and cancellations affecting thousands of passengers. 'BA will have to consider its staffing levels and ask itself how it wasn't able to plan for one of its busiest times of the year,' said a spokeswoman for the Transport and General Workers' Union (T&GWU). 'The union's view is that the staffing levels are too low.'

Source: *People Management* News section, 2 September 2004, p9

As the stages above suggest, the traditional approach to HRP can be highly complex and may require the development of sophisticated HR computer applications to produce accurate and meaningful data. For many organisations, particularly smaller organisations and those operating in very rapidly changing technological environments, traditional approaches to HRP may have less relevance.

Taylor (2005: 105–13) suggests a number of adaptations to traditional approaches which may be relevant to different organisational circumstances. These adaptations include:

- micro-planning – focusing on forecasting the demand and supply of defined occupational groups (eg a chemist may draw up plans to address an expected shortfall in the number of pharmacists following the increase of a pharmacy degree course from three to four years) or specific organisational developments (eg plans to address the extension of the working time directive to junior doctors)
- contingency planning – using computer applications to create new scenarios and to investigate the resourcing implications of possible scenarios (eg a retailer deciding to open a new store and what size it should be)
- succession planning – focusing HRP on the recruitment and development of individuals to fit the top posts in an organisation and to reduce the organisation's vulnerability to losing senior managers
- skills planning – shifting the focus from people to forecasting the skills and competencies required in the future and then deciding the form in which these skills could be obtained (eg through subcontracting).

**ACTIVITY . . .**

To what extent does your organisation carry out human resource planning?

What do you see as the benefits for the organisation in investing in the process of predicting future labour requirements?

What are some of the difficulties associated with human resource planning in practice?

## A SYSTEMATIC APPROACH TO RECRUITMENT AND SELECTION

Having considered the context within which recruitment and selection takes place and how resourcing strategies need to be informed by the wider process of HRP, we move now to focus on the specific component stages of a systematic approach to recruitment and selection. The component elements of a systematic approach are illustrated in Figure 17 on page 158.

### Job analysis

Job analysis represents a crucial stage in the recruitment and selection process because it identifies the nature and scope of responsibilities expected of new recruits. The purpose of job analysis is to break down the job into specific knowledge, skills, and attitude (KSA) requirements for effective performance which can be subsequently assessed. There are a variety of techniques for collecting, analysing and setting out the information required for job analysis. Principal methods of job analysis include observation, work diaries, interviews and questionnaires (Cooper *et al*, 2003: 33–7).

The process of job analysis provides a basis and foundation for the job to be filled and the outcomes of job analysis include job descriptions, accountability profiles, personnel specifications and competence frameworks. These are all considered below.

However, it is important to recognise that a key problem with job analysis is that it assumes the job being reviewed will remain unchanged. The nature of the environment within which many organisations are required to operate means that such assumptions can be inaccurate. As a result there are benefits to be gained from adopting a future-oriented approach to job analysis where the traditional job analysis approach is supplemented by group discussion to identify how existing KSA are likely to change in the future (Newell and Shackleton, 2001: 26).

157

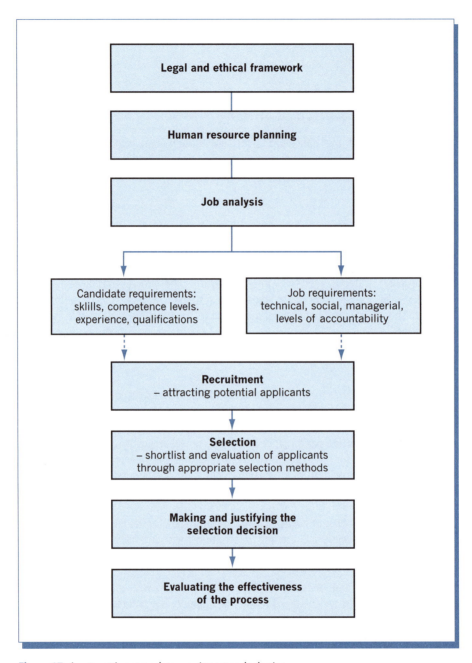

**Figure 17**  *A systematic approach to recruitment and selection*

## Job descriptions and accountability profiles

Job descriptions specify the major duties and responsibilities of a given job and set out the tasks the jobholder is expected to perform. Job descriptions vary in form and content but generally specify job title, location, reporting relationships, job purpose, key responsibilities and any limits on authority or responsibility. They are useful in recruitment and selection in clarifying the nature and scope of responsibilities attached to specific jobs but also in training and development and performance appraisal.

However, job descriptions can quickly become out of date and may lack the flexibility to reflect changes in the job role which may constrain opportunities to reorganise responsibilities and reporting lines. There has thus been a move away from traditional job descriptions to accountability profiles which focus on what the job-holder is expected to achieve rather than what tasks are to be performed. A focus on accountability also sends a clear message about performance expectations in the organisation.

## ILLUSTRATION

### An accountability profile for a front-line customer services position

**Accountabilities**
- Identify and meet a wide range of customer requirements
- Resolve non-routine queries

- Achieve your sales targets

- Analyse, co-ordinate and produce management information
- Build and maintain good working relationships

**Performance measures**
- Meet customer service and compliance standards
- Resolve queries and issues within agreed time scales and quality standards
- Generate quality leads and meet sales targets
- Produce timely, effective and accurate information
- Respond to and provide positive feedback for colleagues and manager

- Develop own skills

- Coach and motivate a team

- Plan and schedule own work and that of colleagues

- Make best use of resources available to meet present and future needs
- Develop improvements to products, processes and services
- Monitor the accuracy of own work

- Achieve your personal development objectives
- Plan, devise and deliver development plans for colleagues
- Meet deadlines without compromising customer service standards – know when to delegate
- Plan the efficient use of time, equipment and budget
- Initiate and present ideas for improvement
- Consistently achieve departmental quality standards

## Person specifications

Whereas the job description relates to the job to be undertaken, the person specification outlines the characteristics and abilities needed for effective job performance. The best-known frameworks are Rodger's (1952) 7-point plan and Fraser's (1966) 5-point plan, illustrated in Table 9. Although dated, these frameworks, or adaptations of them, are still widely used.

**Table 9** *Person specification frameworks*

| Rodger's 7-point plan | Fraser's 5-point plan |
| --- | --- |
| <ul><li>Physical make-up – health, physique, appearance, bearing and speech</li><li>Attainments – education, qualifications, experience</li><li>General intelligence – fundamental intellectual capacity</li><li>Special aptitudes – mechanical, manual dexterity, facility in the use of words or figures</li><li>Interests – intellectual, practical, physically active, social, artistic</li><li>Disposition – acceptability, influence over others, steadiness, dependability, self-reliance</li><li>Circumstances – domestic circumstances, family occupations</li></ul> | <ul><li>Impact on others – physical make-up, appearance, speech and manner</li><li>Acquired qualifications – education, vocational training, work experience</li><li>Innate abilities – natural quickness at comprehension and aptitude for learning</li><li>Motivation – the kinds of goals set by the individual, consistency and determination in following up goals, success in achieving goals</li><li>Adjustment – emotional stability, ability to stand up to stress, ability to get on with people</li></ul> |

A common approach in using frameworks is to specify those characteristics considered essential for effective job performance and those characteristics considered desirable. An advantage of using person specifications is that they help focus on the key attributes required for effective job performance. However, they do suffer from significant shortcomings. As Marchington and Wilkinson (2005: 169) suggest, it is unethical, inappropriate and potentially discriminatory to probe too deeply into areas such as an individual's domestic circumstances or private life.

## Competency frameworks

An alternative to the traditional approach of focusing on job descriptions and person specifications, the so-called 'job-centred' approach, is to focus on the person and the specific competencies required to meet organisational needs. Competencies are behavioural indicators of performance that have been identified as relevant in a particular context (Newell and Shackleton, 2001: 26). The starting-point is an analysis of existing employees and what accounts for effective and superior performance (Taylor, 2005: 142).

There are a number of different approaches to developing competency frameworks but most are focused on identifying both expected 'outputs' or outcomes of individual achievement and the way in which these outcomes are achieved. In other words, individual employees are assessed not just in terms of whether the task was successfully completed but whether it was completed in the right way.

The advantages of using competency frameworks is that they enable the organisation to focus on actual behaviour, what the individual can do or needs to be able to do, rather than making inferences about the personal qualities needed for effective job performance. Roberts (2003: 71–2) identified four types of competency, which can be used as the basis for determining specific behaviours required for job performance:

- natural – made up of the so-called Big Five dimensions of personality (introversion/extraversion, emotional stability, agreeableness, conscientiousness, openness to experience)
- acquired – knowledge and skills acquired through work and experience
- adapting – ability to adapt natural talents and acquired skills to new situations
- performing – observable behaviours and outputs.

There are different models of competence frameworks; some are generic and apply across the organisation, others are focused on the behaviours of specific groups of employee (often referred to as job families). However, most frameworks take the form of a matrix of descriptions or definitions of competence combined with the level or degree of competence. Whiddett and Hollyforde (2000: 14) provide an example of a competency framework which identifies three levels for a role involved in working with people. This is illustrated in Figure 18.

**Competency Framework**

**COMPETENCY CLUSTER**
Working with people

**COMPETENCIES** with levels

- **Managing relationships**
  Level 1: Builds relationships internally
    Level 2: Builds relationships externally
      Level 3: Maintains external networks

- **Teamworking**
  Level 1: Is a team member
    Level 2: Supports team members
      Level 3: Provides direction for the team

- **Influencing**
  Level 1: Projects a positive image
    Level 2: Influences the thinking of others
      Level 3: Changes the opinions of others

**BEHAVIOURAL INDICATORS**
(for Managing relationships)

| Level 1: | Level 2: | Level 3: |
|---|---|---|
| **Builds relationships internally** | **Builds relationships externally** | **Maintains external networks** |
| • Adapts personal style to develop relationships with colleagues. | • Takes account of the impact of own role on the needs of external contacts. | • Takes account of different cultural styles and values when dealing with external organisations. |
| • Adapts form and presentation of information to meet needs of the audience. | • Maintains regular two-way communication with external contacts. | • Actively manages external contacts as a business network. |
| • Identifies and maintains regular contact with individuals who depend on or who influence own work. | • Identifies and nurtures external contacts who can contribute to the business. | • Identifies and makes use of events for developing external network. |

**Figure 18** *A competency framework*
Source: S. Whiddett and S. Hollyforde (2000) *The Competencies Handbook,* CIPD, p14

## EXAMPLES OF THE MOST WIDELY-USED COMPETENCY HEADINGS

- Teamwork
- Communication
- Customer focus
- Results orientation
- Problem-solving
- Planning and organising
- Leadership
- Business awareness
- Decision-making
- Technical skills

Source: CIPD (2005) *Competence and Competency Frameworks* Fact sheet

## Recruitment methods

Sources of recruitment can be broadly categorised as internal and external. Internal recruitment is focused on the organisation's internal labour market as a means of filling vacancies. It is also important to recognise that there are alternatives to recruitment. Rather than automatically replace an individual who has left the organisation it may be possible to reorganise the job, reallocate tasks and even eliminate the job through automation, thus reducing the requirement to recruit.

The CIPD (2005) Recruitment, Retention and Turnover report found that 87 per cent of respondents had a policy of advertising all vacancies internally. The methods used to advertise vacancies internally were predominantly noticeboards and intranets, followed by team meetings and staff magazines.

The external sources of recruitment used by respondents demonstrated significant variation depending on the occupational group being targeted. Advertising and use of agencies were most commonly used for managerial and professional positions. Electronic recruitment through company websites was commonly used for graduate trainees. The Internet has become a more significant recruitment tool, with 75 per cent of respondent organisations using their own websites to advertise vacancies, and there has been a marked increase in the use of commercial websites. Online recruitment brings significant cost savings through saved administration and reducing the time to fill vacancies (Smethurst, 2004).

## ILLUSTRATION

### Targeted recruitment: Cisco Systems

Cisco Systems is a rapidly growing California-based networking firm. Labour shortages among high-tech positions in Silicon Valley have been established as high as 50,000 despite the fact that these are some of the highest paid positions in the USA. Cisco systems have a current vacancy rate in technology positions of only 3 per cent, very low compared to a regional average of 10 per cent. The ability to attract rare talent at a much greater rate than its competitors allows Cisco to continue developing new innovations and to grow at a phenomenal rate.

Cisco has replaced virtually all of its prior recruitment advertising (eg newspapers, radio) with Internet-based recruitment programmes that are specially targeted to the desired applicant population. Cisco treats its recruitment programme as a marketing campaign where it pulls out all the stops to market its jobs to talented outsiders. Targeting passive people who are happy and successful in their present companies, the firm has carefully studied this population to learn the nature of individuals' hobbies, where they would look for work, whose recommendations they would trust in respect of accepting a new position, etc. Cisco's recruiters frequently visit microbrewery and antique shows (identified as hobbies of this target group) and hand out business cards. Based on their market research that most job-related web entries are received from employed candidates searching the Internet during work hours, Cisco provides job browsers with easy access, and fake computer screens in case a boss or co-worker enters the room unexpectedly.

However, web-based recruitment is not Cisco's only foray into non-traditional recruitment sources. The firm routinely acquires between five and six new companies per year in order to fuel its rapid growth with the proven and talented employees of other firms. Recognising that acquisitions in and of themselves do nothing to prevent valued talent from walking out of the door when another employer takes over, Cisco has identified a method of orientation, accommodation and enculturation that allows them to retain virtually the entire technical staffs of it acquisitions.

Adapted from Taylor and Collins, 2000, p319

DIY recruitment can pay dividends for a company and its staff. The employer saves on agency and advertising costs, and the employee who recommends a new staff member receives a reward. Employee referral schemes, where members of staff recommend friends, family or former colleagues for jobs, have proved to be one of the most successful recruitment methods.

**ACTIVITY ...**

Visit the websites of large organisations that regularly advertise job vacancies on their company website and critically evaluate the quality of their recruitment site.

**www.bbc.co.uk/jobs**
**www.nationwide.co.uk/careers/default.htm**
**www.tesco.co/careers/**
**www.mars.co.uk/Careers_at_Mars**
**www.microsoft.co/uk/careers/**

## Selection methods

As suggested earlier, the recruitment and selection process is focused on fitting the right person to the job, team and organisation. The CIPD (2005) Recruitment, Retention and Turnover report found that the selection methods used by organisations varied according to the type of employees being sought. Assessment centres were more commonly used when recruiting managers, professionals and graduates. Online testing was most common when recruiting graduate trainees. However, interviews together with application forms and references, the so-called 'classic trio' (Taylor 2005: 200), remain the most popular and widely used methods of staff selection, as shown in Table 10.

Table 10  *The most widely-used methods of staff selection*

| | Total | Manufacturing and production | Voluntary, community and not-for-profit | Private sector services | Public services | 2004 survey |
|---|---|---|---|---|---|---|
| Interviews following contents of CV/ application form (ie biographical) | 68 | 80 | 56 | 73 | 38 | 66 |
| Competency-based interviews | 58 | 56 | 40 | 61 | 59 | 62 |
| Structured interview (panel) | 56 | 45 | 84 | 45 | 87 | 55 |
| Tests for specific skills | 50 | 39 | 65 | 49 | 61 | 60 |

**Table 10**  *continued*

| | Total | Manufacturing and production | Voluntary, community and not-for-profit | Private sector services | Public services | 2004 survey |
|---|---|---|---|---|---|---|
| Structured interviews (one-to-one and critical incident/ behavioural) | 41 | 40 | 31 | 50 | 25 | 38 |
| General ability tests | 40 | 41 | 51 | 33 | 48 | 53 |
| Literacy and/or numeracy tests | 39 | 40 | 49 | 35 | 42 | 48 |
| Personality questionnaires | 36 | 37 | 35 | 38 | 31 | 46 |
| Employment reference (pre-interview) | 34 | 30 | 25 | 30 | 55 | 31 |
| Assessment centres | 34 | 25 | 38 | 37 | 41 | 43 |
| Telephone interviews | 30 | 25 | 16 | 45 | 13 | 26 |
| Academic reference (pre-interview) | 13 | 10 | 7 | 9 | 29 | 14 |
| Online tests (selection/self-selection) | 5 | 5 | 4 | 7 | 2 | 6 |

Source: CIPD (2005) Recruitment, Retention and Turnover Survey Report, p12

## Selection interviews

Face-to-face selection interviews allow an assessment to be made of the candidate's personality, ability and overall suitability for the job. As Barclay (2001: 81) suggests, selection interviews perform a social function of selling, negotiating and persuading; they are widely acceptable to both managers and candidates and they are more time-efficient and less expensive that other methods such as testing or assessment centres.

However, the interview can take different forms and can vary in design, structure and focus. The design of selection interviews can, for example range from a single face-to-face meeting, through to a panel interview where several interviewers interview a candidate at a single event. Selection interviews can also vary in the degree of structure adopted.

Campion *et al* (1997) have suggested that structure can relate to interview content (ie drawing on job analysis to identify specific questions which are then put to all candidates with limited probing) and to assessment (ie the use of multiple scales and behaviourally-anchored scales to assess responses). As we discuss later, the linking of questions to job analysis combined with a systematic evaluation has resulted in structured interviews having a higher reliability and validity than more traditional interviews.

In relation to content, structured interviews can draw on *situational questions* – ie hypothetical questions where candidates are asked how they would respond in a given scenario – or *behavioural questions*, where candidates are asked to provide examples of how they have responded to specific situations they have had to deal with. For example, where creativity has been identified as a required competence, the candidate might be asked to describe a situation where he or she has solved a problem with an unconventional solution or whether he or she has ever suggested imaginative solutions to business problems.

A study by Barclay (2001) of 174 diverse organisations using behavioural interviews found that their use resulted in better-quality information and generated improved decision-making, fairness, objectivity and consistency.

## Psychometric testing

The term 'psychometric testing' is used to describe a range of tools and instruments designed to measure individual difference in areas such as personality, intelligence and ability. Smith and Robertson (1993: 161) define psychometric tests as

> **carefully chosen, systematic and standardised procedures for evoking a sample of responses from a candidate, which can be used to assess one or more of [his or her] psychological characteristics by comparing the results with those of a representative sample of an appropriate population.**

Testing can take different forms. Tests of achievement measure the skills or knowledge a person possesses. Tests of intelligence measure cognitive skills. Tests of aptitude assess abilities such as verbal, spatial and numerical competence. Tests of personality are based around the measurement of specific personality traits and aim to measure enduring characteristics of behaviour. The aim of tests is to construct profiles which illustrate behavioural tendencies or preferences and which can be compared against published norms or typical scores and profiles of relevant occupational groups. The fundamental premise underpinning testing is that there are certain types of people more or less suited to particular jobs.

## ACTIVITY . . .

Visit the following websites for more information about selection testing.

**www.personneltoday.com/goto/18100** outlines common mistakes in testing

**www.opp.co.uk/index.htm** samples of psychometric materials including Cattell's 16PF

**www.B&Q.co.uk** an online selection activity which allows you to complete a personality profile and receive feedback on characteristics of agreeableness, conscientiousness, conformity, extroversion, emotional stability

**www.shl.com/SHL/uk/Products** a range of psychometric tools for a range of employment situations

**www.support4learning.org.uk/jobsearch/assess.htm** a range of online, interactive resources including job search and work-related assessments

**www.queendom.com** a variety of different psychological tests

## *Assessment centres and ability tests*

Assessment centres and ability tests have both consistently achieved high levels of validity (see Table 11 on page 172). Traditional tests of ability focused on the assessment of specific abilities such as typing and shorthand in order to weed out unsuitable candidates. Increasingly, ability tests are taking the form of observing candidates in a work environment. As the Prêt a Manger illustration below demonstrates, such an approach can bring substantial improvements to the recruitment and selection process.

## ILLUSTRATION

**People**
management

### Pret a Manger

Staff turnover at Pret a Manger hit 98 per cent last year. But Pret's head of recruitment is jumping for joy because her industry average is 150 per cent. 'Turnover was 130 per cent last year, so that's a 30 per cent improvement,' O'Halloran says, 'We are keeping people longer because we are recruiting smarter, and getting the right people in the first place.' Pret employs 2,400 staff of whom 1,900 work as team members in its 118 shops, where they make and serve coffee and sandwiches from 6.30 am to 3.30 pm. It is hard, physical work that depends on good teamwork – and it does not suit everyone. To ensure that it gets people with enthusiasm, Pret uses what is perhaps the ultimate assessment centre – a job-experience day. Applicants first go through a competency-based interview. 'It's about getting the right personality. We want people who are outgoing, have a positive attitude to life, want to work for the company. We aren't necessarily looking for people with experience,' O'Halloran says. If they get through the interview, candidates are asked to attend the on-the-job experience (OJE) day at the shop with the vacancy. Their day begins at the same time as their future colleagues': 6.30 am. A team member will be assigned to act as the candidate's guide for the day but the aim is to get them working with as many other team members and doing as many different jobs as possible. Throughout the process, their future colleagues assess them against core competencies such as enthusiasm and ability to follow instructions. 'It's important that the team makes the decision because they will be working with that person, training them and making them a good person for Pret. When the team buys into a recruit, they take some responsibility for getting them into the team and up to speed,' O'Halloran says.

Source: *People Management*, 16 May 2002, p31

Assessment centres involve a number of candidates being put through a variety of tests and assessments designed to measure specific competencies whilst being observed by trained assessors. Assessment centres thus use a variety of selection techniques and different measures (eg interview, tests, in-tray exercise, role-play, group discussion, individual presentation) which enable assessors to observe candidates in a variety of different situations and make an overall assessment.

## ACTIVITY . . .

Imagine that you have just walked into your office and turned on your PC. The following email messages appear. How would you respond?

*From the Sales Director*
'We're shortly going to be searching for people to work in our new call centre and we think we should be looking for extroverts. However, I thought I'd check with you first. Are we on the right lines, or do you have better advice?'

*From the Production Director*
'I was at a conference yesterday and heard about an investment bank which used to recruit six per cent of its recruits through an employee referral scheme. By increasing

the profile of this scheme, the bank was able to increase this to 23 per cent and cut its recruitment costs by 60 per cent. This sounds pretty powerful to me and could be of value in my area where turnover is quite high. Are there any drawbacks, and if so, how could we overcome them?'

*From the HR Director*

'As you know, we're planning shortly to increase the size of our non-specialist graduate development programme and we'll need at least 100 graduates per year. I want to keep the recruitment process as cost-effective as possible, so can I have your recommendations?'

*From the Company Secretary*

'I was glancing through a management magazine and saw the statement that in an ideal world, rogue employees would be weeded out during the recruitment and selection process. How can we ensure that this is done?'

*From an HR colleague*

'My company is smaller than other supermarkets in the UK and our share price has fallen. We've been making people redundant as we've disposed of unprofitable stores. It's very difficult to recruit and retain staff in retailing and we can't offer the sort of salaries that Tesco and Sainsbury's can give. How do you think we can retain our staff and ensure high levels of performance and commitment?'

*From the Managing Director*

'I know that there is a trend towards the use of competency frameworks but the CIPD themselves say that they can "come across as unrealistic specifications for paragons of virtue on a good day!" What do you think? If competency frameworks are the way forward, how can they be made to work?'

Adapted from Johns and Leatherbarrow (2005) *People Resourcing*, CIPD

## ILLUSTRATION

### Extreme makeover

The Travelodge budget hotel chain is opening on average a new hotel every 10 days – an expansion rate that will create 4,500 new jobs over the next three years and double the size of the company. The company is backed by venture capitalists so targets are very competitive and commercially focused. Travelodge's aggressive expansion plans mean that attracting the right staff is vital. The company has decided to ditch formal competencies for front-desk staff and recruit on personality and personal attributes alone. The group has to be innovative with its recruitment strategy to ensure it attracts and retains the right staff. It has arranged 'speed recruitment' sessions where potential employees sit down for a series of one-to-one brief conversations to find out what the job involves and determine their suitability. The company is also in the midst of a 'Management Idol' talent contest aimed at filling 100 hotel manager positions. Shortlisted candidates attend one-day auditions involving one-to-one interviews and assessment workshops including role plays aimed at bringing out their personalities.

Source: *People Management*, 30 June 2005, pp16–17

## EVALUATING THE EFFECTIVENESS OF RECRUITMENT AND SELECTION

As suggested earlier, the process of recruitment and selection reflects a process of matching predicated on the view that there are clear differences between people and that certain people are more suited to certain jobs than others. In particular, personality and motivation are important influences in determining performance in many customer-facing roles. Changing a person's personality is very difficult but an individual's natural traits and competencies can be built upon and developed. Fitting the right person to the right job ensures personal satisfaction and productivity.

The purpose of recruitment and selection is thus to define requirements, attract suitable candidates and to select candidates by measuring their abilities, aptitudes, skills and competencies against requirements so that individuals and jobs can be appropriately matched.

Recruitment and selection thus involves making predictions about future behaviour so that decisions can be made about a person's suitability for a given job (Newell, 2005: 116). Predications are inevitably problematic and a systematic approach to recruitment and selection is focused on making informed decisions rather than uninformed guesses about a person's future performance in a given role (Newell, 2005: 116).

Concepts of reliability and validity are thus crucial aspects of assessment and selection. Reliability refers to the extent to which any measurement used in the selection process is consistent – ie the degree to which different interviewers agree. Validity refers to the accuracy of the measurement used – ie the degree to which the instrument used accurately predicts job performance, accurately reflects the nature of the work to be undertaken or accurately measures the specific psychological, personality or ability characteristics of applicants (Lundy and Cowling, 1996: 228–9).

In order to achieve reliability and validity, the recruitment and selection process must be objective, fair and free from bias. As Lundy and Cowling (1996: 226–7) put it,

HR selection is a process of measurement, decision-making and evaluation. The goal of a selection system is to select individuals who will perform well on the job. It must be fair. If it is to be fair, it must be as accurate as possible.

**Table 11** *Selection methods and predictive validity*

| | |
|---|---|
| 1.00 | perfect selection |
| 0.65 | intelligence tests and integrity tests |
| 0.63 | intelligence tests and structured interviews |
| 0.60 | intelligence tests and work sampling |
| 0.54 | work sample tests |
| 0.51 | intelligence tests |
| 0.51 | structured interviews |
| 0.41 | integrity tests |
| 0.40 | personality tests |
| 0.37 | assessment centres |
| 0.35 | biodata |
| 0.26 | references |
| 0.18 | years of job experience |
| 0.10 | years in education |
| 0.02 | graphology |
| 0.00 | random selection |

Source: adapted from Robertson I. and Smith M. (2001) Personnel Selection, *Journal of Occupational and Organizational Psychology* Vol. 74. No 4, pp441–72.

Achieving reliability and validity stems from an accurate initial assessment of the component elements of the job to be filled, in other words, from job analysis.

The widespread use of specific selection methods does not guarantee their accuracy or validity in predicting job performance. Marchington and Wilkinson (2005) have summarised the results of research into the predictive validity of different selection methods and found that the most popular techniques are often the least effective in predicting job performance, as illustrated in Table 11.

All selection methods have shortcomings and deficiencies. Traditional interviews can be criticised for their subjectivity and tendency to stereotype people. Anderson and Shackleton (1993: 53–63) summarised the shortcomings of interviews as follows:

- *Primary effect* – interviewers form impressions of candidate's personality very early on
- *Expectancy effect* – interviewers form an expectancy of the candidate from his/her application which strongly affects their final decision
- *Confirmatory information-seeking bias* – interviewers ask questions to actively seek information to confirm their initial impressions
- *Stereotyping and prototyping* – interviewers have notions of stereotypical and prototypical ideal job holders and seek to match candidates to these notions
- *Halo/horns effect* – interviewers interpret information and rate candidates either in a generally positive or generally negative manner
- *Contrast effect* – interviewer decisions are affected by decisions on candidates seen earlier in the day and by pre-set quotas of numbers required
- *Negative information bias* – interviewers are influenced significantly more by negative information than by positive information
- *Clone syndrome* – interviewers prefer candidates similar to themselves in biographical background, personality and attitudes
- *Personal liking bias* – interviewers select candidates they like personally and allow their ratings of ability to be influenced by personal liking.

As suggested earlier, structured interviews have greater predictive validity but nevertheless also have limitations. Situational interviews, where candidates are asked how they would respond in certain hypothetical situations, assume that actual behaviour would be in line with stated behaviour, which may not be the case (Barclay, 2001: 97).

Behavioural interviews are predicated on assumptions that behavioural patterns remain constant over time and that candidates can be fairly compared in this way. However, past behaviour is not always an accurate predictor of future behaviour and this approach marginalises the potential for change on the basis of experience. Equity of comparison can also be challenged on the basis that those candidates with limited experience or poor recall may be disadvantaged in behavioural interview situations (Barclay, 2001: 97).

Psychometric tests also have a number of limitations. There is continuing concern over the ethical use of testing and there are still plenty of poor tests, disreputable providers and untrained assessors (Smith *et al*, 1989: 77–8). Certain tests have been found to contain inherent gender bias and to discriminate against ethic minorities (Newell and Shackleton, 2000: 126). Ability tests are based on specific jobs but often, effective job performance is far more complex than can be captured by a test of ability (Barclay, 2001: 97). Personality tests are based on the questionable assumption that personality is a stable concept and that certain personalities are more suited to certain jobs (Iles and Salaman, 1995: 219–24).

Assessment centres score high on predictive validity because they use a range of measures. However, if the exercises used lack relevance and are poorly designed and assessors lack training they are likely to achieve little. Moreover, assessment centre activities are based on assumptions that the activities undertaken are representative of the job and that the snapshot of observed behaviour is representative of the candidate's behaviour (Barclay, 2001: 97).

The systematic approach to recruitment and selection is valuable in outlining the nature and scope of activities required to ensure that the organisation has sufficient numbers of human resources to meet existing and future needs. However, this approach is predicated on a rational, logical and objective approach to assessment and decision-making. The underpinning rationale is that by following the sequence of defined stages, the organisation will improve the quality of the matching process and ensure that the 'right' person is selected. However, as Taylor (2005: 105) suggests the process of HRP has a low profile in organisations and in practice, planning for human resources is unsystematic and informal.

Moreover, as Newell and Shackleton (2001: 29) suggest, the actual decision-making process is often far removed from the rational normative model. In reality, they argue, organisational recruitment and selection is constrained by perceptual limitations and biases; by limited availability of information on which to base a decision; and by the conflicting goals of different organisational stakeholders which result in personal biases, interpersonal conflicts and power struggles. As a result, irrationality occurs at each stage of the process. For example, whereas the rational, systematic approach suggests that recruitment is about generating the widest possible pool of candidates, in reality it is personal contacts and networks that provide job openings, especially at senior levels. Even where ratings are used to assess candidates, these are often evaluated subjectively and weightings are assigned to justify rather than make decisions (Newell and Shackleton, 2001: 32).

## RETENTION

This chapter has highlighted the challenges faced by organisations in acquiring human resources with the competencies and abilities to support organisational goals and strategies both now and in the future. Having acquired such resources, logic dictates that a primary aim for organisations should be to retain and motivate talented individuals. Managing retention and keeping labour turnover to target represents a key strategic issue for organisations.

Organisations may adopt a policy of segmenting their labour force and adopting different employment strategies for different groups. High levels of labour turnover may be acceptable within peripheral groups where there is a plentiful supply of labour ready to replace those who leave. However, the retention process becomes particularly significant for core employees or knowledge workers. When such employees leave, the organisation loses an essential element of human capital and this loss may be compounded if they join a competitor (Buckingham, 2000: 44).

The CIPD (2005: 23) Recruitment, Retention and Turnover report found that the average level of labour turnover was 15.7 per cent with much higher levels in call centres (35.7 per cent) and hotels, catering and leisure (67.4 per cent). 73 per cent of respondents reported experiencing difficulties in retaining staff and that labour turnover was having a negative effect on organisational performance. Organisations are faced with the prospect of replacing employees, a process which carries significant costs, both direct (eg costs of advertising, agency costs, administrative costs, management time spent on selection) and indirect (eg time taken before new recruit reaches required level of performance, effects of negative employee turnover on existing employees).

The CIPD (2005: 14) Recruitment, Retention and Turnover report estimated that the average direct cost of recruiting a replacement member of staff was £3,950. The average cost of replacing senior managers was estimated at £10,000. The average cost of replacing a manual worker was £1,000.

It is essential therefore to establish why people leave and what may be done to retain them. The CIPD (2005) Recruitment, Retention and Turnover report found that the principal reasons for leaving were opportunities for development, promotion and career advancement outside the organisation and that the most common initiative to improve retention was improving employee communications and involvement. Exit interviews and staff attitude surveys are commonly used methods to understand why people might leave and to gather information to inform retention strategies. The Kwik-Fit example below illustrates how an employee survey can help inform retention strategy.

## ILLUSTRATION

### Employees' ideas boost staff retention: Kwik-Fit

HR initiatives based on employee suggestions have reduced staff turnover by almost a quarter at Kwik-Fit Financial services (KFFS). Turnover at the call centre has fallen to 29 per cent from 52 per cent in 2001 and employee opinion surveys have shown a steady increase in staff satisfaction rates. These improvements have been credited to the introduction of workshops where staff can give their opinions on improving retention and motivation. In 2002 each of the 650 employees attended a one-day workshop, where they were asked for ideas on improving the work environment. Initiatives introduced included a flexible benefits programme and a revised induction scheme. Under consideration is the introduction of a crèche and improved pension provision. Some initiatives are linked to staff performance such as the right to work a four-day compressed week, which is given to staff with a good sales record.

Source: *People Management*, 3 June 2004, p8

Newell and Shackleton (2000: 133) emphasise the importance of recruitment and selection as a process of assessment and socialisation rather than an isolated activity. In this sense, they suggest, there is a need for organisations to consider how recruitment and selection influences candidate expectations and behaviour and to provide reliable information and the opportunity for a genuine exchange of views so that the candidate understands the culture of the organisation, the nature of the job and the opportunities available.

As Newell and Shackleton (2000: 133) put it,

> **Allowing new employees to gain a realistic understanding of the job and organisational culture and using recruitment and selection as a basis for negotiating a robust psychological contract, starts the process of organisational socialisation. It is certainly more likely to lead to the recruitment of individuals who are willing to give long-term commitment to the organisation than is seeing recruitment and selection as a management decision-making process related to a one-sided predication of future, narrowly defined job success.**

Taylor (2005: 350) suggests that the key features of a retention strategy should centre on realistic job previews and effective selection, induction and socialisation strategies. This underscores the importance of job analysis, appropriate selection techniques and the process of socialisation in creating realistic expectations of the job and the organisation and contributing to the development of a robust psychological contract which ensures that the employee remains with the organisation.

Drawing on the work of Hom and Griffeth (1995), Taylor (2005: 350–3) identifies additional features of effective retention strategies as:

- *job enrichment*, or the provision of meaningful and challenging work which reduces the likelihood of the employee becoming alienated and disillusioned
- *leader-member exchange* – Taylor (2005: 351) suggests that the nature of the relationship between the manager and employee can have a significant effect on the development of a high trust employment relationship, especially in the initial stages of employment. Buckingham (2000: 45) suggests that employees, especially knowledge workers, leave managers not companies.
  Such statements underscore the importance of having managers who show care, interest, concern and empathy with employees, who can explain what is expected

of them and provide regular and positive feedback and recognition for work well done. Buckingham (2000) suggests that able managers pay particular attention to the selection and development of their staff and are able to achieve a good fit between talent and work.

■ *managing inter-role conflict* – labour turnover is affected by the conflicting demands of work and family responsibilities. Concern for work–life balance has been fuelled by a number of factors including wider social and economic changes (eg a long hours culture and the impact of 24-hour society) as well as government legislation and initiatives (eg the maternity provisions of 1999 Employment Act, parental leave and new rules on part-time workers).

Specifically, the business case for work–life balance revolves around the potential for a more productive workforce, reduced labour turnover and absence levels, becoming an employer of choice and hence an ability to recruit in competitive labour markets.

There are a range of options available to organisations in creating a work–life balance (part-time working, voluntary reduction in working hours, compressed working week, term-time working, individually tailored working patterns, flexible shiftwork, job-share, flexitime, homeworking). The overall emphasis is on finding creative solutions to tensions between personal circumstances and business demands.

## KEY LEARNING POINTS

■ The resourcing processes of human resource planning, recruitment, selection and retention are critical in ensuring that an organisation has the skills, experience and talent to meet the demands of its environment and adapt to change.

■ HRP is a systematic process of analysing the organisation's HR needs and developing specific, mutually supportive policies to meet those needs.

■ Recruitment and selection is a matching process focused on finding employees who match the job, the team and the organisation. There is a trend towards organisations attempting to match individual values, beliefs and attitudes to the culture and values of the organisation.

■ A systematic approach to recruitment and selection incorporates key stages and activities of job analysis, attracting candidates through appropriate recruitment sources and making selection decisions.

■ Interviews together with application forms and references represent the most popular and widely used forms of selection. There are, however, significant differences in the predictive validity of different selection techniques.

■ Retention is a key strategic issue for organisations. Key features of an effective retention strategy include effective recruitment, selection and socialisation, flexibility and appropriate work–life balance.

## Additional reading

CIPD (2005) *Managing Diversity. Linking theory and practice to business performance*, Change Agenda, May

CIPD (2005) *Managing Diversity: People make the difference at work – but everyone is different*, CIPD Guide, March

CIPD (2005) *Psychological Testing* Factsheet

CIPD (2005) *Online Recruitment* Factsheet

CIPD (2005) *Assessment Centres for Recruitment and Selection* Factsheet

CIPD (2005) *Employee Turnover and Retention* Factsheet

CIPD (2005) *Recruitment* Factsheet

### Web-based sources of information

**www.flexibility.co.uk** discusses the main issues relating to flexibility of working

**www.employersforwork-lifebalance.org.uk** builds a business case for work–life balance

**www.cre.gov.uk** website of the Commission for Racial Equality

**www.eoc.org.uk** website of equal opportunities commission

**www.drc.org.uk** website of Disability Rights Commission

**www.nacro.org.uk** website of organisation dedicated to rehabilitation of offenders

## REFERENCES

Anderson N. and Shackleton V. (1993) *Successful Selection Interviewing*, Oxford, Blackwell

Barclay J. (2001) Improving selection interviews with structure: organisations' use of 'behavioural' interviews, *Personnel Review*, Vol.30, No.1, pp81–101

Buchanan D. and Huczynski A. (2004) *Organizational Behaviour. An Introductory Text*, 5th edition, Harlow, FT/Prentice Hall

Buckingham M. (2001) What a waste, *People Management*, 11 October

Campion M., Palmer D. and Campion J. (1997) A review of structure in the selection interview, *Personnel Psychology*, 50, pp655–702

CIPD (2005) Recruitment, Retention and Turnover Report, London, CIPD: available at **www.cipd.co.uk/surveys**

CIPD (2005) *Competency and Competency Frameworks* Fact sheet

Cooper D., Robertson I. and Tinline G. (2003) *Recruitment and Selection. A Framework for Success*, London, Thomson Learning

Ellis C. and Sonnenfeld J. (1994) Diverse approaches to managing diversity, *Human Resource Management*, Vol.33, No.1, pp79–109

Fraser M. (1966) *Employment Interviewing*, London, McDonald & Evans

Hom P. and Griffeth R. (1995) *Employee Turnover*, Cincinnati, South Western

Iles P. and Salaman G. (1995) Recruitment, selection and assessment, in J. Storey (ed.) *Human Resource Management. A Critical Text*, London, Routledge

IPM (1992) *Statement on Human Resource Planning*, London, IPM

Johns T. and Leatherbarrow C. (2005) *People Resourcing*, CIPD Revision Guide, London, CIPD

Kandola R. and Fullerton J. (1998) *Diversity in Action: Managing the mosaic*, London, CIPD

Kwiatkowski R. (2003) Trends in organisations and selection: an introduction, *Journal of Managerial Psychology*, Vol.15, No.5, pp382–94

Lundy O. and Cowling A. (1996) *Strategic Human Resource Management*, London, Routledge

Marchington M. and Wilkinson A. (2005) *Human Resource Management at Work. People Management and Development*, London, CIPD

Michaels E., Hardfield-Jones H. and Axelrod B. (2001) *The War for Talent*, Harvard Business School Press

Mullins L. (2005) *Management and Organisational Behaviour*, London, FT/Prentice Hall

Newell S. (2005) Recruitment and selection, in S. Bach (ed.) *Managing Human Resources. Personnel Management in Transition*, 4th edition, Oxford, Blackwell

Newell S. and Shackleton V. (2000) Recruitment and selection, in S. Bach and K. Sisson (eds) *Personnel Management A Comprehensive Guide to Theory and Practice*, Oxford, Blackwell

Newell S. and Shackleton V. (2001) Selection and assessment as an interactive decision-action process, in T. Redman and A. Wilkinson (eds) *Contemporary Human Resource Management*, Harlow, Financial Times/Prentice Hall

*People Management*, 16 May 2002, p31

*People Management*, 3 June 2004, p8

*People Management*, 16 September 2004, p13

*People Management*, 30 June 2005, pp16–17

*People Management* News, 2 September 2004, p9

Roberts G. (2003) *Recruitment and Selection. A Contingency Approach*, London, CIPD

Robertson I. and Smith M. (2001) Personnel Selection, *Journal of Occupational and Organizational Psychology*, Vol 74, No4, pp441–72

Rodger A. (1952) *The Seven Point Plan*, London, The National Institute for Industrial Psychology

Smethurst S. (2004) The allure of online, *People Management*, 1, 15, pp38–40

Smith M., Gregg M. and Andrews D. (1989) *Selection and Assessment. A New Appraisal*, London, Pitman

Smith M. and Robertson I. (1993) *Systematic Personnel Selection*, London, Macmillan

Taylor M. and Collins C. (2000) Organizational recruitment: enhancing the intersection of research and practice, in G. Cooper and E. Locke (eds) *Industrial and Organizational Psychology*, Oxford, Blackwell

Taylor S. (2005) *People Resourcing*, London, CIPD

Whiddett S. and Hollyforde S. (2000) *The Competencies Handbook*, London, CIPD

# Developing skills and ability for high performance: training, learning and development at work

---

## CHAPTER 7

## LEARNING OBJECTIVES

- To identify key concepts of learning, training, education and development
- To review key theories of learning and their application at the workplace
- To analyse key features and characteristics of the learning and development process
- To review key trends and developments in learning and development
- To analyse key features of management and leadership development
- To evaluate the contribution of learning and development to organisational performance and effectiveness

## INTRODUCTION

Chapters 2 and 3 evaluated the link between the management of people and organisational performance. The research evidence reviewed was unequivocal in demonstrating that the skills, abilities and motivation of employees can make a difference to organisational performance. This difference can come from the demonstration of discretionary behaviour from employees in customer-facing roles (Chapter 4) or it can come from the ability to retain scarce technical and commercial skills within increasingly tight labour markets (Chapter 6). A willingness to learn and acquire new skills is in itself a form of discretionary behaviour. Where organisations compete on the basis of quality of process it is self-evident that they need to ensure they have staff with the right level and combination of skills, abilities and competencies required by that process.

In a variety of ways, therefore, individual and organisational learning and development can make the difference to the achievement of competitive advantage. As Boxall and Purcell (2003: 143–4) suggest, for firms that have invested in recruitment and selection and have built a labour force with potential, learning and development enables them to maximise this investment and build the firm's agility over the long-term. Learning and development are thus key components of organisational process advantage (Boxall, 1996: 67). As Sloman (2003: 2) puts it,

> Committed individuals who understand the organisation's objectives, and operate in an environment where they have the opportunity to take the appropriate discretionary behaviour, create powerful business advantages which can be very difficult for a competitor to duplicate.

The development of a skilled, creative and able workforce represents a national priority and can be seen as part of a wider political and economic agenda. In 2002, the DTI sponsored research by Michael Porter into levels of UK competitiveness and the persistent gap between UK productivity levels and those of principal competitor nations such as the USA, Germany and France. The resulting report (pp 21, 12) found that

> labour skills continue to be an area of competitive disadvantage for the UK. . . . The UK lags the US in the share of high-skill employees. The UK has a significantly lower share of intermediate-skill employees than Germany and France ... The UK's labour force problem appears to be mainly a problem of the current stock of employees.

There is evidence that persistent skill gaps and deficiencies are creating recruitment problems and affecting the ability of organisations to improve levels of performance. Productivity comparisons between France, Germany, the UK and the USA in terms of the GDP per hour worked (UK = 100) are shown in Table 12.

Table 12  *International productivity comparisons*

|  | UK | USA | France | Germany |
|---|---|---|---|---|
| **1993** | 100 | 137.7 | 125.1 | 106.8 |
| **1998** | 100 | 134.6 | 117.0 | 108.7 |
| **2001** | 100 | 137.5 | 115.3 | 108.8 |

Source: Office for National Statistics, 2002 (**www.statistics.gov.uk**)

Attempts to plug the productivity and skills gap in the UK's national competitiveness can be seen in the current high priority being given to skills development through a range of national initiatives (eg National Vocational Qualifications, Modern Apprenticeships, Investor in People standard) and institutions (eg Learning and Skills Council, Regional Development Agencies, Sector Skills Development Agency, Sector Skills Development Councils, LearnDirect) as well as reforms in the primary and secondary education sector.

'A country's success is achieved through the skills and education of its people – its human capital is its major asset.'                                        Tony Blair, November 2003

'Growing a strong pipeline of talent – that's the critical success factor.'
                                                                Michael Dell, January 2004

'Our Asian rivals are closing the skills gap ... We need a fundamental change of culture so that learning takes place in every workplace.'      Gordon Brown, April 2004

'This country will succeed or fail on the basis of its skills level. In order for Britain to remain competitive and a leading economic power, the skills gap in the British workforce must be addressed.'                                        Tony Blair, May 2004

However, government rhetoric about the transformation of the UK economy into a high skill, knowledge and information economy, though inspirational, obscures the extent of the gap between aspiration and achievement. Notwithstanding the progress being made, current initiatives mask long-standing and systemic weaknesses in UK training and development provision at national and organisational level.

As Taylor (2002: 2) puts it,

**Over many generations Britain has simply not given sufficient priority to the development of training, especially in the use of transferable, intermediate skills that are now believed to be increasingly necessary for the success of modern companies. Too many firms today are trapped in a low-skills equilibrium where they are competing on price in low-value-added product sectors and demanding low-skilled low-cost labour.**

As Chapter 1 has shown, changes in the business and competitive context within which organisations are increasingly being required to operate carry enormous implications for the development of skilled workforces in high-performance organisations producing high-value-added goods and services. As Taylor (2002: 2) suggests,

> **In the face of the globalisation challenge and substantial advances in science and technology in advanced market economies ... Britain's firms will have to raise their efforts and move decisively into the production of high-value/high-quality goods and services and to compete in markets where such goods are in demand.**

The business case for human resource development in the achievement of improved organisational performance is urgent and compelling. However, training and development remains a peripheral and optional activity. Persistent and continuing problems of skills shortages reinforce findings from a wide range of research studies (see Chapter 3) that few organisations are attempting to develop high-performance workplaces producing high-value and -quality goods and services.

Moreover, what training and development does take place is poorly focused and unequally distributed. It is focused primarily on job-related, health and safety and induction training and directed at those with higher levels of education and qualification (Reynolds, 2004: 14). As Westwood (2001: 21) puts it,

> **We seem to spend a lot of money on training that doesn't last and on people who may not need it.**

Just as many organisations pay little more than lip service to the mantra that 'people are our greatest asset', few organisations have fully recognised the contribution of the people they employ to organisational performance. The concept of skill is frequently equated with 'hard' technical skills and abilities whereas 'softer' skills may be equally important in service environments. Certain types of skills, gained through experience, may be essential in the exercise of discretionary effort that results in superior customer service but are frequently under-valued.

Organisations have shown themselves prepared to restructure the work of certain groups of employees (eg railway maintenance, hospital cleaners, call centre work outsourced to India) and to achieve cost savings through outsourcing work to cheaper providers. The implications of such cost-driven measures on service quality are often a secondary consideration.

This chapter explores the processes of training, learning and development in the enhancement of employee skills and abilities and the creation of high-performance working environments where employees can contribute to the full extent of their abilities. It begins with an analysis of the core processes of learning, training and development and their application at the workplace. It goes on to evaluate the role of learning and development in creating and sustaining organisational competence and high performance.

## DEFINING THE TERMINOLOGY OF LEARNING AND DEVELOPMENT

To understand the process of learning and development it is first important to understand the core concepts underpinning the process. Concepts such as learning, training and development are often used interchangeably and although there is a large degree of overlap between them, it is important to be clear on how these terms are being used. The following definitions are provided to demonstrate the distinction between terms and concepts.

### Learning

Buchanan and Huczynski (2004: 110) define learning as 'the process of acquiring knowledge through experience which leads to an enduring change in behaviour.' Learning is a fundamental aspect of our psychological make-up and a vital part of our physical, social and psychological development. We learn through formal, systematic and structured activities at school, college and in the workplace, but also through interaction with other people.

Learning can thus have a formal as well as a spontaneous, automatic and social dimension. As Mullins (2005: 392) suggests, individual learning can be influenced by a wide range of external (relationships, context, methods) and internal factors (perception, motivation, attitudes, ability, emotions, personality). From an organisational perspective, understanding how people learn enables managers to develop strategies to increase individual competence and ability and thus increase organisational flexibility, adaptation and performance. Theories of learning and their implications are reviewed in the section on Conceptualising Learning later in this chapter.

### Training

Training is a specific way in which learning can take place within the organisation. Training can be viewed as a bounded activity focused on equipping employees with the knowledge and skills necessary to perform work roles and responsibilities to satisfactory standards. The Manpower Services Commission (MSC) (1981: 62) defined training as

> **a planned process to modify attitude, knowledge or skill behaviour through learning experiences to achieve effective performance in an activity or range of activities. Its purpose, in the work situation, is to develop the abilities of the individual and to satisfy the current and future needs of the organisation.**

The terms 'attitudes', 'knowledge' and 'skills' are used here in a broad sense. Shaping or changing *attitudes* through training might involve raising awareness of prejudices in order to modify behaviour, developing flexibility and co-operation in team work or courtesy and sensitivity in dealing with customers.

*Knowledge* relates to the way in which we process information and attach sense and meaning to it. A distinction can be made between *explicit knowledge* or knowledge which is quantifiable and hence easily transferred and reproduced, and *tacit knowledge* which is concerned with understanding and application. Tacit knowledge is often combined with experience and interpretation and is therefore far less easy to harness and reproduce.

A similar distinction can be applied to the concept of *skill*. Skills relate to those aspects of behaviour which need to be performed to an acceptable level to ensure effective job performance (Marchington and Wilkinson, 2005: 238). Skills can incorporate a range of abilities including manual or technical skills or the application of specific knowledge and skills to the performance of a discrete task; interpersonal skill or the ability involved in working with and through other people; diagnostic and analytical skills involved in making sense of complex situations and applying judgement and decision-making.

*Tacit skills* are largely instinctive and developed through experience rather than formal instruction. As Harrison (2002: 225) puts it, tacit skills are 'typified in the way in which someone develops their "unique" knack of tackling a job and always does it to a high standard of performance and quality.' Tacit skills are therefore difficult to replicate and can be a source of strategic advantage.

## ILLUSTRATION

### Lorna McKee, Area HR Manager, Hilton Hotel Belfast

*We can't train everyone to do everything. The emphasis is on getting people to learn within the environment where they work, and getting them to adapt and apply that knowledge. Every customer has different expectations. There is no way we can train for every eventuality. We want our staff to be spontaneous and react and respond to guest expectations.*

Source: Sloman (2003) Focus on the learner, CIPD Change Agenda, p3

More recently the term *competence* has gained prominence for aspects of work-related behaviour. There remains, however, some confusion over the use of the term. According to Whiddett and Hollyforde (1999: 5–7) competencies are typical behaviours that individuals demonstrate when undertaking job-relevant tasks to produce job-related outcomes within a given organisational context. Competence and competency are thus person-related and focused on the individual and how they behave in carrying out work-related activities.

Competencies are qualitatively different and relate to specific descriptions of work tasks or job outputs that have to be achieved in order to demonstrate satisfactory job performance. Competency frameworks are used to define the dimensions of a job or activity to be performed and the criteria by which effectiveness of performance will be judged.

## Development

Both training and development can be concerned with the development of knowledge, skills and attitudes but where training is specifically focused on immediate, short-term requirements of the job or task, the concept of development is broader and focused on the longer-term growth and development of the individual in a way that fulfils their potential.

The MSC (1981: 15) defined development as

> **the growth or realisation of a person's ability, through conscious or unconscious learning and development programmes usually including elements of planned study and experience, and frequently supported by a coaching and counselling facility.**

The concept of *coaching* reflects a sporting analogy and is used to describe a one-to-one relationship between a manager and individual employee with the aim of developing or enhancing their performance. Coaching is a more learner-centred activity than instruction. The CIPD (2005) Annual Training and Development Survey found considerable growth in the use of coaching as a development tool.

A related concept is that of *mentoring* which is also growing in popularity as a development tool. Mentoring refers to a relationship where a senior, experienced individual provides support, advice and friendship to a younger less experienced member of staff. Mentoring can be both formal and informal and can take different forms – for example, some organisations use mentoring arrangements for new recruits or as a key aspect of diversity management.

187

## Education

The concept of education is broader in scope than training and is concerned with learning over an extended period that develops the individual's knowledge, social understanding and skill and intellectual capacity. The MSC (1981) says:

> **Education is defined as activities which aim to develop the knowledge, skills, moral values and understanding required in all aspects of life rather than a knowledge and skill relating to only a limited field of activity.**

## CONCEPTUALISING LEARNING – AN OVERVIEW OF KEY THEORIES

Learning is a common theme underpinning concepts of training, education and development. How people learn and how they acquire skills and abilities for effective job performance are important considerations for the design and implementation of learning and development strategy and practice. Knowing how people learn can help managers to effectively diagnose performance problems and identify corrective actions. This section therefore summarises key theories of the learning process and outlines their implications for learning and development design.

Theories of learning have their roots in the study of psychology and initial theories were developed from research studies into animal behaviour and learning. From these early studies different perspectives have been developed which provide insights into the nature of individual learning. It is generally recognised that there are four broad perspectives based on behaviourist, cognitive, social learning and humanist psychology.

## Behaviourist perspectives on the learning process

As the term suggests, the behaviourist perspective was concerned with the study of behaviour and those actions that could be observed, measured, quantified and controlled (Mullins, 2005: 403). A fundamental concept of the behaviourist approach is that of *conditioning* or the process whereby certain events become associated with certain outcomes; in behaviourist terms, between *stimulus* and *response*.

Pavlov's (1927) experiments with dogs demonstrated how certain instinctive reflexes such as salivation could be 'conditioned' to respond to different stimuli. Skinner's (1948) experiments with rats and pigeons demonstrated the effects of reward and punishment on learning. Skinner showed that a particular response could be learned when associated with a reward, whereas behaviour associated with punishment would be discontinued.

The behaviourist perspective thus suggests that learning is the result of experience and that we use knowledge of our past behaviour to change, modify and improve behaviour in the future (Buchanan and Huczynski, 2004: 112). Moreover, we learn to repeat behaviour which has favourable consequences and avoid behaviour that leads to negative consequences.

Behaviourist approaches have been very influential in highlighting specific elements in the process of learning which need to be taken into account when designing or facilitating learning events. It demonstrates how behaviour can be 'shaped' through appropriate reinforcement techniques.

As Stewart (2002: 126) suggests, learning and development programmes based on behaviour modification can be used in a variety of organisational settings and for a variety of knowledge, skills and attitudes outcomes such as sales training, VDU operation, call centre work and professional management development. It can be especially important in induction where it is important that new employees learn appropriate stimulus–response associations. This approach can also underpin performance management systems designed to shape employee behaviour to conform to organisational goals and priorities.

The shortcomings of the behaviourist approach stem from its restrictive and mechanistic approach. The range of stimuli in the workplace may make it difficult to identify a 'correct response' (Marchington and Wilkinson, 2005: 239). Moreover, as Mullins (2005: 409) suggests, it fails to sufficiently acknowledge the complexity of social interaction and the influence of internal factors such as personality, perception and attitudes on behaviour.

## Cognitive approaches

In contrast to the restrictive, reactive and mechanistic approach of behaviourism, cognitive approaches emphasise the use of proactive mental processes in learning whereby individuals process information, gain insight and understanding and consider alternative ways of achieving their goals (Buchanan and Huczynski, 2004: 111). Mental models such as attitude formation thus result from our experience of interacting with our environment and processing the information received about that environment. Cognitive approaches also emphasise the informal nature of learning.

Cognitive approaches stem from the work of Kohler (1925) who researched how animals solved problems and that of Piaget (1926) whose work was focused on child development. Many cognitive theorists view learning as a sequence where information about the environment is processed in distinct stages; an active perception stage which gives attention to stimuli from the environment; a mentally active stage which makes sense of this information; and a restructuring and storage stage where the information is internalised (Mullins, 2005: 411).

A related aspect of the cognitive approach is the concept of *schema* or *cognitive maps* which suggests that we create personal representations of our understanding of our environment and our experiences within that environment (Stewart, 2002: 179). Kelly's (1955) Personal Construct Theory argues that we create our own mental models of the world and our place within it based on our experiences, beliefs, values and feelings. Such mental models and constructs are likely to vary between individuals and hence the process of learning will also vary.

Cognitive learning theory has significant implications for organisational HR strategy and practice. Models of training, learning and development (as outlined in the next section) are informed by a view of learning as a series of stages incorporating motivation, insight, information processing, understanding, memory and emotion. At a broader level, Stewart (2002: 179) argues that cognitive learning theories provide a theoretical foundation for culture change programmes whereby organisations define (for instance through mission and values statements) the types of behaviours employees are expected to demonstrate.

A theme of cognitive learning theory is that learning does not just occur in formal structured situations and that learning can be informal and spontaneous. The dynamic, continuous and cyclical nature of learning is best exemplified by the experiential learning approach illustrated by Kolb's (1983) learning cycle (Figure 19).

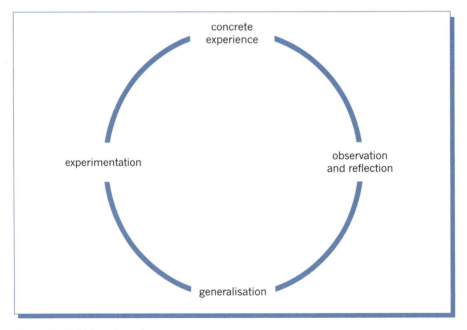

**Figure 19** *Kolb's learning cycle*

According to the model, effective learning results from progression through the four stages. Kolb's model sees learning as goal-directed and thus recognises that as individual goals may vary, so individuals will pay attention to different stages of the cycle (Stewart 2002: 180). Honey and Mumford's Learning Styles Questionnaire (LSQ) (1986) measures and describes these different orientations and preferences as follows (Marchington and Wilkinson, 2005: 242):

- *Activists* learn best by active involvement in concrete tasks, and from relatively short tasks such as business games and competitive teamwork exercises.
- *Reflectors* learn best by reviewing and reflecting upon what has happened in certain situations when they are able to stand back, listen and observe.
- *Theorists* learn best when new information can be located within the context of concepts and theories, and they are able to absorb new ideas, distanced from real-life situations.
- *Pragmatists* learn best when they see a link between new information and real-life problems and issues, and from being exposed to techniques that can be applied immediately.

The experiential approach sees learning as a cyclical, dynamic and continuous process. It also underscores learning as an active process in which learners are not passive recipients of 'training' but actively seek out opportunities to apply their behaviour in new situations. The experiential approach and the concept of learning styles have implications for learning and development design and learning methods. It underpins organisational initiatives such as action learning sets (small groups working on 'live' organisational problems and issues). The emphasis on reflection has obvious links to the 'thinking performer' concept and Continuous Professional Development (CPD).

## ACTIVITY . . .

Why is it important for an HR manager to understand different learning theories?

How can this knowledge be applied to learning and development initiatives within an organisation?

## Social learning

A refinement of behaviourist and cognitive approaches is so-called Social Learning Theory or *observational learning* (Stewart, 2002: 177) which suggests that learning is a social activity and that individuals learn through observing and imitating the behaviour of others.

This approach incorporates the concept of 'role model' which suggests that individuals will seek to 'model' themselves on others who they perceive to be successful and therefore imitate their behaviour (Stewart, 2002: 177). Role modelling underpins mentoring-type initiatives within organisations. Marchington and Wilkinson (2005: 240) argue that many basic, and social and interpersonal skills are learned in this way and that observational learning is an effective way of transferring tacit skills. The drawback is however, that individuals may also learn inappropriate behaviours – eg bullying, racist and sexist behaviour.

## Humanist perspectives on learning

A third approach to learning has been categorised as the humanist perspective. Key aspects of the humanist approach can be seen in the work of Carl Rogers (1969) who argued that individuals have a natural aptitude for learning and have control over their own learning processes and outcomes. As Reynolds *et al* (2002: 22) put it,

> **Knowledge is a personal, subjective issue, not an external commodity waiting to be internalised through the absorption of content.**

A key focus of this approach is that it is learner-centred. It takes the view that individuals cannot be taught but can learn if the environment is supportive. The role of the trainer in this scenario shifts to that of a learning facilitator while the responsibility for learning rests firmly with the learner.

Facilitation involves the creation of an environment in which people are motivated to think, contribute ideas, listen to others and evaluate their contribution. Humanist approaches thus emphasise a shift from traditional, instructor-led, content-based training interventions to self-directed, work-based learning processes and to the creation of an organisational culture that embeds individual and collective learning and embraces change (see the section later in this chapter entitled *Creating a climate conducive to learning and development*).

## IMPLEMENTING TRAINING, LEARNING AND DEVELOPMENT

The learning theories reviewed above have identified broad principles of learning which in turn underpin organisational processes of training, learning and development.

Principles of learning thus provide a useful framework for the design and implementation of training, learning and development activities. The most widely used framework is the systematic training cycle which comprises four key stages of identifying training needs, designing training, learning and development solutions, implementing training and learning solutions and evaluating their effectiveness.

Harrison (2005: 117) provides a variation on these four broad stages and identifies a cycle of learning and development delivery which comprises eight component elements, as illustrated in Figure 20.

The structured, systematic approach provides a useful framework for the design and implementation of learning and development. However, as Marchington and Wilkinson (2005: 243) suggest, learning and development in organisations rarely follows a logical and structured path and is more likely to be characterised by ad hoc and reactive approaches. A further drawback of the systematic approach is that learning and development becomes isolated from other HR initiatives and wider business goals and priorities. Moreover, a systematic approach is focused on the development of specific knowledge rather than building core learning abilities (Reynolds, 2004: 6).

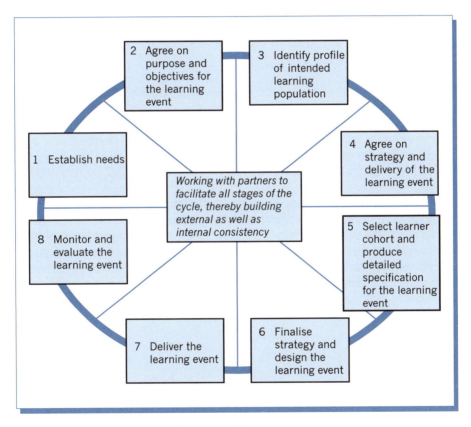

**Figure 20** *Eight-stage process to facilitate planned learning events*
Source: R. Harrison (2005) *Learning and Development*, p117

**ACTIVITY . . .**

You have been asked to design a learning event to improve the networking and presentation skills of senior HR professionals.

How would you structure the learning event?

What learning methods would you use?

How would you evaluate the effectiveness of the event?

## KEY TRENDS AND DEVELOPMENTS IN LEARNING AND DEVELOPMENT

As stated earlier, the UK has a poor record on vocational education and development compared with competitor countries and numerous reports and research studies have criticised the quantity and quality of vocational education and training (Constable and McCormick, 1987; Handy, 1987).

The UK continues to adopt a voluntarist approach where employers are seen as the key beneficiaries of training and development, and thus in control of levels of training provision, while the government's role is to encourage training through a range of national and local initiatives. This contrasts with other European countries, principally France and Germany where the responsibility is shared. (For an account of UK national VET policy and practice see Marchington and Wilkinson, 2005; Harrison, 2002; Stewart, 1999.)

However, the structure of UK financial markets and the resulting pressure on organisations has inhibited the development of a long-term strategic approach to VET. As Harrison (2002: 32) has suggested, 'In the UK, short-termism still dominates the financial base of most organisations and the structure of industry generally, and there is a persistent over-reliance by employers on market forces to provide their skills supply.' A lack of investment in training and development is seen as a key contributory factor to persistent skills shortages. The following section examines the nature, scope and causes of skills shortages as well as evaluating recent trends and developments in organisational learning and development.

### Skills shortages

The National Employers Skills Survey (2003) was based on a large-scale and comprehensive analysis of skills across sectors and occupations and highlighted continuing and persistent skills shortages which were in turn contributing to recruitment problems and inhibiting improvements in organisational performance.

The survey found high levels of sectoral and regional variation. London, the South-East and the West Midlands were the most severely affected areas, and retailing, health and social work were particularly affected sectors. Overall, however, 22 per cent of employers reported skills gaps in their workforces. One of the survey's findings was that 'In total, 2.4 million employees were described by employers as not being fully proficient in their current job. This is equivalent to 11 per cent of total employment in England' (National Employers Skills Survey, 2003: 10). More recently the CIPD Recruitment, Retention and Turnover Report (2005) found that 85 per cent of organisations were experiencing recruitment difficulties due to a lack of specialist skills and experience.

Figure 21 illustrates the distribution of employment, vacancies and recruitment problems. The National Employers Skills Survey (2003) found that so-called elementary skills occupations (ie clerical, personal services, cleaning services, security, sales-related services) had a disproportionately high share of skills gaps. The 2005 CIPD survey reported that 45 per cent of organisations were experiencing recruitment difficulties for managerial and professional staff.

Figure 22 illustrates the causes of skills gaps. Although a proportion of skills gaps were attributed to a lack of experience some were more structural in nature reflecting a lack of

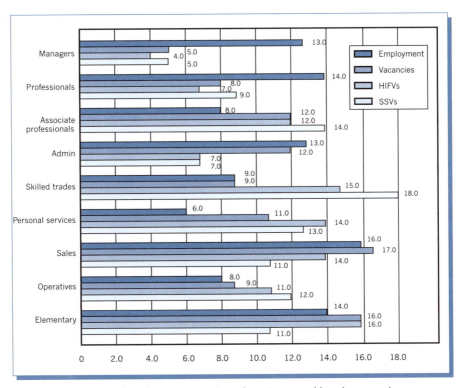

**Figure 21**  *Distribution of employment, vacancies and recruitment problems by occupation*
Source: LSC National Employers Skills Survey, 2003 (IFF/IER)

training or failure to keep up with change. More specifically, a third of skills gaps were identified as stemming from employers' failure to provide sufficient training.

Figure 23 illustrates the impact of skills shortages. Overall the impact on organisational performance was significant both on short-term profits through increased costs and loss of business and on long-term success of the enterprises through delays to new product launches and failing to meet customer service and quality standards. Actions taken by employers to address skills shortages centred predominantly on increased recruitment effort and activity.

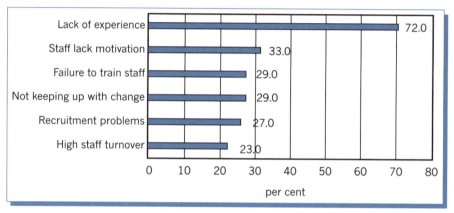

**Figure 22** *Causes of skills gaps*
Source: LSC National Employers Skills Survey, 2003 (IFF/IER)

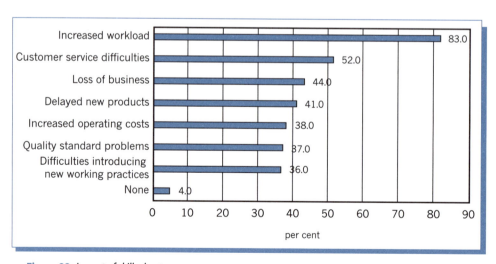

**Figure 23** *Impact of skills shortages*
Source: LSC National Employers Skills Survey, 2003 (IFF/IER)

There is evidence that skill shortages persist and are likely to get worse. The CIPD Training and Development annual survey report 2005 found a high level of awareness among organisations of changing skill requirements and the expectation of higher and broader skill-level requirements in the future. The key drivers of changing skills needs were identified as organisational strategy (79 per cent) and quality improvements (56 per cent). Other reasons included technological change (53 per cent) and the need to respond to legislative requirements (51 per cent). A significant proportion (41 per cent) reported cost reductions as a driver of changing skills needs which, the CIPD suggests,

**will come as unwelcome news to those who believe that UK employers should be competing on added value rather than cost.**

## ILLUSTRATION
### Current skills shortages

The media industry is saturated with people wanting to get in, but still there are always areas that are currently experiencing a shortage of skilled, qualified candidates. Skills shortages occur in the media industry for different reasons; current technicians/personnel get older and retire, with not enough new people entering the industry to take their place; in new media and new technology areas, the demand for certain equipment knowledge, or types of work exceeds the current practitioners trained in these fields.

Source: Skillset, Sector Skills Council for Audio Visual Industries, 2005, **www.skillset.org**

## ILLUSTRATION
### Olympic shortages predicted

Skills shortages in the construction industry could hamper preparation for the Olympic Games and slow down building projects outside London. In total £8.3 billion of capital works are planned to support the games, and it's estimated that 12,000 jobs will be created, many of which will be in construction. 'The risk is that we will fail to get the necessary influx of skills into the industry to cope with increased demand,' said Barry Stephens, chief executive of the National Federation of Builders. Michael Brown, deputy chief executive of the Chartered Institute of Building, said that its research backed this up, with 91 per cent of its 40,000 members anticipating a skills shortage beyond 2005. The institute found that 79 per cent had experienced recruitment problems during 2004–5.

Source: *People Management*, 1 September, 2005

## The nature of training and development provision

Figures on the amounts spent on training and development activities vary and reflect variations in the methodology and sampling of different surveys. Training activities are also sensitive to employer assessments of economic conditions and aggregate figures may mask sectoral variations. The National Employers Skills Survey (2003) reported an average provision of five days' training per employee at an average cost of £206 per employee. The majority of the training provided was specifically related to the employee's job, although other aspects of training provision focused on health and safety training, training in new technologies and induction. The CIPD (2005) Training Survey findings indicated an average of 5.8 days' training per employee at an average cost of £607.

Despite the stated intention of employers to increase training budgets in order to upskill their workforces, the CIPD (2005) Annual Training survey found evidence of continuing short-termism and a focus on immediate operational issues rather than a proactive longer-term view of training as an investment. Although organisations were aware of changing skill requirements, the focus of their activities was on immediate rather than future skill requirements.

Moreover, constraints to the development of a more strategic long-term proactive approach were noted. Although 94 per cent of respondents stated that upskilling their workforce was central to achieving their objectives, 39 per cent reported a lack of interest by senior management as a barrier to achieving the improvements needed. 81 per cent of respondents cited business pressures as the main reason for the lack of managerial support for learning and development. Only 17 per cent of organisations rewarded and recognised managers for developing and improving the skills of employees, which may account for poor management commitment to training and development. Such findings demonstrate a prevailing view of training as an optional, peripheral, reactive activity and point to an urgent need to build management support for training.

## Changing use of learning and development practices

Traditional forms of learning – eg formal education courses and instructor-led training – are still the most popular and widely-used methods of training and development. This is despite evidence that employees prefer active on-the-job methods of learning, and highlights something of a mismatch between organisational practice and employee preference (CIPD 2005: 15). Figure 24 illustrates the proportion of organisations that use different training methods.

However, more traditional methods are predicted to grow at a much slower rate in the future as organisations increasingly use alternative methods of learning and development. Expected changes in training and development methods point to a growth in e-learning and coaching by line managers. Mentoring and more on-the-job methods are also predicted to increase in use.

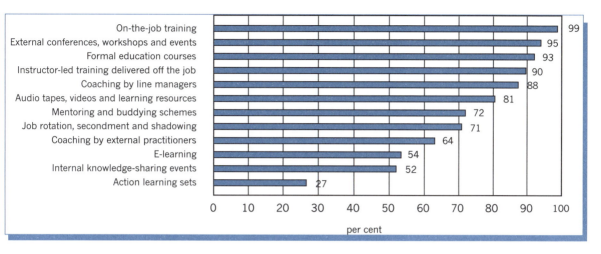

**Figure 24** *Percentage of organisations that use different training methods*
Source: CIPD Training and Development Annual Survey Report, 2005, p8

## MANAGEMENT AND LEADERSHIP DEVELOPMENT

There is widespread recognition of the importance of leadership to organisational performance. As Hutchinson *et al* (2004) found in their research,

> **The role of the front-line manager in bringing (HR) policies to life and in leading was among the most important of all factors in explaining the differences between success and mediocrity in people management.**

However, research has found that UK managers receive less training than managers in the USA, Japan, Germany and France (Keep and Westwood, 2003). The CIPD (2005) Training Survey found that 85 per cent of organisations undertook leadership development activities. The main drivers behind such initiatives were identified as organisational change (63 per cent) and business strategy (62 per cent). In addition, internal skills gaps – principally people management skills and the ability to manage organisational change – were identified as drivers by 57 per cent of organisations. The most common leadership development activities undertaken by organisations include incorporating development needs into performance reviews, in-house development programmes and external seminars and conferences.

Management development can, however, encompass a very wide range of activities, and techniques such as coaching and mentoring are increasingly being recognised as more effective in management development.

## THE CONTRIBUTION OF LEARNING AND DEVELOPMENT TO ORGANISATIONAL EFFECTIVENESS

There is considerable evidence of extensive variation in organisational approaches to training, learning and development. Research by the Ashridge Group (Hall 2002: 201) categorised three broad approaches to organisational training and development reflective of different environmental conditions and pressures. Organisational training and development can be categorised as fragmented where training, learning and development is ad hoc, unplanned and unstructured. More formalised approaches demonstrate a closer integration of learning and development with organisational and individual goals. Focused approaches adopt a long-term view of learning and development and encompass a wide range of activities to develop knowledge, skills and attitudes.

Although the categories may reflect different time-frames and different environmental pressures on organisations, it is nevertheless possible to discern aspects of organisational practice within all three categories within contemporary organisations.

### ACTIVITY . . .

Analyse your organisation's approach to learning and development. What factors influence the approach adopted? Compare your analysis with that of a colleague from another organisation.

### ILLUSTRATION

#### Learning leads the way at INA Bearing

When managers and workers at manufacturing firm INA Bearing Company embarked on a three-year change programme in 2001, they knew that the future of their company was at stake. 'This was not only a change programme, this was our fight for survival,' says Adrian Roberts, personnel manager.

Low-cost competition from Eastern Europe meant that the factory, which makes engine components, had lost more than 500 jobs since the late 1990s, cutting its workforce to 360. 'People felt that closure was imminent. The grapevine was rife with rumour,' Roberts recalls. 'We knew that we needed to differentiate ourselves to safeguard the plant, but we couldn't compete with Eastern Europe.' Instead, the management decided to transform the factory into a 'production location of choice' for high-tech products by boosting the skills of the remaining employees. With this came the recognition that the plant required a huge investment in training and development to create a culture of continuous improvement. As Roberts says, 'We switched investment from machinery to people and focused on making the rate of learning greater than the rate of change.'

To involve the whole workforce in the culture change the firm bought in a 'five-S' (sort, straighten, sweep, standardise and self-discipline) training programme for all employees to improve the work environment. This led to immediate improvements in productivity, quality and health and safety.

The next step was to launch an NVQ programme for all operators in performing manufacturing operations. This runs alongside a team leader's programme in business improvement techniques. Senior managers are involved in delivering training. The company has also developed a learning centre at the plant where employees can use computers to access LearnDirect courses.

The effects of the change programme have been widespread and tangible. Staff turnover has dropped to 2.5 per cent from 8.1 per cent, and absence rates have been cut in half. Productivity and health and safety have improved. Cost reduction projects undertaken by employees have resulted in savings of more that £324,000. Quality has also improved and the defect rate has dropped from 53 per million to 6.5 per million.

Source: Z. Roberts and R. Watkins (2003) Learning leads the way, *People Management*, 6 November 2003, pp34–5

The view of learning and development as an investment in human capital for competitive advantage highlights a range of new approaches to learning and development and a challenge to develop and implement new models of learning and development for current conditions. As Reynolds *et al* (2002, px) put it,

> **Greater experimentation with alternative processes is needed – in particular, blends of self-directed, experiential and socially-mediated learning.**

Sloman (2003: 29) argues that in a period of uncertainty and turbulence, learning and development processes should be marked by a shift of focus from training to learning. As he puts it,

**Interventions and activities which are intended to improve knowledge and skills in organisations will increasingly focus on the learner. Emphasis will shift to the individual learner (or team), and he or she will be encouraged to take more responsibility for his or her learning. Efforts will be made to develop a climate which supports effective and appropriate learning. Such interventions and activities will form part of an integrated approach to creating competitive advantage through people in the organisation.**

A shift from instructor-led, content-based to self-directed, work-based approaches carries considerable implications for the nature and scope of learning and development provision. As Reynolds (2004: x) suggests,

**It implies a need to re-evaluate the way we design interventions, leading to methods that consciously deepen the learning capabilities of employees, allowing them to take greater responsibility (individually and collectively) for their learning.**

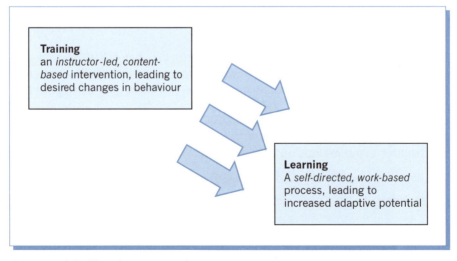

**Figure 25** *Shift of focus from training to learning*
Source: Reynolds (2004) *Helping People Learn*, p26

Implicit in such a shift is a blurring of the balance between formal and informal learning, the creation of communities and networks of practice rather than classrooms and a focus on self-directed learning. Learning activities such as coaching, e-learning and blended learning are important features of self-directed, work-based approaches.

## COACHING

As highlighted earlier, coaching is becoming an increasingly popular and widespread tool in learning and development, with executive coaching becoming particularly widespread. The main reasons organisations use coaching are to improve individual performance, deal with under-performance and improve productivity (CIPD, 2005). A CIPD (2004) factsheet has identified the key features of coaching as:

- Coaching is a relatively short-term activity (except with executive coaching which tends to have a longer time-frame).
- It consists of one-to-one developmental discussions.
- It provides people with feedback on both their strengths and weaknesses.
- It is aimed at specific issues/areas.
- It is time-bounded.
- It focuses on improving performance and developing/enhancing individual skills.
- It is used to address a wide range of issues.
- Coaching activities have both individual and organisational goals.
- It works on the premise that clients are self-aware and do not require clinical intervention.
- It focuses on current and future performance/behaviour.
- It is a skilled activity.
- Personal issues may be discussed but the emphasis is on performance at work.

Despite the widespread popularity and growth of coaching, there are issues about the management and delivery of coaching in an organisational setting. Few organisations have a policy, with the result that coaching can be an ad hoc activity with a concentration on senior management (Marchington and Wilkinson, 2005: 251).

Coaching may be delivered by a wide range of individuals including external providers and line managers, and it is important that coaches are selected in line with organisational requirements and the needs of individuals. It is important therefore that coaches have appropriate skills and are trained for their coaching role. Coaching is a widespread tool but there is a lack of established standards, professional bodies and qualification frameworks (CIPD, 2004).

## E-LEARNING

E-learning has been defined by the CIPD (2001) as

> **Learning that is delivered, enabled or mediated by electronic technology, for the explicit purpose of training in organisations.**

The CIPD Annual Training and Development Survey (2005) found that e-learning accounted for under 10 per cent of total training time but was expected to increase dramatically. 54 per cent of respondents reported using e-learning, 39 per cent were planning to introduce it in the coming year. E-learning is primarily associated with IT training (70 per cent), technical training (45 per cent), health and safety training (34 per cent) and induction (33 per cent), and is mainly aimed at technical activities.

The benefits of e-learning rest in its 'just-in-time' availability, flexibility and accessibility and the opportunity it provides for interaction with course content and with other learners and tutors (Reynolds *et al*, 2002:53). However, as Reynolds *et al* (2002:x) suggest, the notion that e-learning would deliver efficiency gains by simply replacing face-to-face training by technology has been discredited because of shortcomings of technology infrastructure and the time necessary to participate. So-called blended learning approaches are seen as more effective in capturing the flexibility of e-learning in integrating work, learning and community at the workplace.

## BLENDED LEARNING

Blended learning is an approach to training design that involves the use of a combination of delivery methods and suggests that e-learning will be most effective when it forms part of a wider strategy of learning which involves both the classroom and on-the-job, work-based learning (Sloman, 2003: 57).

Blended learning programmes combine a variety of different training methods within one programme in order to maximise individual learning and development opportunities in a cost-effective way. As Reynolds *et al* (2002: 59) suggest,

> **Blended approaches can encourage participants to make better use of face-to-face contact in the knowledge that preparations and follow-up can be conducted online. Totally online course should be reserved for those contexts in which it is impossible for learners to come together.**

# CREATING A CLIMATE CONDUCIVE TO LEARNING AND DEVELOPMENT

Reynolds (2004: 13) identifies three key stages for the development of a climate where learning, development and improvement can flourish. Each stage carries reciprocal responsibilities for employees and managers, as illustrated in Table 13.

**Table 13** *Responsibilities of managers and employees in creating a climate of learning*

| | Managers | Employees |
|---|---|---|
| **Sense of purpose** *Develop and share a vision* | Keep abreast of the changing conditions in which your organisation operates<br>Contribute to the development of the organisation's strategy and vision<br>Bring the vision to life by expressing it in ways that are clear to employees | Be aware of the organisation's vision and strategic needs<br>Confirm your understanding of its vision and strategy with others<br>Participate fully in group decisions<br>Fulfil commitments to your group |
| **Freedom to learn** *Empower employees and lead by example* | Enable and encourage, rather than control. Develop coaching capacity<br>Encourage reflection. Unlock enquiry skills rather than teach staff how to behave<br>Maintain and demonstrate personal commitment to learning | Take control of your learning and development<br>Look on work challenges as learning opportunities, and practise critical reflection on work outcomes<br>Contribute to team development as much as your own |
| **Supportive environment** *Encourage networks and align organisational systems* | Encourage employees to share their knowledge.<br>Champion the use of peer-to-peer networks<br>Ensure that such networks are effective through 'light touch' facilitation<br>Ensure that the organisation's policies and systems remain in alignment with its vision | Identify the networks in which you operate<br>Support them by contributing ideas and knowledge for others<br>Offer support for improvements in the design of policies and systems |

Source: J. Reynolds (2004) *Helping People Learn. Strategies for moving from training to learning*, CIPD Research report, p13

Sloman (2003) identifies the following features as facilitating a shift in focus from training to learning as a realisable long-term business goal.

- High-level commitment must be secured by making an effective business case. At the heart of the case is the argument that investing in the self-development of people will be less costly in the long run.
- The central argument in the business case is that more learning is a deliverable, and that this must be achieved in a real environment if it is to be implemented in the workplace.
- Three activities comprise the transition agenda: the development of coaching capacity, the introduction/extension of competency frameworks, and the modularisation of training activities.
- E-learning may emerge as an enabling mechanism to assist the transition.
- Wider measures and metrics which indicate the links between learning and performance are needed.
- New attitudes and approaches will be required, not least from those who work in the training function.

Source: M. Sloman (2003) *Focus on the Learner*, CIPD Change Agenda, p14

## ILLUSTRATION

### Singapore Airlines – training a key to competitive advantage

*In SIA we spend a lot of money on training. We believe that there is no moment, regardless of how senior you are, when you cannot learn something. So for all of us, senior vice presidents included, we're sent for training regularly. We all have a training path. Training is a necessity, not an option. It is not to be dispensed with when times are bad. Training is for everybody. It embraces everyone from the office assistant and baggage-handler to the CEO. We do not stint on training. We'll use the best in software and hardware that money can buy. Because we take a long-term view of training, our investments in staff development are not subject to the vagaries of the economy. Training is forever. No one is too young to be trained, nor too old.*

Taken from J. Wirtz and R. Johnston (2003) *Singapore Airlines: what it takes to sustain service excellence – a senior management perspective*, p10, reprinted with permission from The Emerald Group Publishing Ltd

## THE LEARNING ORGANISATION

The concept of the learning organisation emphasises the need for organisations facing an uncertain and turbulent environment to create a climate that enhances knowledge and learning. The learning organisation model generated a considerable degree of interest in the 1990s following the publication of a book entitled *The Fifth Discipline* by Peter Senge. In it Senge argues that those organisations which value, encourage and facilitate the learning and development of all employees acquire the ability to learn and react more quickly and effectively than their competitors to changed environmental conditions.

Senge (1990: 1) defined a learning organisation as a place where

> **people continually expand their capacity to create the results they truly desire, where new and expansive patterns of thinking are nurtured, where collective aspiration is set free, and where people are continually learning how to learn together.**

An alternative and more prosaic definition of the learning organisation has been suggested by Pedlar *et al* (1991: 1) as

> **an organisation that facilitates the learning of all its members and continuously transforms itself.**

Senge (1990) identified five component elements as essential in building organisational learning and adaptation capabilities, as illustrated in Table 14.

The learning organisation represents an aspirational ideal rather than an empirical reality and is thus offered as a journey towards an ideal or as a goal for organisations to aspire to. As Mullins (2005: 399) puts it,

> **The learning organisation sounds ideal; the kind of company in which we might all like to work!**

However, the learning organisation remains a nebulous, ill-defined and ambiguous concept. Although there may be general agreement that learning is a positive thing, and that individual and collective learning should be promoted and supported, there is a lack of consensus as to how this might be achieved in practice.

More recently, interest has centred on the concept of knowledge management or the production and formalisation of workplace learning in a way that aligns learning with business needs. As Harrison (2005: 152) puts it,

> **Knowledge management means using the ideas and experience of employee, customers and suppliers to improve the organisation's performance.**

**Table 14** *Senge's five learning disciplines*

| Learning discipline | Explanation |
|---|---|
| 1 Personal mastery | a discipline of *aspiration*, concerning what you as an individual want to achieve |
| 2 Mental models | a discipline of *reflection and inquiry*, concerning the constant refinement of thinking and development of awareness |
| 3 Shared vision | a *collective* discipline, concerning commitment to common sense of purpose and actions to achieve that purpose |
| 4 Team learning | a discipline of *group interaction*, concerning collective thinking and action to achieve common goals |
| 5 Systems thinking | a discipline which concerns *understanding, interdependency and complexity* and the role of feedback in system development |

Source: Senge P. (1990) *The Fifth Discipline. The Art and Practice of the Learning Organisation.*

Knowledge can be seen as a source of competitive advantage and many organisations are beginning to identify and formalise workplace knowledge on the basis that creating new forms of knowledge and translating this into innovative action creates core competence and hence competitive advantage. Harrison (2005: 153) suggests that knowledge management can be used in three broad ways: to provide banks of information that enable employees to record and access explicit knowledge across the organisation; to provide access to data across boundaries; and to allow groups of people to interact and create new knowledge through virtual communities where they can share expertise and tacit knowledge.

## PAUSE FOR THOUGHT . . .

Peter Senge (1990) has suggested that 'A learning organisation harnesses the full brainpower, knowledge and experience available to it in order to evolve continually for the benefit of all its stakeholders.'

What key characteristics would you expect to find in an organisation that claimed to be a learning organisation?

## EVALUATING THE LEARNING AND DEVELOPMENT CONTRIBUTION

Chapter 3 evaluated the concept of human capital and emphasised the need to develop a range of metrics to demonstrate the effectiveness of HR initiatives in supporting organisational goals and priorities. Assessing the effectiveness of learning and development is a key part of this process. Moreover, the shift from instructor-led, content-based to learner-centred, work-based approaches requires a re-think of the evaluation process and its appropriateness to new learning and development interventions. However, although it is becoming more and more necessary to demonstrate the cost-effectiveness of providing learning opportunities, the evaluation of learning and development remains nebulous, unsystematic and inadequate. Where the output of training is clear, such as reducing the number of errors in a production process, the return on an investment in training can be calculated and demonstrated. It is, however, much more difficult to establish the impact of management and leadership training and development activities on individual and business performance.

A widely-known framework for evaluating learning and development interventions is that of Hamblin (1974) who identified five levels of evaluation:

- *reactions level* or evaluation of the training, most commonly through post-course evaluation forms
- *immediate level* or evaluation of the extent to which learning objectives have been achieved
- *intermediate level* or the impact of training on job performance and whether learning has been transferred to work performance
- *departmental effect* – has the training improved the performance of the department?
- *ultimate level* or the extent to which organisational performance has improved.

Kirkpatrick's (1976) framework offered four levels of evaluation:

- *reaction* – did the participants enjoy the programme?
- *learning* – what knowledge, skills were gained?

- *behaviour* – what changes in job behaviour can be traced to the training?
- *results* – has the training improved organisational performance in terms of reducing costs, improving quality or quantity of work?

A broader framework, the so-called CIRO framework (Harrison 2002: 313), suggests evaluation of the **C**ontext within which the learning event has taken place; the **I**nputs into the learning event; the **R**eactions to the learning event; and the **O**utcomes of the learning event. More recently, Phillips (2005) has developed a Return on Investment (ROI) level of evaluation which involves:

- collecting data – both hard (eg output, quality, time, cost) and soft (eg customer satisfaction levels)
- isolating the effects of training – through techniques to pinpoint the improvements stemming from training as opposed to other variables (eg control groups, trends lines, forecasting models)
- converting data to monetary values – using techniques to calculate the monetary value of training
- tabulating the cost – identifying costs related to the training
- calculating the return on investment – dividing net training benefits by training costs, expressed as a percentage
- identifying intangible benefits – such as increased job satisfaction, improved team working, reduced complaints
- reporting – using appropriate communication techniques to disseminate information.

## KEY LEARNING POINTS

- The development of a skilled, creative and able work force represents a national goal, but evidence remains of widespread and persistent skills shortages which are hampering organisational growth and improvements in performance.
- It is generally recognised that there are four broad perspectives on learning which impact on training and learning design. These have been categorised as behaviourist, cognitive, social learning and humanist approaches.
- There is evidence of a shift from instructor-led, content-based approaches to learning and development interventions to self-directed, work-based approaches. Although such a shift is in its infancy, it carries considerable implications for the nature and scope of learning and development provision.
- Trends in learning and development point to a decline in traditional forms of learning – eg formal education – and a growth in alternative methods, in particular coaching, mentoring and e-learning.
- Individual and collective learning are core elements in high-performance working systems and important aspects of investment in human capital for competitive advantage. However, the methodology for evaluating the contribution of investment in learning and development interventions is poorly developed.

## Additional reading

CIPD (2005) Reflections on the 2005 training and development survey

CIPD *Inclusive Learning For All*. Why accessible e-learning makes business sense

CIPD *Training to Learning*, Change Agenda

CIPD *Basic Skills in the Workplace. Opening doors to learning*, Change Agenda

CIPD (2005) *Who Learns at Work? Employees' experiences of training and development*, Survey report, March 2005, available at **www.cipd.co.uk/surveys**

### Web-based sources of information

**www.e-learningcentre.co.uk**

**www.dfee.gov.uk/skillsforce/1.htm** statistics and reports

**www.lsc.gov.uk**

**www.iipuk.co.uk**

## REFERENCES

Boxall P. (1996) The strategic HRM debate and the resource-based view of the firm, *Human Resource Management Journal*, Vol.6, No.3, pp59–75

Boxall P. and Purcell J. (2003) *Strategy and Human Resource Management*, Basingstoke, Palgrave

Buchanan D. and Huczynski A. (2004) *Organizational Behaviour. An Introductory Text*, 5th edition, Harlow, FT/Prentice Hall

CIPD (2001) *Training and Development 2001*, Survey Report, London, CIPD

CIPD (2004) *Coaching* Factsheet, London, CIPD, available at **www.cipd.co.uk**

CIPD (2005) *Recruitment, Retention and Turnover* Report, London, CIPD

CIPD (2005) *Training and Development* Annual Survey Report, London, CIPD, available at **www.cipd.co.uk/surveys**

Constable J. and McCormick R. (1987) *The Making of British Managers*, London, British Institute of Management

Hall R. (2002) The Context and Practice of Employee Development in Leopold J. (ed.) *Human Resources in Organisations*, Harlow, FT/Prentice Hall

Hamblin B. (1974) *Evaluation and Control of Training*, Maidenhead, McGraw-Hill

Handy C. (1987) *The Making of Managers*, London, MSC/NEDO/BIM

Harrison R. (2002) *Learning and Development*, 3rd edition, London, CIPD

Harrison R. (2005) *Learning and Development*, 4th edition, London, CIPD

Honey P. and Mumford A. (1986) *The Manual of Learning Styles*, Maidenhead, Peter Honey

Hutchinson S. and Purcell J. (2004) *Bringing Policies to Life: The vital role of line managers in people management*, Executive Briefing, London, CIPD

Keep E. and Westwood A. (2003) *Can the UK Learn to Manage?* London, The Work Foundation

Kelly G. (1955) *The Psychology of Personal Constructs*, New York, Norton

Kirkpatrick D. (1976) Evaluation of training, in Craig R. and Bittel L. (eds) *Training and Development Handbook*, New York, ASTO/McGraw Hill

Kohler W. (1925) *The Mentality of Apes*, Harcourt, Brace and World

Kolb D. (1983) *Experiential Learning: Experience as the source of learning and development*, Hemel Hempstead, Prentice Hall

LSC, *National Employers Skills Survey. Key Findings* (2003) Institute of Employment Research/IFF Research Ltd, available at **www.lsc.gov.uk**

Manpower Services Commission (MSC) (1981) *A New Training Initiation*, Sheffield, MSC

Marchington M. and Wilkinson A. (2005) *Human Resource Management at Work*, 3rd edition, London, CIPD

Mullins L. (2005) *Management and Organisational Behaviour*, 7th edition, Harlow, FT/Prentice Hall

Office for National Statistics 2002 **www.statistics.gov.uk**

Pavlov I. (1927) *Conditioned Reflexes*, Oxford, Oxford University Press

Pedlar M., Burgoyne J. and Boydell T. (1991) *The Learning Company. A Strategy for Sustainable Development*, London, McGraw-Hill

*People Management*, 1 September 2005

Phillips J. (2005) Measuring up, *People Management*, 7 April, p42–3

Piaget J. (1926) *The Language and Thought of the Child*, Harcourt, Brace

Porter M. and Ketels H. (2003) *UK Competitiveness: Moving to the next stage*, DTI Economic Paper No.3, ESRC

Reynolds J. (2004) *Helping People Learn: Strategies for moving from training to learning*, Research report, London, CIPD

Reynolds J., Caley L. and Mason R. (2002) *How do People Learn?*, London, CIPD

Roberts Z. and Watkins R. (2003) Learning leads the way, *People Management*, 6 November, pp34–5

Rogers C. (1969) *Freedom to Learn*, Ohio, Merrill

Senge P. (1990) *The Fifth Discipline. The Art and Practice of the Learning Organization*, New York, Doubleday Currency

Skinner B. (1948) *Walden II*, London, Macmillan

Sloman M. (2003) *Focus on the Learner*, London, CIPD, available at **www.cipd.co.uk/changeagenda**

Stewart J. (1999) *Employee Development Practice*, Harlow, FT/Prentice Hall

Stewart J. (2002) Employee development, in Leopold J. (ed.) *Human Resources in Organisations*, Harlow, FT/Prentice Hall

Taylor R. (2002) Skills and innovation, in *Modern Workplaces*, ESRC Future of Work Programme Seminar Series

Westwood A. (2001) Drawing a line – who is going to train our workforce?, in *The Future of Learning for Work*, London, CIPD

Whiddett S. and Hollyforde S. (1999) *The Competencies Handbook*, London, CIPD

Wirtz J. and Johnston R. (2003) Singapore Airlines. What it takes to Sustain Service Excellence – A Senior Management Perspective, *Managing Service Quality*, Vol 13, No.1 pp10–19

# Managing and rewarding performance at work

## Kevin Lamb

## LEARNING OBJECTIVES

- To explain and discuss the main components of performance management systems
- To explore the potential influence of various contextual factors on the design and operation of performance management systems
- To analyse the main employee development issues relating to effective performance management
- To evaluate the implications of individual differences for reward and motivation strategies
- To analyse the potential relevance of individual performance-related pay for improving performance

## INTRODUCTION

In a summary of the research on performance management in the past decade or so Williams (2002: 10) notes that there is no real agreement on a definition of the process. He sets out the three main perspectives as primarily concerned with:

- managing organisational performance
- managing employee performance

or

- integrating both organisational and employee performance.

Armstrong and Baron (1998: 7) define the process as

**a strategic and integrated approach to delivering sustained success to organisations by improving the performance of the people who work in them and by developing the capabilities of teams and individual contributors.**

The CIPD base their Factsheet (August, 2004) on this definition which in common with most others is a holistic one drawing together various HR processes.

Torrington and Hall (2005: 262–3) state that

> **Performance management tends to be tailor-made and produced in-house (which is why there are so many different versions), with an emphasis on mutual objective-setting and on-going performance support and review. The term, therefore, remains beyond precise definition, and rightly so, as it is critical that the system adopted fits with the culture and context of the organisation.**

Williams (2002: 30) concluded his review of recent research by commenting that

> **formal employee performance management of the holistic, comprehensive, integrative kind that is advocated in much of the literature is rare. The dominant approach to managing employee performance still rests on objective-setting and annual appraisal.**

We should note Boxall and Purcell's contention at this point as they suggest that although appraisal systems 'can be used effectively when they are well led and well resourced' (2003: 146), it is even more important for managers to focus their available energies on ensuring that good quality selection and retention decisions are adopted(2003: 144). These are seen as a more efficient way of attaining high levels of performance.

The main ingredients in most performance management systems are processes that seek to integrate the key elements of organisational strategy and goals with employee inputs and outputs, training and development and financial and non-financial rewards. Thus employee direction is stimulated in the direction the organisation seeks to travel.

Lawson (cited in Walters, 1995: 13) has called this the attempt to achieve 'connectivity' by

> **identifying, building upon, and strengthening the connections that link the organisation, its managers and its employees with its customers and markets.**

Drawing on the work of Guest and Hoque (1994) concerning linkages between business and HR strategies we can say that the chances of an integrated, holistic model of performance management will be maximised where the organisation has:

- appropriately designed HR processes in performance management, employee development, reward and communication.
- integration between these processes and other HR practices and clear links with the main elements of organisational strategy (horizontal and vertical integration)
- a supportive management culture.

Although Guest and Hoque rightly admit that achieving this is a 'tall order', it nevertheless remains the goal of numerous HR professionals in partnership with business managers in an endeavour to seek strategic alignment. While performance management may be seen as a daily and on-going process, it is apparent that certain systems must be in place if the full advantages are to be realised.

Armstrong and Baron (1998: 85–100) have provided a succinct and telling summary of research findings criticising the operation of performance management and appraisal systems. In particular, criticisms have been focused on the misuse of authority by managers and the inherent problems of one person assessing the performance of another in an objective manner. Other common problems relate to misunderstandings over the purpose, conflicting objectives, lack of preparation, overwhelming paperwork, decisions allegedly being made prior to the interview, the 'halo and horns effect', lack of appraisee involvement, inadequate training and support for line managers, and a lack of follow-up actions.

Having signalled the main thrust of performance management and discussed definitions, this chapter now focuses on appraisal system design and contextual considerations before moving to a brief discussion of interview issues and follow-up requirements. We then examine the main considerations concerning links between employee development and performance management before investigating the reward implications of individual differences and the relationships between intrinsic and extrinsic motivators and performance. Finally, we evaluate individual performance-related pay in terms of its effects on employee performance.

## DESIGNING APPRAISAL SYSTEMS

The lifeblood of performance management practices flows into and out of the appraisal system and the design of such a system is therefore an essential starting point. As Fletcher (1993: 48) has written:

**Many of the problems of appraisal systems arise out of the design process. Get it wrong here and it is likely to stay wrong.**

Using off-the-shelf systems will rarely produce good or lasting results because the main considerations in design are of a contextual nature. The variables are likely to be concerned with organisational culture, occupational composition of the workforce, organisational size and competitive pressures, the nature of the product or service, customer expectations, technology, labour market pressures, general business plans – especially with regard to expansion or contraction – and the pace and type of change required.

Although these variables will influence the type of system most appropriate, they will not necessarily determine it due to other influences such as senior management values, internal politics and the notion of choice. In turn these factors may help or hinder the effectiveness of performance management.

In their book devoted purely to the design and implementation of appraisal systems, Mohrman *et al* (1989) suggested that six stages were critical:

1   Select the right people.
2   Decide on a process to guide your design.
3   Assess the current organisational situation.
4   Establish the system's purpose and objectives.
5   Design the performance appraisal system.
6   Experiment with implementation.

It is often helpful for the purposes of explanation to separate out the general key issues into (a) system type and pre-interview actions, (b) interviewing, and (c) post-interview actions.

## Types of appraisal systems

There are a number of different appraisal systems any of which may be appropriate for an organisation, although that is largely dependent on the type of contextual factors outlined above. Major questions when assessing which type to adopt will be 'What will best fit our existing and desired culture?' and 'What is likely to work best, given our specific aims and objectives for performance management?'

The aims of performance management may be quite varied and conflicting as well as misunderstood within the organisation. Mohrman *et al* (1989) cited their experience in America:

> **In every organisation we have studied, we have found the same results: Appraisal systems invariably have multiple purposes, and appraisers and appraisees invariably and systematically have different views of their purpose.**

This highlights the importance of clearly thought-out aims and thorough communication of them.

Whereas it is perhaps not difficult to see why the type of system may vary between organisations due to occupational composition or the sophistication and maturity of HR processes, a strategic approach to design may well seek to change the prevailing culture, patterns of behaviour and attitudes, making the fit less obvious.

We discuss below some of the more popular approaches to appraisal and explore their strengths and weaknesses before making some comments about which types of system may best fit different organisational contexts.

## Objective-setting systems

Performance is assessed against the achievement of pre-set objectives and future objectives are agreed for the period ahead. Some organisations require objectives to be set for specific areas. An example is Elida Fabergé who require three work targets to be agreed that link with overall business objectives, and a further three related to skill and competency development (IDS *Study 748*, April 2003: 30).

Although most guides to appraisal make clear the desirability of objectives being mutually agreed, a central issue is clearly the extent to which over-zealous appraisers impose them on others in terms of the number and nature of objectives. Use of self-appraisal forms, central monitoring of the content of forms and having an appeal system in place can partly guard against these problems.

Unless objectives are regularly reviewed and amended during the appraisal period, it is likely that they will become irrelevant due to the changing internal and external environment and new objectives will surface which may not then be recorded for discussion at the following review. Such problems tend to discredit the process if not kept in check.

The acronym SMART is often used to describe the requirements for good objective-setting. To this we may add 'mutually agreed' and 'challenging'.

**PAUSE FOR THOUGHT . . .**

If you have recently been set objectives in the context of appraisal, evaluate the extent to which they meet each of the following criteria:

- Specific
- Measurable

- Achievable
- Relevant
- Time-bound.

In addition, consider whether they were

- mutually agreed

and

- challenging.

Compare your answers with a colleague's answers.

Are there acceptable reasons to explain your findings, or are any weaknesses related to an area that needs improvement in the way managers set objectives? If so, what should be done to bring about these improvements? Can you relate this framework to your own organisation?

We would be right to ask whether an objective-setting/results-based system can be motivational. Assuming that the appraiser is capable of conducting the interview competently, the idea of setting objectives sits well with Locke's (1968) goal theory mentioned in Chapter 5. The key issues here are the extent to which the objectives are reasonably challenging and measurable, the provision of regular feedback and the commitment (as opposed to mere acceptance) of the appraisee.

We can take this concept further perhaps by applying questions that could arise from the AMO equation (Boxall and Purcell, 2003: 20).The employees may be committed or motivated (M), but do they possess the ability (A) to meet the objectives to the standard required? How much attention will be given in the appraisal interview to discussing the most suitable methods to enable new skills and knowledge to be developed? Will any agreed measures on this issue be actioned? In addition will there be adequate support and resource allocation to ensure that the opportunity (O) for achievement is present? These questions are partly relevant to the style adopted by the appraiser in the interview, as we shall later discuss.The main strengths and weaknesses of objective-setting systems are presented in Table 15.

## Behaviourally-anchored rating scales (BARSs)

Whereas an objective-setting approach is mainly concerned with outputs, a BARS system is more concerned with inputs in terms of the way employees display certain kinds of

**Table 15**  *Strengths and weaknesses of an objective-setting system*

| Strengths | Weaknesses |
| --- | --- |
| 1  Gives a clear target to aim at. | 1  Some managers may have difficulties ensuring objectives are SMART. |
| 2  Helps focus attention on what is seen as important to both the employee and the organisation. | 2  Objectives may be too easy or too hard. |
| 3  Assists the employee in prioritising work. | 3  Objectives can lose relevance over time. |
| 4  Helps minimise role ambiguity. | 4  More important activities may arise during the review period but not be taken account of. |
| 5  Enables input and participation by the employee. | 5  The processes involved in achieving objectives may be important but not considered. |
| 6  Enables evaluation of success at a later date. | 6  Other important work activities may be given less attention if not seen as relevant to the objectives. |

desired behaviours. An inherent feature of many BARS systems is the assumption that the desired behaviours will result in higher levels of individual and organisational performance, although actual output results are not normally measured except in more sophisticated versions. Several different methods can be used to decide which BARS to use. In summary these involve:

- identifying the key behaviours or competencies required for effectiveness in the job
- distinguishing between effective and ineffective performance for each behaviour required. The behaviours considered are then rated as a range across categories using either numbers such as 1 to 5 depicting levels of performance or several descriptions such as 'Always behaves this way' to 'Never behaves this way'
- focusing the interview on discussing and agreeing where the employee's behaviour fits with each of the categories.

One of the main reasons for the introduction of BARS was to get away from the old appraisal practice of rating employees on traits such as 'conscientiousness', 'enthusiasm' and 'open-mindedness' because these are notoriously hard to define, measure and agree upon. Their connection with performance also appears dubious.

Armstrong and Baron (1998: 40) suggest that modified versions of BARS are sometimes utilised as the 'dimensions' in a differentiating competency framework.

The value of both BARS and competency frameworks are heavily dependent on the way they are arrived at. Employees have to have the necessary training and support in developing appropriate behaviours. The specific requirements of each role must be effectively communicated, and those displaying the desired behaviours need to receive regular praise and recognition. Competency approaches can be a tool for achieving horizontal integration across the crucial HR areas of selection, appraisal, rewards and development. Rankin (2001) found that of those organisations with competency frameworks, 82 per cent made use of them for performance management. The CIPD Survey of Performance Management (September 2005) found that 31 per cent of respondents utilised a competency-based approach.

Even if behaviour can be accurately measured we may question the extent to which it can be influenced or changed. The role of rewards may be significant here, as our later discussion will consider.

A fundamental question for all adherents of behavioural performance management systems is not only the extent to which human attitudes and behaviour can be influenced but also the time, effort and costs involved. We may reflect again on Boxall and Purcell's contention that it is wise to ensure that the right selection decisions are made in the first place.

Table 16 *Strengths and weaknesses of behaviourally-anchored rating scales*

| Strengths | Weaknesses |
|---|---|
| 1  Ratings are based on clearly documented examples of behaviour. | 1  Time-consuming to establish and keep up to date. |
| 2  Ample documentation of different dimensions of behaviours provides wide scope for discussion. | 2  An employee may not display consistent behaviour, making ratings hard. |
| 3  If the appraiser works closely with the appraisee and has plenty of regular contact there should be enough evidence to produce accurate ratings. | 3  Employees who receive lower ratings than colleagues may become demoralised if ratings are shared and transparent. |
| 4  The system is normally based on some form of job analysis. | 4  The behaviours may lose relevance over time. |
| 5  If ratings are consistent it enables comparisons between employees to be made. | 5  Managers may fear or dislike rating employees and therefore manipulate assessments. |
| 6  Can facilitate integration of HR practices. | 6  There may be a heavy reliance on self-assessment unless the appraiser can observe behaviour or gather evidence from reliable sources. |

Although it is apparent that such systems may assist in highlighting desired organisational values, it is less clear how they will assist in the achievement of organisational strategy and goals. Perhaps to try and overcome this problem some organisations combine a BARS or competency approach with an objective-setting one, and while this may help measure both inputs and outputs, it may also unduly complicate matters for both appraisers and appraisees. It is nevertheless apparent that given the changing requirements of an increasing number of jobs, an ideal approach to managing performance would encompass discussion, support, development and measurement of both inputs (or behaviours) and outputs (or objectives/results). The practicality of designing, implementing and operating this type of system in the decade ahead is perhaps one of the major challenges facing organisations that wish to treat people as their 'greatest asset'.

Williams (2002) noted that evidence for the use of behaviour-based assessment for performance management in the UK (whether via BARS, competencies, or any other method) was relatively weak, citing data from the studies of the then IPD (1998) and the Industrial Society (1994). An online survey of 'around 900 businesses' conducted jointly by *Personnel Today* and PeopleSoft in 2004 found that less than 1 per cent said they used a competency-based approach to performance management. Almost 90 per cent of respondents with a system said they used targets or objective-setting. The same survey found that as many as 27 per cent of organisations had no performance management system at all.

## PAUSE FOR THOUGHT . . .

To what extent do you believe that the attitudes and behaviour of employees in critical areas of their work can be influenced?

Identify two areas where different attitudes and behaviour may be needed among any employees in the future, and consider what HR or other processes can be utilised for influencing this.

## Simple rating systems

A simple rating approach to performance management enables employees to be rated against any criteria regarded as of significance by managers, although it is highly desirable that employees and/or their trade union representatives are involved in determining the criteria. A key aspect of this type of system is the degree to which the chosen criteria impact upon performance and employee perceptions of fairness in its administration. Job analysis rarely underpins such a system. An example of a simple rating system is one of several given in the ACAS Advisory Booklet on Employee Appraisal (2003). The areas in which performance is rated consist of volume of work, quality of work, knowledge of job, dependability, innovation, staff development, communication and teamwork. Performance in each of these areas is rated as either high, medium, low or not acceptable, and then an overall rating is given.

## Critical incident systems

This approach draws upon the most critical aspects of a job, which are determined by job analysis. The appraiser then records examples of how the appraisee performs in tackling each critical incident throughout the review period. This record forms the basis for appraisal. Examples of critical incidents for an employee in retail sales might include:

- identifying specific customer needs
- relating the key product benefits to these needs in a clear and convincing manner
- answering customer queries in a polite and thorough way
- dealing with difficult customers as appropriate
- leading and participating in stocktaking exercises as and when necessary
- closing sales effectively.

The method can encourage managers to be less subjective due to the need for recording evidence as the basis of assessment, but the time this takes is possibly its biggest drawback. As with BARS, this approach can also assist in the development of competencies due to the analysis of what constitutes effective and ineffective behaviour.

## Blank sheet appraisal

The use of rating criteria and structured forms is dispensed with in a blank sheet approach because this relies on simple paperwork with few, if any, headings for guidance. Instead, the subject of discussion is left for the appraiser and appraisee to determine. Inevitably, this may lead to control by the former, albeit to a lesser degree in organisations with flat structures or those composed of experienced professionals.

## DECIDING WHO TO INVOLVE

The above types of appraisal systems are all open to different ways of involving people. However, there are other formal ways of gaining differing perspectives, the two main ones being self-appraisal and 360-degree feedback.

## Self-appraisal

There appears universal agreement among practitioners and academics alike as to the value of some type of self-assessment exercise being conducted by appraisees. In view of this it is surprising that the CIPD's 2005 report based on 560 respondents found that self-appraisal was used by only 30 per cent of organisations. Self-appraisal is normally carried out prior to the appraisal interview via a form that largely mirrors that completed by the appraiser after the interview. By encouraging reflection on the past and contemplation of the future, the prospects of a more informed interview and joint dialogue are enhanced.

## 360-degree appraisal

A 360-degree approach can utilise all the systems mentioned above and is often seen as a panacea representing a 'best practice' approach. Research findings are nevertheless problematic. In their discussion of the characteristics, advantages and disadvantages, Armstrong and Baron (1998: 313–28) state that a number of the HR specialists they visited whose organisations were using 360-degree appraisal 'strongly believed that it should be used only for development purposes'.

Williams (2002: 170) quotes figures from an Ashridge survey, from those conducted by SHL and also from the Industrial Society (now the Work Foundation) to show the slow but steady growth of the method. The CIPD's 2005 report found the method used in 14 per cent of organisations. Use of a multi-rater approach is more powerful as a feedback tool and therefore more likely to be accepted. Raters can include managers, peers, subordinates, customers, clients and others involved in the network of work activities.

---

### ACTIVITY . . .

Questionnaire: how ready is your organisation for 360-degree appraisal?

Respond to statements 1 to 12 according to whether you

**strongly agree** ................................................ *score 5*
**agree** ............................................................ *score 4*
**neither agree nor disagree** ...................... *score 3*
**disagree** ...................................................... *score 2*
**strongly disagree** ...................................... *score 1*

When you have completed the questionnaire, add up your total score.

| | | |
|---|---|---|
| 1 | There is common understanding about what constitutes high performance | |
| 2 | There are high levels of trust and openness between employees and managers | |
| 3 | People are interested in learning | |
| 4 | People are receptive to the views and opinions of others | |

| | | |
|---|---|---|
| 5 | People are willing and able to provide criticism in a constructive manner | |
| 6 | People tend to prefer finding solutions to problems rather than allocating blame | |
| 7 | People rarely engage in in-fighting and internal politics | |
| 8 | There is support, resources and training available to help people learn | |
| 9 | People are willing to invest time and effort in appraisal | |
| 10 | The actions arising from appraisal are followed up | |
| 11 | Confidentiality is respected | |
| 12 | People value the outcomes of appraisal | |

Total: _____

Your score may vary from a minimum of 12 to a maximum of 60. The higher the score, the more potential there is for 360-degree appraisal. However, an organisation is only likely to be able to benefit from this approach if the score exceeds 40.

Before introducing such a system, careful consideration must be given to ensuring that the conditions are right. The Activity questionnaire above provides an example of some of the matters that require consideration.

## APPRAISAL IN CONTEXT

We emphasised earlier that the relevance of any performance management system depends on various contextual factors and we now give brief attention to this.

Employees whose jobs have a high degree of freedom and discretion, who use specialised and complex skills and who often work in physical isolation from their managers are probably suited to a system in which self-appraisal plays a large role but which is linked to mutually agreed objectives. Such employees probably have greater knowledge of their job requirements and their strengths and weaknesses in fulfilling them than their managers, who will rarely observe them or be in a position to gather hard data on performance. In this instance an *objective-setting* system is likely to be of most value. A key role for managers in this situation will be to explain current organisational strategy, goals and priorities so that the objective-setting discussion can take full account of them.

*Behaviourally-anchored rating scales* may be appropriate to an organisation where employees carry out varying tasks for which relationships and interactions with others are crucial and where emotional intelligence and impression management are highly valued due to their influence on job success.

In contrast, if employees are performing largely mechanical tasks requiring minimal discretion with predominantly quantifiable outputs, then a simple *merit rating* system may be preferable.

It is more difficult to see where a blank sheet system has potential, but we should remind ourselves of the vast number of small organisations with no HR presence and few links with employers' associations or consultants. If there is a desire to establish some HR processes, and roles are flexible and informal, a *blank sheet* system may be much more helpful than any of the other systems. In this context this 'system' may act as a short-term measure which serves the purpose of bringing together employees and their managers and enables the discussion of issues of concern that would otherwise be left to fester and have a de-motivational effect. Similar points can be made for small, start-up businesses.

Given the complexity of modern organisations, one implication of this discussion is that some may benefit from being flexible and having different systems for different sections of the workforce.

Hartle (1995: 129–44) has provided a useful introduction to the factors that require consideration when seeking to fit a system to organisational culture. A narrower but deeper insight is provided by Verweire and Van den Berghe (2005: 786) whose

> **central proposition is that apart from strategic alignment, an organisation also needs to align different components of the integrated performance management framework in correspondence with its maturity level.**

In terms of international organisations, Mendonca and Kanungo (2005) have produced an intriguing paper attempting to relate Hofstede's four cultural dimensions to 'state-of-the-art performance management techniques and practices' used in North American organisations. They conclude that these techniques can be effective in non-Western developing countries provided that interventions and adjustments are made at two levels. These are seen as concerning (a) internal organisational work cultures and constraints, and (b) leadership and empowerment considerations.

At Microsoft UK the main contextual influence is said to be its 'people vision', which is about 'creating an environment where great people can do their best work and realise their full potential' (IDS *Study 748*, April 2003: 17). The organisation prides itself on its open, honest culture and encourages employees to seek an appropriate work–life balance. According to the IDS research (as cited above):

## THE APPRAISAL INTERVIEW

Appraisal interviewing requires a much wider range of skills than does selection or disciplinary interviewing. Although the legal pitfalls are comparatively fewer, an appraiser may require skills involved with:

> **Microsoft attempts to engage employees in terms of their physical, emotional and intellectual environment.**

- active listening and establishing rapport
- motivating
- providing constructive feedback
- seeking agreement
- persuasion
- receiving and giving constructive criticism/feedback
- negotiation
- giving praise and recognition
- formulating objectives
- ranking or assessing performance
- identifying and agreeing training and development needs.

Not only does the effective appraiser require these type of skills but each appraisee must be treated as a separate entity because of his or her individual differences. Ideally, therefore, the development of appraisal skills should be an on-going activity rather than being undertaken at a one-off training event. According to Mumford (1996: 76):

> **One of the difficulties for many bosses is that effective appraisal for improvement and development purposes requires them to behave in a way foreign to their normal managerial style. They are required to be reflective and analytical and to be good listeners rather than authoritative immediate decision-takers leading a discussion.**

We can postulate three different styles of appraisal interviewing as being

- autocratic
- participative
- joint learning.

In the *autocratic* approach the appraiser takes on the role of judge and expert, regarding the appraisee as passive and able to benefit from the passing on of advice, direction and knowledge. This one-way dialogue is at odds with motivation theories but may be of use in countries or cultures where there is a high acceptance of authority and status relationships. It is, however, still likely that employees in some UK organisations will recognise this style as being adopted by their own appraisers especially where a command-and-control culture operates.

The *participative* approach is characterised by a proactive attempt to involve appraisees and seek out their opinions. This approach is not easy for managers whose natural style is directive or those who work in a macho-type environment. The participative approach is the one favoured and suggested in most appraisal training programmes, and if followed up by a supportive management style may well motivate many employees and produce positive feelings in the post-interview phase.

The *joint learning* approach goes further than the participative one in terms of the information and opinions sought and the topics of conversation. Rather than focus solely on the performance and development of the appraisee (as in the other two approaches), feedback is openly sought on the role the manager/appraiser plays in supporting, coaching, advising and managing the appraisee throughout the review period. Although the interview is primarily about the past and future role of the appraisee, the outcome of the appraisal should be of value to both parties. This style is therefore intended to influence the performance relationship between the two, although as with 360-degree appraisal it is only likely to work well in a high-trust culture.

## PAUSE FOR THOUGHT . . .

Which of the three roles outlined above most closely resembles the interview style adopted by the person conducting your last appraisal interview?

What were the implications of the style used for (a) the way you felt immediately afterwards, and (b) its influence on your later performance?

In reviewing the literature on the characteristics of effective appraisal interviews, Anderson and Barnett (1987) state that the key features are:

- a substantial element of employee participation in the appraisal process
- a positive and supportive approach by the interviewer
- identifying and analysing problems affecting the employee's job performance
- the setting of goals to be achieved by the employee
- that the balance of the interview is focused more on performance than on personality.

Although the absence in the above list of any reference to discussions of employee development needs is perhaps indicative of the way appraisal has evolved in the past 20 years or so, Anderson and Barnett's factors are nevertheless still central to the success of the interview process in many organisations.

## POST-INTERVIEW FOLLOW-UP

Weaknesses concerning lack of follow-up have long been reported in surveys (see for instance Gill, 1977) and appear to remain a problem underlining the need for the continual nature of the process to be embedded in other organisational policies and activities. The development of an action plan as an outcome of appraisal can help overcome this problem if dates are agreed for follow-up and review meetings however formal or informal these may be. Some organisations set objectives and/or measure the performance of their managers in operating performance management and wider HR processes. This assists horizontal integration and helps in gaining managerial commitment to their broader people management tasks within the organisation.

Regular evaluation of the process, by seeking opinions of both appraisers and appraisees and disseminating results to all stakeholders, helps both improve the process and sends out an appropriate message. Action plans emanating from appraisal will vary depending on the aims, but should normally cover:

- employee goals and objectives
- development needs and possible ways of meeting them
- personal and career development plans
- responsibilities and time-scales
- interim review dates to provide support and progress updates.

There may also be implications for reward and specific performance improvement programmes, although matters directly relating to discipline are best kept out of the process.

## INTEGRATING EMPLOYEE DEVELOPMENT WITH PERFORMANCE MANAGEMENT

We have emphasised the critical importance of integration between various HR processes in order to maximise the effectiveness of performance management. In terms of employee training and development there are a number of key questions that will require addressing. These include regularly asking the following:

■ Are the training and development needs that are agreed in appraisals clearly linked to organisational priorities as arrived at via analysis of strategic goals?
■ To what extent will we take account of the personal development needs of employees when they are not directly relevant to strategic goals?
■ How will we ensure that we consider long-term development needs and not just immediate ones?
■ How capable are our managers of identifying development needs and ways of meeting them?
■ To what extent do we want to utilise the appraisal process as a vehicle for evaluating past training and development experiences?
■ How easily can the training and development needs most likely to influence performance be actioned and resourced?
■ To what extent are we making use of all the learning opportunities available to us, and is our definition of development broad enough?

Many texts on appraisal have noted the difficulty in some contexts of discussing both development and performance in the same meeting. These difficulties are magnified if pay is also on the agenda because employees will be reluctant to admit to what might be seen as 'deficiencies' for fear that they may be used as a reason to defer pay awards.

In discussing ways of meeting needs it is best to avoid the trap of simply looking through lists of training courses (unless perhaps internal capacity to help others learn is very weak). It is worth devoting time and attention to ways in which an employee has learned best in the past, to his or her learning styles and preferences as well as cost considerations. Such discussions can involve exploring the potential of well recognised learning methods such as coaching, mentoring, shadowing, computer-based training, job instruction, the delegation of challenges, directed reading and professional networking, etc, as well as utilising less recognised ones. With regard to management development, for instance, Mumford (1997) has suggested that provided the right processes are in place, there are often genuine opportunities to learn from a host of everyday workplace activities including mergers and acquisitions, meetings, managing a change, questioning, reviewing and auditing, walking the floor and observing. Much of Mumford's work over the past decade has been devoted to explaining ways in which organisations can build their capacity to make use of and manage these types of opportunities.

Microsoft deploy a rather unusual way of segmenting the way development needs are met by suggesting that they ought to be apportioned into (a) on-the-job experience, comprising 70 per cent; (b) coaching and mentoring, 20 per cent; and (c) online and classroom-based formal training, 10 per cent (IDS *Study 748*, April 2003: 17).

In deciding on how best to meet priority development needs we suggest that the key issues concern the following (priority in the order stated):

1   the likely effectiveness of the method in meeting the need
2   the direct and indirect costs involved
3   the ease of accessing the resources or putting the method into operation
4   the learning preferences/style of the employee
5   the motivational effects of the learning process and outcomes
6   the differences between available methods with regard to the time the employee may be away from the job and not be fully productive.

The prioritisation of these six factors will vary between organisations largely depending on their learning philosophy, managerial values, organisational goals and short-term operational priorities. In turn, this will influence the likely added value of the training/development undertaken to both the employee and organisation.

## PAUSE FOR THOUGHT . . .

What is the normal order of priority of the six factors above when deciding how to meet the training and development needs of employees in your organisation?

Have these changed over the past few years, and if so, in what way?

Are there other factors that you can add to the list, and if so, what are they?

The appraisal interview also presents an ideal opportunity to assess the extent to which any learning undertaken has been transferred to the workplace. There can be few organisations that would not benefit from reflecting on what has helped or hindered learning transfer in the past and thereby put themselves in a position to consider 'What can we do to maximise learning transfer to the workplace in future?'

## FINANCIAL AND NON-FINANCIAL REWARDS

The Taylorist view that the best way to maximise efficiency and individual performance is via a 'carrot and stick' approach has lost much of its relevance and credibility in recent decades for a variety of reasons. Among these are the changing nature of work, changing and diverse employee expectations and values, as well as research findings such as those from the Hawthorne studies and the theories developed by Maslow and Herzberg, as outlined in Chapter 5. The notion and consequences of individual differences are also central to any analysis of why generalisations about influencing workers purely via financial incentives are best avoided.

Some people will be very motivated by the prospect of earning more money, whereas others may at best be indifferent. Our discussion of individual differences will seek to shed light on the reasons for this.

## Individual differences and rewards

### ACTIVITY . . .

Questionnaire: what rewards do you most value?

Below is a list of what we can term 'rewards'.

As **Task 1**, in column 1 number the three forms of reward that are most important to you in order of priority. Compare your answers with those of a colleague.

As **Task 2**, find out or estimate what the top three rewards are for *two* other people you know. If possible, try to select two people in a different age-bracket from yourself, such as a parent or older relative. Use columns 2 and 3 for this.

| Type of reward | 1 | 2 | 3 |
|---|---|---|---|
| High wages or salary | | | |
| The chance of promotion | | | |
| Career development prospects | | | |
| Challenging work | | | |
| Status (people 'look up to you') | | | |
| Social relationships with work friends | | | |
| Achieving excellent results consistently | | | |
| The power to control resources and people | | | |
| Good opportunities to learn | | | |
| Having varied and interesting work | | | |
| Pride at being a member of the organisation | | | |
| Getting as much free time as possible | | | |
| Having an easy job in a low pressure environment | | | |
| The satisfaction of producing high quality work | | | |
| Helping those less fortunate than you in your work | | | |

Dessler (2005: 439) has stated that

> **different people react to different incentives in different ways ...
> People differ in personality, ability, values, and needs, and these
> differences manifest themselves in different desires and different
> reactions.**

Rowntree (2000) has provided a simple yet useful checklist to assist managers in thinking through what may motivate their employees. The Activity on page 233 is largely based on this. Close scrutiny of this list outlines the diverse nature of the rewards people may want from their work.

One implication of individual differences is that when an organisation is designing its reward strategy, a survey into employee attitudes is essential if the aim is to try and motivate employees. It may also imply that some organisations should adopt different approaches to reward for different sections of the workforce – something that many traditional HR (or 'personnel') practitioners would regard as anathema. In this connection we must take cognisance of Adam's theory (1963) regarding the weight that people put on comparisons, and Jacques' 'felt fairness' principle (1962). Both theories suggest that unless the rationale for such differences is well explained it may offend employees' sense of justice and prove counter-productive.

We have noted that employees are motivated in different ways. The reasons for this are complex and hard to pin down. Among them are influences of age (Finegold *et al*, 2002), family considerations (Rynes *et al*, 2004), gender (Ameudo-Dorantes and Mach, 2003), career expectations, peer pressure, personal values, personality, and professional and occupational cultures. Moreover, employee needs and motivators do not remain static and are likely to change throughout a person's life.

The views held by managers as to what motivates may be wide of the mark. Kovach (1987) found that although managers regarded their employees as primarily motivated by money, when these same employees were asked to rank various rewards, the financial incentives were placed in fifth place on a list of ten, behind intrinsic motivators.

Although it may not be possible to satisfy the diverse needs of all employees, a strategic approach to human resource management would take account of the match between employee orientations to work and the existing reward system in initial selection decisions. Knowing the trade-offs different employees are willing to make between various rewards can assist in satisfying needs, provided that both the reward system and management decision-making is flexible. Using such a flexible approach is likely to be more problematic in the voluntary and public sectors than in the private sector.

Table 17 presents some of the major intrinsic and extrinsic motivators. Whereas extrinsic rewards may be the prime motivator for some, they may also motivate most employees for a limited period before losing their appeal and becoming seen as the norm or as a right. Intrinsic motivators are more enduring and can act as a differentiator between organisations from an employee perspective. Many of the intrinsic motivators in Table 17 relate closely to features of Hackman and Oldham's Job Characteristics Model (1980) outlined in Chapter 5.

**Table 17**  *Intrinsic and extrinsic motivators*

| Intrinsic | Extrinsic |
| --- | --- |
| Challenging and enjoyable work | Pay and financial incentives such as: |
| Receiving praise and recognition | ■ the level of salary on offer |
| Sense of pride in the job | ■ premium overtime rates |
| Feelings of self-esteem and worth | ■ team or group bonuses |
| Earning respect and trust | ■ performance-related pay |
|  | ■ commission |
|  | ■ profit-related pay |
| High involvement in decisions affecting the job | Benefits such as: |
| Opportunities for personal growth | ■ company car |
| Enhanced freedom, autonomy and control over work processes | ■ pensions |
|  | ■ health insurance |
|  | ■ discounted gym membership |
|  | ■ life insurance |
| Making a personal contribution to a better society through work | Awards and prizes such as: |
|  | ■ a weekend away with your partner |
|  | ■ a trip to a major sporting event |
|  | ■ gold watch/ jewellery |
|  | ■ a flight in an air balloon |

In terms of managing performance, the key issue with reward systems is determining which strategies will encourage high levels of team and individual performance while at the same time being likely to have a positive effect on other HR goals (such as selection and retention) and on other business goals (such as speed, quality, product/service costs and return on investment). How much it is possible to make use of motivators specific to an organisation's workforce will differ between organisations due to various contingencies. These may present opportunities or constraints and might include considerations about the technology in use, the employee relations climate, the nature of the work, market and competitive pressures, the education and skill levels of the

## PAUSE FOR THOUGHT . . .

On 5 June 2005, the *News of the World* reported that professional footballer and England international Ashley Cole was preparing to leave his club even though he did not want to. Cole is 24 years old, one of the top left-backs in the world, and has been at Arsenal since he was a boy. Unfortunately for him, during 2005 he was found by the Football Association to have been involved in secret talks about a possible transfer to rivals Chelsea, for which they fined him £75,000. This row over alleged 'tapping up' seemed to have been the catalyst for a breakdown in his negotiations with Arsenal about the terms of a new contract and for what he alleges was bad treatment by the Club Vice-Chairman, David Dein. Cole is reported to earn around £25,000 a week at present (ie £1,300,000 per annum).

Cole is quoted as saying, 'I feel betrayed, confused, and badly let down. If there's no future for me at Highbury, then it's all down to them. It's no exaggeration to say that they've broken my heart. Can I ever forgive them? I really don't know. I've supported Arsenal since I was seven, but they have hurt me. . . . Dein didn't show me any respect and treated me like a little kid.'

Cole said that despite his highly-publicised contract negotiations his main concern had not been his salary.

'It's not about money – it's about decency and the principle of treating people fairly,' he said. 'If they offered me £100,000 or £200,000 a week now, I wouldn't accept it. Even though I knew many of my team mates were earning much more than me I never demanded equal pay. I can look at myself and say: "Ashley, you loved Arsenal and you never let them down." Can the board say the same? I don't think so.'

Although we cannot be sure exactly what went on behind the scenes at Arsenal, it does show that although money is important, it is no guarantee that a person will be happy – and that everyone has his or her own sense of pride and justice. Organisations that want to retain high-performers ignore this principle at their peril. Shortly after the above report Cole seemed to have settled his differences with the club, but ' fair treatment and respect' together with being made to feel wanted seem to have been as important as money.

Source: *News of the World*, 5 June 2005.

workforce and cost implications. Those organisations that take a strategic perspective in relation to encouraging high performance through utilising the reward system will reap the benefits and provide a comparatively more satisfying work environment for employees at all levels.

## Expectancy theory and performance management

Porter and Lawler's development of expectancy theory (1968) postulates that if a specific reward is to be effective in influencing behaviour, four conditions must come into play.

The reward must:

1   *be valued by the employee (and valued above alternative rewards)*
    This can be determined for each employee via regular formal and informal discussions as well as via the appraisal and review meetings. Attitude surveys can inform management about the more general feelings of employees regarding different rewards.

2   *be seen as attainable via effort*
    Employee confidence and any concerns, anxieties or other factors felt to hamper the chances of goal attainment can be discussed at appraisal and via regular on-going contact with managers. Good leadership can build confidence and inspire action.

3   *be seen as attainable provided the employee does what is expected of him or her*
    Goal-setting and clarification of expectations is an essential feature of many appraisal systems, specifically those based on objective-setting. Again, good practice in leadership, delegation and communication together with feedback ensures clear focus.

4   *be seen as attainable because the employee has the necessary skills and knowledge*
    We have made reference in the previous section (*Integrating employee development with performance management*) to how crucial it is that employee development practices are well managed and fully considered in appraisal and as an on-going task.

The above brief discussion of expectancy theory indicates that all four elements can be brought together via the crucial integrating processes of appraisal, development, communication and reward.

## Individual performance-related pay

Armstrong and Baron have provided a useful chapter in their most recent text which reviews some of the issues to consider when linking performance management with reward (Armstrong and Baron, 2005: 103–14). A full description and analysis of different financial reward methods is outside the scope of this chapter, but because of its potential relevance we conclude this chapter by analysing the significance of individual performance-related pay (IPRP).

The CIPD's survey in 1999 into various types of performance-related pay obtained responses from over 1,100 organisations. In terms of IPRP some of the main findings were:

- IPRP was being used for 40 per cent of managers and 25 per cent of non-managers.
- Larger organisations were much more likely to be using IPRP than smaller or medium-sized ones.
- In the small minority that had abandoned it, the main reason was employee discontent.
- 23 per cent of awards exceeded base pay by more than 10 per cent, but 35 per cent of awards were less than 4 per cent of base pay.
- Organisations felt that IPRP had influenced the behaviour of high performers more than average or poor performers.
- The biggest impact was seen to be on those nearer the top of the managerial scale.
- The major problems were seen to be (a) that pay awards were too small to motivate employees, and (b) a number of weaknesses relating to the abilities of managers to conduct assessments competently and fairly.

The authors concluded the section on IPRP by commenting (CIPD, 1999: 11) that

> **Overall, these findings on the success of IRPR indicate useful but not startling gains. IPRP is certainly not seen as a panacea but, consistent with the fact that its use is growing, it is typically seen as a practice which adds value to the organisation.**

If IPRP is to stimulate improvements in performance, its design must be geared to that. Yet studies have shown that although enhanced performance is often the main goal of IPRP, it is by no means the only one.

Kessler and Purcell (1992) found that the objectives of IPRP in the nine organisations they studied included those frequently cited in the literature – recruitment, retention, motivation and performance – but there was also an agenda (partly hidden) which sought to promote culture change, weaken trade unions, personalise the employment relationship, provide better value for money and force managers into more direct relationships with employees. After interviewing 60 managers they presented a rather pessimistic picture showing the main problems experienced to be difficulties in assessment, increased workload and time pressures due to interviews and paperwork, a tendency to rate employees near the middle ground even when performance did not justify it, the frequent levelling of allegations of bias, and an increased difficulty in discussing development needs at the same time as pay.

An even more pessimistic view emerged from Randle's (1997) investigation into the effects of IPRP in a large pharmaceutical company. The scheme was unpopular among scientists who felt their work was hard to assess. A lot of energy and effective work went unseen and was not rewarded, whereas employees who were highly visible and who frequently raised issues with managers, talked a lot at meetings and had skills in impression management benefited most. This had led to points-scoring activities, secrecy and less willingness to share information where it would not be noticed. Randle concluded that the scheme had failed to influence attitudes as intended and had proved dysfunctional for performance.

If employees are to receive additional pay for good performance, there must clearly be an objective way of measuring performance and distinguishing between those whose performance is ranked in categories such as 'Excellent' ,'Good', 'Satisfactory', or 'Below the expected standard', etc. The level of ease or difficulty in doing this not only depends on reasonably accurate measurement criteria and management objectivity, but also on the nature of the roles themselves. Evaluating the performance of call centre workers, traffic wardens, production operatives or fast food outlet managers is certainly less problematic than that of journalists, zookeepers, research scientists or solicitors.

When considering the relevance of an IPRP scheme, the questions in the box below require addressing as a starting-point before the technicalities are worked out.

## ASSESSING THE POTENTIAL VIABILITY OF IPRP

1 What are the main motivators for our employees in each role/dept or unit, etc?
2 What will employees think about a IPRP scheme, and how will we consult them?
3 How will we ensure that the amounts we pay out are worth striving for?
4 How precisely are we going to measure the performance of employees?
  – Can the key aspects of jobs be easily identified and isolated?
  – Can the differences in performance levels be easily observed and detected?
  – Will the assessment criteria be accepted as fair?
  – Are the factors we will measure within the control of each employee?
5 Should we have a pilot scheme, and if so, who should be involved?
6 To what extent can we utilise other ways of influencing performance to complement IPRP?
7 What do line managers think about conducting pay assessments?
8 How should we give the awards – monthly, quarterly, annually?
9 How likely is it that performance will improve if we introduce IPRP, and by how much?
10 Are we doing all we can to motivate employees at present?
11 Is there a way we will be able to control the costs of IPRP and link it to our ability to afford it?

A comprehensive OECD report (2004) into the characteristics and impact of IPRP among civil servants in all member countries concluded that the effect on motivation was 'ambivalent' and observed that IPRP had not motivated the majority of staff. The strongest motivators for civil servants were seen to be 'the content of jobs and career development opportunities'. However, in common with several other studies, IPRP was still deemed to be of value due to other outcomes such as facilitating wider organisational changes. Within the Civil Service these were said to involve

> **effective appraisal and goal-setting processes, clarification of tasks, acquisition of skills, creation of improved manager–employee dialogue, more teamwork, and increased flexibility in work performance.**

In a similar vein a study of IPRP in an Irish multi-divisional company by Kelly and Monks (1997) found no major criticisms; three quarters of the 70 respondents believed the scheme 'had inspired increased performance'. However, as the authors asserted,

> **this does not necessarily indicate that it was the monetary element which created the incentive. Improved communication with superiors, increased focus on set objectives and a clear picture of how individual work fits into overall company goals were observed as associate characteristics of motivation.**

In this instance it did appear that the IPRP scheme had assisted in enhancing individual performance – but perhaps due to the wider elements mentioned as much as the financial incentives.

The OECD report and the work of Kelly and Monks both appear to indicate that IPRP can have positive benefits in the right environment, but the extent to which the financial incentives are responsible for this is unclear.

There is perhaps the longer-term prospect that the comparatively new concept of 'contribution-based pay' may evolve into an appropriate tool for the integration of performance management with reward strategies. As yet, few organisations seem to utilise this approach and so further evidence is required on its effectiveness. According to Armstrong (2002: 311) contribution-based pay involves 'paying for results plus competence and for past performance as well as future success'.

The way performance management as a whole will develop is uncertain but it is worth concluding with Williams' (2002: 252) observation that

> **The core of performance management practice, for many organisations, would appear to be traditional performance appraisal, perhaps with appraisal-related pay tacked on to it. The organisational context and aspects of the work system seem, on the face of it, to be taken for granted.**

## KEY LEARNING POINTS

- Performance management is the major HR process for achieving horizontal integration.
- Provided that senior managers cascade the key business goals downwards and demonstrate commitment to performance management, the potential exists for achieving the integration of employee development and the work priorities and objectives of employees with organisational strategies.
- Performance appraisal is at the heart of performance management, and the design of an appropriate system must take account of a range of contextual issues.
- Managers require training and support so that they can develop the skills, knowledge and confidence to conduct interviews and the necessary follow-up activities effectively throughout the year.
- Actions plans, based on joint agreement between appraiser and appraisee, should be flexible and include both development and work objectives derived from an open and informed dialogue.
- A broad view should be taken as to what constitutes the methods for employee training and development based on what is likely to work best, and taking advantage of work-based learning opportunities when appropriate.
- The range of factors that may motivate an employee is wide and complex yet worthwhile researching in order to provide a sound basis for stimulating enhanced levels of performance.
- The extent to which individual performance-related pay (IPRP) may stimulate improvements in motivation and performance is heavily dependent on the environmental context in which it is introduced. The value of IPRP as a method for bringing about higher levels of performance remains subject to much debate.
- There appears to be considerable scope in many organisations for greater consideration to be given to utilising intrinsic motivators to provide a more enduring base for managing performance.

# REFERENCES

ACAS (February, 2003) *Appraisal*, Advisory booklet, ACAS

Adams J. S. (1963) Towards an understanding of inequity, *Journal of Abnormal and Social Psychology*, Vol.67, pp 422–36

Ameudo-Dorantes C. and Mach T. (2003) Performance pay and fringe benefits: work incentives or compensating wage differentials?, *International Journal of Manpower*, Vol.24 (6), pp672

Anderson G. C. and Barnett J. G. (1987) Characteristics of effective appraisal interviews, *Personnel Review*, Vol.16 (4) pp18–25

Armstrong M. (2002) *Employee Reward*, London, CIPD

Armstrong M. and Baron A. (1998) *Performance Management: The new realities*, London, IPD

Armstrong M. and Baron A. (2005) *Managing Performance: Performance management in action*, London, CIPD

Boxall P. and Purcell J. (2003) *Strategy and Human Resource Management*, Basingstoke, Palgrave Macmillan

CIPD, Performance Management Factsheet, August 2004

CIPD Survey Report on Performance Management, September 2005

Dessler G. (2005) *Human Resource Management*, Harlow, Pearson Prentice Hall

Guest D. E. and Hoque K. (1994) Yes, Personnel does make the difference, *Personnel Management*, November, pp40–4

Finegold D., Mohram. S. and Spreitzer G. M. (2002) Age effects on the predictors of technical workers' commitment and willingness to turnover, *Journal of Organisational Behaviour*, Vol.23 (5), p655

Fletcher C. (1993) *Appraisal – Routes to Improved Performance*, London, IPM

Gill D. (1977) *Appraising Performance: Present trends and the next decade*, London, IPM

Hackman J. R. and Oldham G. R. (1980) *Work Redesign*, Addison Wesley

Hartle F. (1995) *How to Re-engineer your Performance Management Process*, Kogan Page

Incomes Data Services (2003) *Performance Management*, IDS study 748

Institute of Personnel and Development (1999) *Performance Pay Trends in the UK*, London, IPD

Jacques E. (1962), Objective measures for pay differentials, *Harvard Business Review*, January–February, pp133–7

Kelly A. and Monks K.. (1997) Performance-related pay: what makes a successful scheme? Research Papers Series, No.19, Dublin City University Business School

Kessler I. and Purcell J. (1992) Performance-related pay: objectives and applications, *Human Resource Management Journal*, Vol.2 (3) pp16–33

Kovach K. A. (1987) What motivates employees? Workers and supervisors give different answers, *Business Horizons*, 30, pp58–65

Mendonca M. and Kanungo R. N. (1996) Impact of culture on performance management in developing countries, *International Journal of Manpower*, Vol.17 (4/5), pp65–75

Mohrman A. M. Jr, Resnick-West S. M. and Lawler E. E. (1989) *Designing Performance Appraisal Systems*, San Francisco, Jossey-Bass

Mumford A. (1997) *Management Development: Strategies for action*, 3rd edition, London, CIPD

OECD, (October, 2004) *Performance-related Pay Policies for Government Employees: Main trends in OECD member countries*, OECD

Porter I. W. and Lawler E. E. (1968) *Managerial Attitudes and Performance*, Irwin

Purcell J., Kinnie K., Hutchinson S., Rayton B. and Swart J. ( 2003) *Understanding the People and Performance Link: Unlocking the black box*, London, CIPD

Randle K. (1997) Rewarding failure: operating a performance-related pay system in pharmaceutical research, *Personnel Review*, Vol.26 (3) pp187–200

Rankin N. (2001) Raising performance through people: the eighth competency survey, Competency and emotional intelligence, Annual Benchmarking Survey 2000/2001, pp2–21

Rowntree D. (1999) *The Manager's Book of Checklists*, Harlow, Pearson Education

Rynes S. L., Gerhart B. and Minette K. A. (2004) The importance of pay in employee motivation: discrepancies between what people say and what they do, *Human Resource Management*, Vol.43 (4), pp381–94

Torrington D., Hall L. and Taylor S. (2005) *Human Resource Management*, London, FT/Prentice Hall

Verweire K. and Van den Berghe L. (2003) Integrated performance management: adding a new dimension, *Management Decision*, Vol.41 (8), pp 782–90

Walters M. (ed.) (1995) *The Performance Management Handbook*, London, IPM

Williams R. S. (2002) *Managing Employee Performance: Design and implementation in organisations*, Thomson Learning

# Managing individual and collective relationships at work

*Dorothy Foote*

## CHAPTER 9

> **LEARNING OBJECTIVES**
> - To explain the nature of the employment relationship and the different interests of employers and employees
> - To assess the impact of contextual factors on the employment relationship
> - To compare and contrast individual and collective approaches to the management of the employment relationship and their relevance in different organisational contexts
> - To evaluate different approaches to employee involvement and participation and their relative impact on the development of employee commitment strategies

## INTRODUCTION

Previous chapters have emphasised the importance of people as a resource for competitive advantage in organisations and the need to have well developed and appropriate strategies for people resourcing and retention. This chapter builds on these discussions and explores the importance of positive relationships in the workplace.

In its 1997 position paper *Employment Relations Into the Twenty-First Century*, the Institute of Personnel and Development (subsequently the CIPD) recommended that all employers should conduct an in-depth review of their approach to employment relations. This was supported by the positive link that their research had shown (IPD, 1997: 1) between

> **managerial strategies on employment relations and employees' identification with, and support for, performance improvement and organisational change.**

The paper went on to say that

> **successful organisations are increasingly those which have a constructive relationship with employees and a management approach which enables them to develop and draw on the full potential of their people.**

The development of constructive relationships requires a focus on both the formal and informal relationships that occur at work between employer and employee. The organisation and the people working in it will have different agendas and different interests. These interests can often be of a conflicting nature, but the success and very survival of the organisation represents a crucial common interest that can provide a basis on which to build understanding and ultimately lead to constructive compromise and agreement. Effective and harmonious employee relations can only be achieved if differences are reconciled: only then can the organisation grow, prosper and add value across its activities. This chapter will focus on the use of managerial strategies of employee involvement and participation (EIP) as mechanisms for the development of employee commitment. It will also look at conflict-management strategies that can help to minimise the risk of conflict and provide mechanisms through which conflict can be handled constructively for positive outcomes.

## DEFINING RELATIONSHIPS AT WORK

Organisations take many different forms, as do the people management functions within them. Just as organisations are influenced by the environments in which they operate, so are the practices of people management. The effectiveness of organisations is a result of the way in which they integrate the various parts of the internal system with the external environment. According to Marchington and Wilkinson (2005: 28), 'Integration is at the heart of HRM.' They identify two forms of integration:

*vertical*, which refers to

> **the links between HRM and both wider business strategies and the political, economic, social and legal forces that shape (and to some extent are shaped by) organisations**

and *horizontal*, which refers to

> **the 'fit' between different HR policies and practices, and the degree to which they support or contradict one another.**

The extent to which an organisation successfully integrates its activities will impact on the nature of its relationship with its employees.

---

**ACTIVITY . . .**

Consider the case of Company A, a manufacturer of high-tech components for the computer industry. It is located in an old coalmining area of South Wales and many of its employees were once employed in the mining industry before its demise. Unlike other branches of the company in Japan, Company A recognises a trade union for collective bargaining purposes and also consults with its workforce through a system of works councils and employee representatives who represent both union and non-union employees. Manufacturing is done on a team basis with production and performance bonuses paid when targets are met. Jobs are graded on a job family basis and a skills development programme supports career development throughout all levels of the company.

Analyse this case study and identify examples of horizontal and vertical integration and the impact of each of these examples on the employment relationship.

---

At a fundamental internal level, integration is needed between the social systems (the ways in which work groups are organised and the processes of interaction) and the technical system (how work is organised and carried out to deliver products or services to customers). The key role played by people in the ability of an organisation to achieve this integration and deliver its objectives makes the human resource potentially very powerful. Strategies for managing the employment relationship must, therefore, recognise the different interests that exist between employer and employee: employers seek to employ people at the lowest cost to the organisation whereas employees seek to earn as much as possible for their efforts. This might seem like an irreconcilable difference in economic interest, but there is one outcome that is important to both sides – the success of the organisation.

It is this common interest that makes the relationship viable and provides a basis on which differences can be addressed and resolved. The challenge is to develop a relationship that gives each party a reasonable and mutually acceptable return on their investment. This can be achieved through a range of processes and procedures that formalise the relationship and seek ways of reaching agreement on areas of difference. Organisations therefore develop agreements, rules and procedures relating to the key aspects of the employment relationship that set standards of behaviour for everyone in the organisation. They also ensure that when conflict arises, it is dealt with fairly and reasonably.

## PERSPECTIVES ON THE EMPLOYMENT RELATIONSHIP

The way in which managers approach the employment relationship, and the strategies they develop and apply, will be influenced by their own frame of reference. In other words, their attitudes, presumptions and psychological influences will determine how they perceive issues and events and the decisions that they make and actions they take. There are a number of different potential perspectives on employment relations, as set out in Table 18.

Table 18  *Theories in employee relations*

| Perspectives | Features in workplace | Manifestations |
|---|---|---|
| Unitary | Omnipotent management exercising unilateral control | Unilateral PRP (performance-related pay), emphasis on communication and performance evaluation |
| Pluralist | Limited power-sharing between major interested parties | Negotiations with interest groups, stakeholder perspective |
| Marxist | Focus on exploitation and structured inequalities | Conflict absenteeism, false consciousness and consumerism |
| Systems | Institutions in equilibrium governed by rules. Open systems, inputs and outputs affected by environment | Refinement of descriptive tool. Scope for international comparisons |
| Feminist | Male advantages embedded in institutions, culture, and hence workplace | Agitation to improve policies and conditions of employment |
| Post-modern | Belief in post-industrial world of work where meanings disputed by ambiguity and ambivalence | Adoption of a rhetoric of HRM plus associated ideologies |

Adapted from G. Hollinshead, P. Nicholls and S. Tailby (1999) *Employee Relations*, FT/Pitman Publishing, p14

These theories give an indication of the degree of complexity of the employment relationship and the range of views and approaches that can be taken. No one theory provides an answer to or explanation for what we observe in the workplace. As Hollinshead *et al* (1999: 15) point out, each theory makes sense of some portion of the employment relationship; an understanding of social, political and historical contexts provides us with a set of lenses to make sense of the differing aspects of the employment relationship.

Much of the discussion about management perceptions in UK employment relations has focused on the unitary and pluralist perspectives which were first distinguished by Fox (1966). A unitary perspective assumes that the organisation is an integrated group or team of people with a single authority/loyalty structure and a common set of values. Conflict is seen as irrational, unnecessary, exceptional and counter-productive to team prosperity, the product either of mistakes or mischief. It argues for the right of management to manage on behalf of the team and regards bodies such as trade unions as an intrusion, competing with management for employee loyalty. The emphasis is on conflict avoidance, through such methods as paternalism, informing and consulting the workforce.

## ILLUSTRATION

### Alpha Company

The Alpha Company is a long-established family business. The Chairman is the original owner, whose son and daughter hold the positions of managing director and operations director respectively. The latter also includes responsibility for 'personnel issues'. The company prides itself on providing good working conditions for its employees including heavily subsidised meals, a visiting chiropodist, regular social events and an open-door policy (managers' doors are always open to staff with issues to discuss). It does not recognise a trade union because that is viewed as unnecessary by management because employees are happy. The Chairman describes the workforce as his 'second family'. In the unlikely event that employees have a problem or concern, they know that they can discuss it with their manager and it will be dealt with on their behalf.

A pluralist perspective, on the other hand, assumes that organisations are composed of individuals who may in many instances share the same goals with the organisation, but may also have some divergent goals. Even where goals are shared between employer and employee, there may be different views on how these goals should be achieved. This produces tension that must be managed in the interests of maintaining a viable collaborative structure. Conflict is seen as a rational manifestation of such differences with a high potential for its occurrence. The potential for conflict arises from a variety of sources including personal, industrial and organisational factors.

Within the pluralist perspective, trade unions are viewed by employers as a rational employee response, and a useful institution within the employment framework. The basis of control still rests with management through negotiated and agreed rules and procedures, giving rise to shared decision-making over certain issues. The extent to which decision-making is shared is determined by the organisation's employee relations policy.

## ILLUSTRATION
### Beta Council

Beta Council is a local authority operating in the south of England. It employs 3,000 staff across the range of its activities. Beta recognises three different trade unions representing clerical, manual and technical employees. It consults employees through its Joint Consultative Committee, and employer and employee representatives negotiate its terms and conditions of employment nationally. Unions and employer do not always see eye to eye but management likes to know what it is dealing with and feels that the established structures help it to anticipate problems and manage conflict through the mechanisms that exist. As well as the JCC, the Council has a series of detailed procedures that have been negotiated and agreed with its trade union representatives.

Management has an important role to play in shaping the employment relationship and its implicit right to manage, or 'managerial prerogative', is a principle that has been dearly held over the years. Embedded in this belief is a pressure to resist any sharing of decision-making responsibility and power with employees and their representatives. Where senior management hold a unitarist perspective, the upholding of this prerogative would be paramount, and although communication and consultation may take place, management would always make the final decision. Where management holds a pluralist perspective, there is still a belief in managerial prerogative, but recognition that if differences are to be resolved, some sharing of decision-making power may be necessary. This may mean that certain procedures require agreement between an employer and union representatives before a decision can be reached.

Research has attempted to categorise management styles in employment relations (eg Fox, 1974; Purcell and Sisson, 1983). Lewis, Thornhill and Saunders (2003) provide a helpful summary of the typology of management styles based on that developed by Purcell and Sisson (1983) – see Table 19.

Although the authors acknowledge these as ideal types that oversimplify reality, they do provide us with a structure and framework for analysis. As Lewis *et al* (2003: 105) state, 'concluding what something is not may allow us to define what it is'.

**Table 19** *Management styles in employee relations*

| Title | Characteristics | Most likely to occur in | Possible examples |
|---|---|---|---|
| Traditionalists | Exploit employees<br>Treat labour as a factor of production<br>Driven by cost minimisation<br>Little attention to employee involvement<br>Anti-union | Hotel and catering<br>Garment manufacture | Reports to TUC 'bad bosses hotline' |
| Sophisticated paternalists | Non-union<br>Generous treatment of employees<br>Sophisticated HR policies<br>Unitarist | High-technology<br>Creative industries | Marks & Spencer<br>Hewlett Packard |
| Sophisticated moderns (constitutionalists) | Reluctantly recognise unions<br>Formal, detailed collective agreements<br>Win–lose attitude to bargaining<br>Pluralist | Manufacturing<br>Engineering | Ford |
| Sophisticated moderns (consulters) | Willingly recognise unions<br>Unions enjoined in management of employment relationship<br>Bargaining seen as a joint problem-solving exercise<br>HR policies to engender employee commitment | Companies with relatively low labour costs as a proportion of total costs<br>Japanese-owned companies | ICI<br>Hitachi<br>Nissan<br>Dupont |
| Standard moderns | Recognise unions albeit with ambivalent attitude<br>Fire-fighting approach to employee relations | Heavy manufacturing and engineering companies, long tradition of unionisation<br>Conglomerate, multi-product companies that have grown through acquisition and diversification | Lucas<br>British Aerospace |

Source: Lewis, Thornhill and Saunders (2003: 106), adapted from Purcell and Sisson (1983), Purcell and Gray (1986), Blyton and Turnbull (1998)

It has previously been acknowledged that context influences employee relations strategy and action and a particular management style may be more relevant to particular circumstances. On this basis it could be argued that an understanding of the above typology of management style provides the scope for flexibility and adaptability of style. In a rapidly changing external environment a key management skill would therefore be the ability to anticipate change and adapt management style and strategy appropriately.

## ACTIVITY . . .

*In which of the categories listed in Table 19 would you place your organisation?*

*What do you see as the major employee relations challenges facing your organisation over the next five years? How might these influence management style?*

## COLLECTIVISM V INDIVIDUALISM

We have already noted that management philosophy, beliefs and style influence policies, procedures and strategies. An important aspect of policy development is the stance taken on a collective versus individual approach to the management of the employment relationship. In other words, does management seek agreement from employee representatives on terms and conditions of employment matters, or does it decide unilaterally? Does it communicate to the workforce via elected employee representatives, or does it communicate with employees on a one-to-one basis? Issues of individualism/collectivism underpin the development and scope of employee involvement and participation strategies. Perspectives on the employment relationship will influence that decision, as will structural factors. For example, in a large organisation it is difficult to deal directly with every employee and collective arrangements can bring advantages of economies of scale.

## ACTIVITY . . .

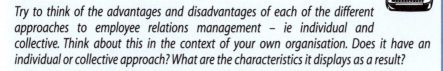

*Try to think of the advantages and disadvantages of each of the different approaches to employee relations management – ie individual and collective. Think about this in the context of your own organisation. Does it have an individual or collective approach? What are the characteristics it displays as a result?*

One might think that union recognition is an inherent part of a collective approach to employee relations, but this is not necessarily the case. Employees may group together for employee relations purposes on a temporary basis, perhaps to air a complaint to management, or on a more permanent basis through a staff association. See below for an example of a staff association.

## ILLUSTRATION

### Nene Building Society Staff Association

Over 75 per cent of the employees of the Nene Building Society belong to its staff association. The association was set up by the employer ten years ago to give its employees a voice in the organisation. It is financed by the employer and by member subscription and is allowed to use employer premises for meetings and functions at a reduced cost. A formal agreement exists, signed by the managing director and the Chairperson of the staff association, which sets out specific matters for consultation with the association. These include business developments, working environment and health and safety matters. Employees elect representatives to consult with management on their behalf. Nene is convinced that the climate of involvement that this arrangement creates contributes to staff motivation and the company's high performance in its market.

## PAUSE FOR THOUGHT . . .

*How does a staff association differ from a trade union?*

Legislation also means that organisations which previously had no collective representation of employees now have to be prepared to provide this facility in the eventuality of redundancies, transfer of undertakings or health and safety issues. The law requires employers to consult with employees collectively on these issues, whether a union is recognised or not, if the organisation employs more than 20 people. So the decision not to formally recognise a trade union does not mean that an employer can avoid all collective relationships with its employees, but for some employers union recognition provides a more predictable and structured way of managing employee relations.

## UNION RECOGNITION

Union recognition has until recently been a voluntary option for employers, and statistics clearly show that levels of recognition declined from a peak of 13.2 million members in 1979 to 7.8 million people in 2000 (Lewis *et al*, 2003: 152). This represents a decline in membership of approximately 40 per cent. Since the Employment Relations Act 1999, however, trade unions have had a legal right to recognition. In organisations with over 20 employees, a union can seek recognition from the employer. The result of such a request could be either formal recognition by the employer or a failure to agree on recognition, in which latter case the Central Arbitration Committee (CAC) may intervene and seek to help both sides reach an agreement or a recognition ballot of the of the workforce may be held. If a voluntary agreement cannot be reached, statutory minima are applied. Since the legislation has been implemented, cases of union recognition have increased. In particular, there is clear evidence of a preference on the part of employers to reach voluntary recognition agreements rather than resist and find themselves forced into recognising a union via the statutory process. This gives the employer and union the flexibility to negotiate terms that suit both parties, rather than be constrained by the legal provisions. Lewis *et al* (2003: 159) adapt TUC data to show this trend as in Table 20.

**Table 20** *Union recognition 1996–2001*

| Period | No. of months | No. of voluntary agreements | Average no. per month during period |
|---|---|---|---|
| Jan–Dec 1996 | 12 | 110 | 9.2 |
| Jan 97–Feb 98 | 14 | 81 | 5.8 |
| March 98–Oct 99 | 20 | 109 | 5.5 |
| Nov 99–Oct 2000 | 12 | 159 | 13.3 |
| Nov 2000–Oct 01 | 12 | 450 | 37.5 |

Source: Lewis et al (2003) p159

The maintenance of this trend depends on the ability of trade unions to sustain the level of efforts and resources that are invested in recruitment campaigns. From an employer perspective, this trend sends a clear message that organisations must be union-aware and be proactive in developing a policy and position on union recognition that fits with the needs and objectives of the business. How will it deal with a request from a union for recognition? If more than one union seeks recognition rights, how should it proceed? Some organisations may choose to actively fight against union recognition and remain union-free. For organisations that already recognise a union, issues also arise. For example, is the existing union the most appropriate to represent the workforce? Does it have low or high membership? If it has low membership, there is a risk that a rival union may build up membership, reach the statutory threshold and claim recognition rights.

## ACTIVITY . . .

*What strategies might be adopted by an organisation to ensure that it remains union-free?*

*How can management minimise the risk of a rival union threatening an existing union recognition agreement?*

The policy position adopted must, if it is to be successful, integrate vertically and horizontally with other policies and procedures. It must be a coherent part of HRM and employee relations policies and reflect the wider psychological contract.

## THE PSYCHOLOGICAL CONTRACT

Previous chapters have referred to the importance of the psychological contract and the associated expectations that employees may hold of their organisation and their managers and vice versa. In the management of relations with employees this process of aligning expectations is particularly pertinent in the drive for employee hearts and minds. Minimising the risk of conflict and gaining employee commitment will depend on having focused strategies in place. Our original economic model of the employment relationship takes us only so far along this road. In a changing world the pressures on the employment relationship must be understood and taken account of in strategy development. Sparrow and Cooper (2003) identify key challenges for HR professionals in managing employee expectations and behaviour in a changing environment. They identify in particular the impact of international competition, new forms of work organisation and changing individual expectations and behaviours as key drivers for change in the approach that managers take to employment relations. Table 21 provides a comparison of the past and emergent form of the psychological contract in an employee relations context.

Sparrow and Cooper (2003: 16–17) speak of

> **a shift from relational aspects in the employment relationship to more transactional components. The old deal was stereotyped as one in which promotion could be expected, and when granted was based upon time-served and technical competence. As long as the company was in profit and you did your job, then you had no cause to fear job loss. The organisational culture was paternalistic, and essentially encouraged an exchange of security for commitment.**

This is contrasted with the new employment contract in which change is continuous and promotion is harder to gain. People are 'empowered' to take on more responsibility not just for their job but also for their learning and development within that job. Sparrow and Cooper (2003: 18) argue that a 'new and very different psychological contract' has emerged as a result of the following factors:

- globalisation
- downsizing

Table 21  *Past and emergent forms of psychological contract*

| Characteristic | Past form | Emergent form |
| --- | --- | --- |
| Focus | Security, continuity, loyalty | Exchange, future |
| Format | Structured, predictable, stable | Unstructured, flexible, open to (re)negotiation |
| Underlying basis | Tradition, fairness, social justice, socio-economic issues | Market forces, saleable, abilities and skills, added value |
| Employer's responsibilities | Continuity, job security, training, career prospects | Equitable (as perceived) reward for added value |
| Employee's responsibilities | Loyalty, attendance, satisfactory performance, compliance with authority | Entrepreneurship, innovation, enacting changes to improve performance, excellent performance |
| Contractual relations | Formalised, mostly via trade union or collective representation | Individual's responsibility to barter for his/her services (internally or externally) |
| Career management | Organisational responsibility, in-spiralling careers planned and facilitated through personnel department input | Individual's responsibility, out-spiralling careers by personal reskilling and retraining |

Source: P. R. Sparrow and C. L. Cooper (2003: 17), a composite from Hiltrop (1995) and Anderson and Schalk (1998)

- increased levels of flexibility
- more short-term contracts
- greater reliance on virtual workers
- boundaryless careers.

This makes the challenge of gaining and maintaining employee commitment even greater.

## GAINING AND BUILDING EMPLOYEE COMMITMENT THROUGH EMPLOYEE INVOLVEMENT AND PARTICIPATION

The goal of achieving a committed workforce has focused management attention on processes of employee involvement and participation (EIP). A variety of terms have been developed to describe and categorise the roles that employees play in influencing decision-making in organisations. As with many topics in the study of the employment relationship there is no one agreed set of definitions. Whereas in practice the two terms are often used interchangeably, researchers and writers in this field provide characteristics by which differentiation can be achieved, particularly in the consideration of drivers and objectives. Lewis, Thornhill and Saunders (2004: 248) argue that to view the two terms as synonymous is to oversimplify, and offer a number of differences between the two. They argue that involvement and participation differ in terms of the exercise of power in the relationship, the locus of control, the nature of employee influence and the driving force behind each approach in practice. Each can also differ in terms of the purpose, scope, level of adoption and the form or forms in which they manifest themselves. If we accept this argument, it is possible to characterise each process using Lewis *et al*'s factors – see Table 22.

Such distinctions can help us understand what is happening in organisations, and why, but clearly the reality will reflect the specific circumstances within an organisation. Issues of power and control are crucial in the employment relationship and the location of power and control will be influenced by a number of environmental factors. For example, in a situation of high unemployment and recession, the balance of power and control will be in favour of management in any EIP-type encounter and the willingness to share decision-making could be undermined.

**Table 22** *Characteristics of involvement and participation*

| Characteristic | Involvement | Participation |
| --- | --- | --- |
| Exercise of power | Management | Shared |
| Locus of control | Management | Shared |
| Nature of employee influence | Information, feedback only – no agreement needed | Shared decision-making – agreement needed |
| Driving force | Management | Employees |
| Purpose | Employee commitment | Employee power |
| Scope | Determined by management | Agreed with management |
| Level of adoption | Job/task level | Organisation level |
| Forms taken | Direct with employees | Indirect via employee representatives |

Based on Lewis, Thornhill and Saunders (2003) p248

## ACTIVITY . . .

*Using the PESTLE framework of analysis, identify the key external environmental influences on the locus of power and control in the employment relationship. What impact do these factors have on the nature of participation in organisations?*

Fundamentally, involvement can be seen as a range of management-initiated processes reflecting managerial interests where the needs of the business and the contribution of employees to the success of that business are paramount. Involvement strategies have emerged over the past 20 years in response to a number of environmental influences. We have already noted that influences in the economic environment have led to increased competition for organisations and a need to respond effectively and quickly to changing markets. The growth of the HRM approach has also contributed to an acknowledgement that people are key to an organisation's ability to respond effectively. As a result, management initiatives have focused on maximising the contribution of this resource. If we think back to the issue of managerial prerogative, we can see that this might pose a dilemma for management: how can involvement of employees be achieved while retaining decision-making power in management hands? Involvement initiatives are therefore designed to engage the support, understanding and optimum contribution of employees in an organisation and their commitment to its objectives. They do not involve sharing decision-making or power and tend to focus on the task-related activities of the individual or workgroup. Examples of such involvement might include job design and enrichment, semi-autonomous group-working, team briefing, newsletters, corporate videos and other communication tools. Hyman and Mason (1995: 77) provide a useful categorisation of such processes in relation to the related goals of management – see Table 23.

Participation, while undoubtedly related to involvement, is more power- than business-centred. Whereas involvement has been management-driven, trade unions, governments and European statutory measures have driven participation. Whereas involvement focuses on sharing information, participation is designed to allow employees to take part in decision-making on matters that affect them. Gennard and Judge (2005: 180) include in their consideration of participation methods such processes as joint consultation, collective bargaining and board-level worker representation.

Joint consultation is the subject of some debate as to whether it can really be considered to be true participation. Salamon (2000: 343) defines joint consultation as

**Table 23** *Employee involvement processes*

| Method | Communication | |
|---|---|---|
| | **Flow** | **Goal** |
| *Group* | | |
| Briefing groups | Downward | Team communication |
| Chair's forums | Downward | Information dissemination |
| Semi-autonomous work groups | Upward | Group responsibility |
| Quality circles | Upward | Quality ethos, diagnostic improvements |
| *Individual* | | |
| Counselling/mentoring | Upward | Employee welfare/development |
| Appraisal and development | Upward | Career development |
| Suggestion schemes | Upward | Diagnostic improvements |

Source: Hyman and Mason (1995)

> **a process wherein management not only determines issues on which it wishes to seek the views and opinions of employees but also retains the discretion to decide the final outcome without subjecting it to joint agreement with employees or their representatives.**

The absence of the need to reach agreement means that the power to decide rests completely with management. As Figure 26 shows, joint consultation can sit on either side of the line between involvement and true participation. Its location depends on the extent to which it is reacting to information rather than merely being provided with it (Guest and Fatchett, 1974). The reality of what is called joint consultation in UK organisations varies from the provision of information at one end of the spectrum to a process of joint decision-making at the other, and it is therefore important in any analysis and evaluation of the process to be aware of these differences. In addition, employee participation can be characterised by its representative nature whereby employees elect representatives who are often, but not always, trade union representatives to participate in these activities on their behalf.

Ramsay (1996) organises the different approaches to involvement and participation into four main categories:

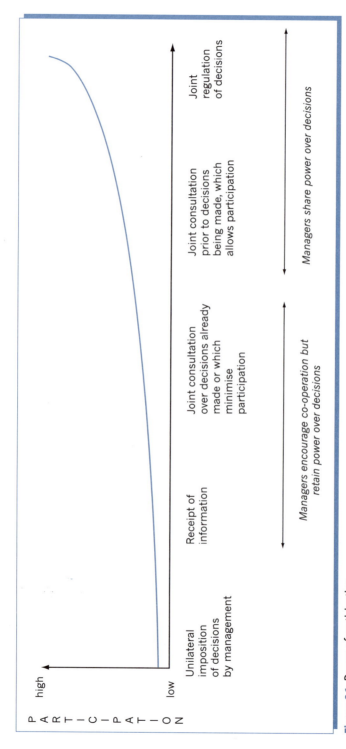

**Figure 26** *Degree of participation*
Source: Lewis, Thornhill and Saunders (2003) p253

1 communications and briefing systems – downward and upward
2 task and work group involvement – including teamworking and total quality management programmes
3 financial participation – including profit-sharing, profit-related pay and share ownership
4 representative participation – including collective bargaining and joint consultation.

Collective bargaining is a process of joint regulation towards the top end of Figure 26. Rose (2004) defines it as

> **the process whereby representatives of employers and employees jointly determine and regulate decisions pertaining to both substantive and procedural matters within the employment relationship. The outcome of the process is the collective agreement.**

So the process basically determines the rules by which the employment relationship will be put into operation. It is a representative process, often but not exclusively involving trade union representatives, and can lead to agreed outcomes on a variety of topics, typically hours of work, pay and holidays as substantive issues. Agreements may also be reached on the content of procedures such as grievance- and discipline-handling. Reaching agreement is inherent in the process and a failure to agree could lead to a dispute situation. As a form of participatory power-sharing, therefore, collective bargaining displays the characteristics of shared decision-making.

The history of involvement and participation in the UK has largely been one of shifting emphasis between joint consultation and collective bargaining at particular points in time. The 1998 Workplace Employment Relations Survey statistics (Millward *et al*, 2000: 109) show that in the UK 29 per cent of all organisations were engaged in collective pay bargaining *and* that 29 per cent reported having a consultative committee in place (although only 23 per cent of organisations were considered to have a 'functioning committee' that met at least once every three months as opposed to 'window dressing' committees that did not meet regularly). So, having experienced fluctuations between the levels of use of these two approaches throughout the latter part of the twentieth century, the UK entered the new millennium in a situation where both are being reported in equal numbers.

However, as with all statistics, we must be cautious in drawing sweeping conclusions. Both processes have shown a decline in the past 20 years. WERS again shows the presence of collective bargaining declining from 60 per cent of organisations in 1984 and joint consultation from 34 per cent in the same year. The decline in collective bargaining can be linked to a number of factors, not least the decline in trade union membership and recognition. Although the trade union recognition provisions of the 1999 Employment Relations Act have led to some increases in membership and recognition levels, there is not yet evidence to suggest anything more than a small increase, and an upward swing is not necessarily imminent. Overall, we have seen a decline in the traditionally popular methods of participation and a 'significant shift to forms of employee involvement in the UK over the past two decades' (Lewis *et al*, 2003: 272) reflecting managerial responses to the changing external environment.

## *EIP* AND THE PERFORMANCE LINK

The link between involvement, commitment and organisational performance underpins the above shift in emphasis from participatory methods to management-driven involvement practices. In its position statement *Employment Relations Into the Twenty-First Century* (1997) the CIPD presents research evidence to demonstrate how employment relations impacts on business performance (Guest and Conway, 1997; Patterson, West, Lawthom and Nickell, 1997). This evidence shows that:

- Key elements of good people management practice are job design, skills development and a climate of regular, systematic involvement.
- Good people management practices are associated with a positive psychological contract based on trust, fairness and delivery of the deal.
- An organisation culture in which employees believe their employer will look after their interests has a positive outcome for work performance.

The resultant conceptual framework provides a basis for organisations to review their practices and strategies in order to more finely tune them to a high-performance agenda. An important outcome of such a review would be the development of an employee commitment strategy. Gennard and Judge (2005: 181) discuss the importance of an employee commitment strategy based around Walton's (1985) thinking.

> **The commitment strategy involves employees contributing their own ideas on how their performance and the quality of product and service they provide can be improved. There is clear evidence that employees want to be part of a successful organisation which provides a good income, and an opportunity for development and secure employment.**

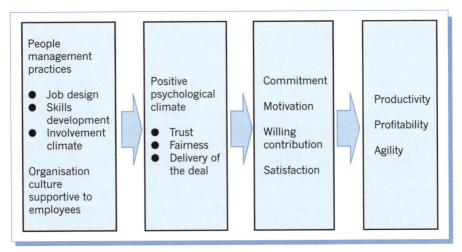

**Figure 27** *A conceptual framework for reviewing employment relations within organisations*
Source: CIPD, 1997

For the organisation, a key outcome of a commitment strategy is high-performing people creating a high-performing organisation. This is supported by the findings of the CIPD's *Understanding the People and Performance Link* (2003), in which the researchers report that HR policies which engage staff through involvement in decision-making, job influence, performance appraisal and teamworking can be linked to job satisfaction and motivation (Purcell *et al*, 2003).

Recent research by Marchington, Wilkinson, Ackers and Dundon (2001) reinforces the importance being placed by businesses on the employee contribution, and uses the term 'employee voice' to encompass the variety of mechanisms now used in organisations to encourage and support communications. This research shows that employee voice contributes to business performance through better employee contributions, improved management systems and productivity gains. Rose (2004: 383) uses the term 'voice' as a

> **'catch all' ... to cover a wide range of processes and structures which allow and even empower employees, directly or indirectly, to contribute to decision-making within the organisation.**

Indeed, a voice perspective could be seen as providing a helpful way forward in exploring the future development of EIP mechanisms in an environment in which management-driven and employee-driven strategies for EIP appear to be in a state of transition. The more traditional definitions and models increasingly require caveats in order to be applied to changing organisational contexts

Further complexity arises with the introduction of the Information and Consultation of Employees Regulations 2004. As of April 2005, this legislation gives employees new rights to be informed and consulted about issues that affect their employment and the prospects of the business. Although initially applying to organisations with 150 employees or more, it will by 2008 apply to all organisations with more than 50 employees (CIPD, 2005) and will inevitably lead to an increase in the number of joint consultative committees in the UK. In its recent policies and procedures document, the CIPD notes that this legislation poses a significant challenge to the UK involvement and participation system. Its specific requirement for representative arrangements is in direct contrast to the recent 'overwhelming trend within the system … towards arrangements for direct (ie employee-based) information disclosure and consultation' (Beaumont and Hunter, 2005a: 3). The legislation does not explicitly require unions to be involved, and Metcalf (2005: 31) sums up the challenge that this legislation poses for trade unions:

> **The tough job for unions is to build on these schemes and expand their role within them so that they are seen as the legitimate voice of employees. Alternatively, this institution may crowd them out.**

How employers respond to this within their existing involvement-oriented strategies remains to be seen, but an integrated model of employee voice could be a helpful way forward.

## MANAGING CONFLICT

Generating commitment is a major challenge for organisations, and maintaining high levels of commitment is an on-going challenge. A coherent and sustained commitment strategy will help, but the human resource is the least predictable of all the resources that an organisation has to manage. Unlike other resources, humans have the capacity for thought and emotion, and however many procedures are in place, there is always the risk that someone will behave and react in a way that could not have been anticipated. This makes it very difficult to maintain a harmonious working environment all of the time. In order to make EIP and commitment strategies work, therefore, organisations also need a strategy for handling conflict and channelling it in a constructive direction. This section will examine conflict in the work environment and explore how managers can anticipate potential conflict and put mechanisms in place both to minimise the risk of conflict and to resolve any issues that arise.

As we learned earlier in this chapter, the management view of conflict will depend on the frame of reference held. If a unitarist view is taken, conflict will be seen as a bad and undesirable thing. A pluralist view, on the other hand, would see certain types of conflict as being a positive force that can be managed in order to produce constructive outcomes. If conflict is supportive of the goals of a group or organisation and improves its performance, then it may be seen as good or functional. If, on the other hand, it hinders group or organisational performance, it may be seen as bad or dysfunctional. Schmidt's (1974) research (cited in Mullins, 2002: 814) into practising managers identified a number of positive and negative outcomes of conflict:

*Positive*
- better ideas produced
- people forced to search for new approaches
- long-standing problems brought to the surface and resolved
- clarification of individual views
- stimulation of interest and creativity
- a chance for people to test their capacities

*Negative*
- some people felt defeated and demeaned
- distance between people is increased
- development of a climate of mistrust and suspicion
- individuals and groups concentrate on their own narrow interests
- resistance develops, rather than teamwork
- an increase in employee turnover.

## ACTIVITY . . .

*From your own experience try to think of a conflict situation that had a positive outcome. Identify those aspects of the conflict-handling approach that helped achieve the positive outcome.*

Whatever view we might take of conflict, whether we see it as a bad or good thing, understanding it is the first step in managing for a positive outcome.

## SOURCES AND MANIFESTATIONS OF CONFLICT

As Hatch (1997: 308) explains, conflict is hard to explain because it does not always manifest itself in an overt way. People 'employ numerous psychological defence mechanisms and conscious strategies in order to disengage from overt conflict'. This makes the prediction of the occurrence of overt conflict difficult. In an adaptation of Walton and Dutton's research findings (1969), Hatch offers a helpful model to aid prediction and understanding based on a view of conflict as 'embedded in local conditions which are even more deeply rooted in the environment and organisational context':

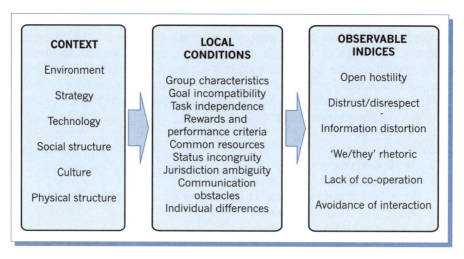

| CONTEXT | LOCAL CONDITIONS | OBSERVABLE INDICES |
|---|---|---|
| Environment | Group characteristics | Open hostility |
| Strategy | Goal incompatibility | Distrust/disrespect |
| Technology | Task independence | Information distortion |
| Social structure | Rewards and performance criteria | 'We/they' rhetoric |
| Culture | Common resources | Lack of co-operation |
| Physical structure | Status incongruity | Avoidance of interaction |
| | Jurisdiction ambiguity | |
| | Communication obstacles | |
| | Individual differences | |

**Figure 28** *A model showing the possible sources of interdepartmental conflict*
Source: Hatch (1997), p308, Walton and Dutton (1969)

Although the basis of this model is 'inter-unit conflict', there is a relationship between the 'observable indices' above and other potential sources of conflict as summed up by Bryans and Cronin (1983: 103, cited in Mullins, 2002: 817). They categorised sources of conflict under six headings:

- Differences between corporate and individual goals
- Conflicts between different departments or groups within the organisation
- Conflict between the formal and informal organisation
- Conflict between manager and managed
- Conflict between individual and job
- Conflict between individuals.

Armstrong (2003: 260) sums up more concisely by saying that

**conflict is inevitable in organisations because they function by means of adjustments in their structure and membership. Conflict also arises when there is change, because it may be seen as a threat to be challenged or resisted, or when there is frustration ...**

Understanding the range of potential sources is helpful, but if we accept Hatch's view of the difficulty in predicting manifestation of conflict, then managers must have strategies in place for handling conflict effectively when it does occur. Understanding the potential causes helps develop appropriate strategies. Recognising conflict when it rears its head also helps in dealing with issues when they are small-scale and localised to prevent them from becoming major issues that are harder to manage. This has been a key underpinning principle of the traditional UK approach to conflict-handling.

Broadly, conflict can take one of two forms: individual and collective. Individual conflict tends to be more random than collective conflict. Often it is a spontaneous response to some perceived deprivation or mistreatment. Blyton and Turnbull (2004: 350) describe such action as 'spontaneous, reactive, and above all not born out of any calculative strategy'. Sometimes it is immediately expressed, but often it is suppressed until an event causes it to become apparent or a build-up of frustration causes the individual to give emotional expression to his or her disquiet. Individual conflict can manifest itself in a range of ways including absenteeism, labour turnover, sabotage, accidents, poor performance or inappropriate behaviour. Sometimes a one-to-one approach can lead to an individual solution, as in the example below.

## ILLUSTRATION

### John

John had worked in his current role for three years and had performed so well that he was promoted to supervisor of his department. It was clear to John from the start that his new role was much more demanding. He needed to seek advice from a number of different colleagues on a regular basis and was increasingly feeling inadequate and a failure. He started to feel angry that he was not getting the support that he needed to fulfil his role to his own high standard of performance. After months of putting up with his bad moods, his wife suggested that he make an appointment with his line manager and get his concerns on the table. John was initially reluctant to do this, as he believed that he was promoted to a level at which he was expected to be able to cope, and that talking to his manager would be a sign of failure. However, he did as suggested. His manager was surprised to learn of John's concerns. He thought John was doing a good job. After a long discussion, it became clear that there were some key skills that could be enhanced, particularly in delegation and time management, so a development plan was agreed and implemented over a three-month period, much to John's relief. At his next six-month review, he had achieved his targets and was feeling much more confident in his managerial competence.

Collective conflict involves a number of people coming together to express dissatisfaction. It implies a degree of organisation on the part of those involved and usually has a plan of action and a specific and articulated objective. While such action tends to be associated with trade unions, it is possible for collective action to occur in non-union situations, although it can be more difficult for employees to organise collectively without the structures that union membership and employer recognition provide. Collective conflict can take a number of forms including output restrictions, go-slows, overtime bans, working-to-rule and withdrawal of labour (strike).

The dividing line between organised collective conflict and unorganised individual conflict is, however, not as clear-cut as has just been suggested (Blyton and Turnbull, 2004: 350). Some collective conflicts are spontaneous and lacking in focused objectives; some individual conflicts manifest themselves as individual events, such as sickness absence, but could be part of an organised protest. Blyton and Turnbull report a 'blue flu' day when all the officers from the New York Police Department reported themselves sick on the same day – an example of organised individual action with a collective impact.

It would be wrong to assume that the absence of collective conflict shows a harmonious working environment for individual conflict can, in fact, exist but be hidden like a time-bomb waiting to explode. This underlines the importance of the existence of EIP strategies that facilitate open discussion and resolution of issues.

## ILLUSTRATION

### The hotel manager

A large hotel chain was suffering from high employee turnover, absenteeism and an increasing number of guest complaints about the negative attitude of staff. A new manager was brought in from one of the more successful hotels in the chain to effect improvements. Over a period of months, she worked alongside employees in all of the key departments and listened to their views and concerns. It was clear that employees felt isolated in their roles. They did not identify with the company or the hotel and had many complaints about the working environment, most of which were very minor in themselves but had combined to create a serious morale problem. 'Nobody listens to us' was a common complaint. The manager decided to introduce a staff consultation process and set up an employee forum. Each department within the hotel was asked to nominate a representative to attend a meeting every three months with the manager. Lunch was provided and an informal and open atmosphere was encouraged although action points were circulated to all staff via noticeboards. At first things were difficult. No one except a few loud characters spoke. However, as time went on and actions were seen to be taken as a result of the meetings, the discussions became more inclusive. Over a two-year period, employee absence declined and customer complaints reduced in number. Typically for the hotel sector, employee turnover is still high, but the manager is confident that given more time she can make improvements here too.

## CONFLICT RESOLUTION STRATEGIES

A strategic approach to conflict resolution requires integration with other HRM and business strategies – eg to be horizontally integrated with involvement and participation strategies, and vertically integrated with the business strategy and the external environment. Over the last 80 years or so good practice standards in UK conflict resolution have been provided for employers and employees by the Advisory, Conciliation and Arbitration Service (ACAS). This has resulted in an approach based on codes of practice which provide guidance in developing grievance and dispute procedures and their implementation (ACAS, 2005). Adherence to these guidelines provides employees with a level of protection in the face of the actions of an unscrupulous employer, and supports employers who find themselves facing accusations of discrimination or unfair dismissal. This procedural approach provides clarity and consistency but has also been criticised for being time-consuming and adversarial, not least by the UK Government in its consultations on dispute resolution in 2001 (DTI, 2001). Concern was growing that too many disputes were not being resolved within the workplace and were being brought into the public domain through unfair dismissal and discrimination claims. This in turn was perceived to be leading to problems of congestion in the employment tribunal system and high public cost (Foote, 2004: 4). As a result of this review, new provisions have been introduced via the Employment Act 2002. These were designed to encourage the disputing parties to resolve their differences at a local and preferably informal level within the organisation. Statutory minimum grievance procedures are now laid down and employees must raise grievances with their employer and follow the procedure before making a claim to an employment tribunal.

### Web resources

*For further information on the ACAS guidelines, log on to **www.acas.org.uk**. Supporting information can also be obtained from **www.cipd.co.uk**.*

The two types of statutory grievance procedure brought in by the 2002 Act are shown below. They comprise (a) the standard version, and (b) the modified version which would apply only after the employee had left the organisation (eg in constructive dismissal cases).

### *Employment Act 2002 Standard Grievance Procedure*
*Step 1: statement of grievance*
The employee must set out the grievance in writing and send the statement or a copy of it to the employer.

*Step 2: meeting*
The employer must invite the employee to attend a meeting to discuss the grievance. The meeting must not take place unless a) the employee has informed the employer what the basis for the grievance was when he or she made the statement under Step 1 above, and b) the employer has had a reasonable opportunity to consider his response to that information.

The employee must take all reasonable steps to attend the meeting.

After the meeting the employer must inform the employee of his decision as to his response to the grievance and notify the employee of the right to appeal against the decision if the employee is not satisfied with it.

*Step 3: appeal*
If the employee does wish to appeal, he or she must inform the employer.

If the employee informs the employer of his or her wish to appeal, the employer must invite the employee to attend a further meeting.

The employee must take all reasonable steps to attend the meeting.

After the appeal meeting the employer must inform the employee of his final decision.

### Modified Grievance Procedure
*Step 1: statement of grievance*
The employee must a) set out in writing (i) the grievance, and (ii) the basis for it, and (b) send the statement, or a copy of it, to the employer.

*Step 2: response*
The employer must set out his response in writing and send the statement or a copy of it to the employee.

Source: Rose (2004), p545

The Government's intention in implementing the 2002 Act was to encourage people within organisations to develop an approach to conflict resolution which utilises internal resources and maximises their effective use. An increasingly popular response to this driver has been the use of mediation within organisations to resolve conflict in its very early stages. This approach makes use of the services of a trained third party to facilitate the resolution of the problem through a process of structured discussions. In some organisations, external mediators are used, but in others members of staff are trained as mediators and form a pool of expertise which is drawn on to mediate conflict issues as they arise. There is growing evidence to support this method of conflict resolution as one way of achieving resolution within the organisation and reducing recourse to tribunal (Foote, 2004).

In cases of collective conflict, a number of formal mechanisms can be developed to prevent or manage such situations:

- informal discussions between management and employee representatives
- collective bargaining in order to reach agreement on potentially contentious issues
- consultation through which management can communicate proposals, gain employee feedback and if necessary revise proposals to accommodate employee views
- negotiation – a process of constructive compromise through which specific skills are used to reach an agreement between initially divergent opinions
- advice from third parties, employers' association or ACAS.

As with individual conflict, the implementation of a formal procedure can bring advantages to both sides in the event of a collective dispute: shared understanding, clarity and consistency of approach, predictability of outcome, fairness and equity of treatment.

Within individual and collective procedural frameworks, there is scope for the use of different management styles in different types of conflict situation. Thomas (1976) developed a categorisation of five main types of conflict-handling management styles: competition, collaboration, avoidance, accommodation and compromise. He observed that rarely is one style appropriate for all situations. The adoption of a particular style will depend not only on one's own preferred management style but on an appreciation of the needs of different situations and a willingness and ability to modify one's own conflict resolution style to suit. Three specific factors are significant here:

- power – who has it, where does it lie, and how is it balanced across parties?
- urgency of resolution
- specificity of the goal or concern.

In conclusion, therefore, the potential for conflict is an important feature of the employment relationship but it need not be seen as occurring in opposition to co-operation. As Hatch (1997: 323) puts it,

> **Conflict and cooperation are only opposed when conflict is defined as destructive; when its constructive aspects are in focus, conflict and co-operation are seen as complementary processes.**

The development of EIP strategies that are based on this understanding provide the means of encouraging co-operation and commitment. Focusing thinking on common interests and understanding between employer and employee in turn helps minimise the risk of conflict arising.

## KEY LEARNING POINTS

- Strategies for managing the employment relationship must recognise the different interests that exist between employer and employee. The one common interest is the success of the organisation, and this provides the basis on which differences can be addressed and resolved.
- The way in which managers approach the employment relationship, and the strategies they develop and apply, will be influenced by their own frame of reference comprising their attitudes, presumptions and psychological influences.
- Context influences employee relations strategy and action, and a particular management style may be more relevant in specific circumstances. In a rapidly changing external environment a key management skill would, therefore, be the ability to anticipate change and adapt management style and strategy appropriately.
- Organisations need to consider the relative benefits of an individual and collective approach to EIP strategy development. Although an individual approach may be preferred, legislation requires a collective approach in certain prescribed situations – eg redundancies, transfer of undertakings and health and safety.
- The concept of the psychological contract can be useful in understanding the expectations of employees and employers in an analysis of the employment relationship. Changes in terms of globalisation, downsizing, flexibility, short-term contracts, virtual workers and portfolio careers make the challenge of gaining and maintaining employee commitment even greater.
- In seeking to differentiate between involvement on the one hand and participation on the other, it is helpful to consider factors such as the exercise of power in the relationship, the locus of control, the nature of employee influence, the driving force behind each approach in practice, purpose, scope, level of adoption and form.
- Over the past 20 years we have seen a decline in the traditionally popular methods of participation, such as joint consultation and collective bargaining, and a significant shift towards forms of employee involvement – eg job enrichment, team briefing, quality circles – reflecting a managerial response to the changing organisational environment.
- Conflict can be categorised according to whether it is individual or collective in nature, and good practice guidelines for handling conflict in the UK have been procedural in nature, based on codes of practice from ACAS.
- Successful management of the employment relationship is based on an appreciation of the key characteristics of conflict and cooperation and the development of appropriately integrated EIP strategies.

## Additional reading

Blyton P. and Turnbull P. (2004) *The Dynamics of Employee Relations*, 3rd edition, London, Palgrave Macmillan

– a text that critiques thinking and challenges the reader to take a more critical approach to traditional employee relations thinking

Lewis P., Thornhill A. and Saunders M. (2003) *Employee Relations: Understanding the employment relationship*, London, FT/Prentice Hall

– a useful textbook providing a detailed insight across the range of employee relations topics

Sparrow P. R. and Cooper C. (2003) *The Employment Relationship: Key challenges for HR*, Oxford, Butterworth-Heinemann

– an interesting analysis of the issues of change and how they impact on the employment relationship, bringing together contemporary issues related to the psychological contract, work–life balance, individualisation of the employment contract and the consequent challenges for HRM professionals

Two useful reports from the CIPD provide research findings and valuable case study information exploring the organisational response to consultation legislation and practical implications for practitioners:

Beaumont P. B. and Hunter L. C. (2005a) *Information and Consultation: From compliance to performance*, Research Report, London, CIPD

Beaumont P. B. and Hunter L. C. (2005b) *Making Consultation Work: The importance of process*, Research Report, London, CIPD

---

### Web-based sources of information

There are many useful websites that provide useful information on employee relations in general and in specific aspects of the subject. Some useful starting-points are:

**www.acas.gov.uk** – a source of employment advice, codes of practice and practical guidance
**www.cac.gov.uk** – a source of information on conflict-handling processes
**www.tuc.org.uk** – (for individual union sites, insert union name in place of 'tuc') – union perspectives on employee relations
**www.cbi.org.uk** – employer perspectives on employee relations
**www.dti.gov.uk** – government perspective and practical guidance on and interpretation of employment legislation
**www.cipd.co.uk** – useful site for CIPD members seeking practical tools, research and guidance across the whole spectrum of HRM and employee relations.

---

# REFERENCES

Advisory Conciliation and Arbitration Service (2004) *Discipline and Grievances at Work*, London, ACAS

Anderson N. and Schalk R. (1998) The psychological contract in retrospect and prospect, *Journal of Organisational Behaviour*, 19, pp637–47

Armstrong M. (2003) *A Handbook of HRM Practice*, London, Kogan Page

Beaumont P. B. and Hunter L. C. (2005a) *Information and Consultation: From compliance to performance*, Research report, London, CIPD

Beaumont P. B. and Hunter L. C. (2005b) *Making Consultation Work: The importance of process*, Research report, London, CIPD

Blyton P. and Turnbull P. (2004) *The Dynamics of Employee Relations*, 3rd edition, London, Palgrave Macmillan

Blyton P. and Turnbull P. (1998) *The Dynamics of Employee Relations*, 2nd edition, London, Macmillan

Bratton J. and Gold J. (2003) *Human Resource Management Theory and Practice*, 3rd edition, Basingstoke, Palgrave

Bryans P. and Cronin T. P. (1983) *Organization Theory*, London, Mitchell Beazley

Buchanan D. and Huczynski A. (2004) *Organisation Behaviour: An introductory text*, 5th edition, London, FT/Pitman Publishing

CIPD (2005) *Information and Consultation of Employees Policies and Procedures fact sheet*, April 2005

DTI (2002) *High-Performance Workplaces. The role of employee involvement in a modern economy. A discussion paper*, London, DTI

Foote D. (2004) A new route to conflict resolution in the workplace?, *Human Resources and Employment Review*, Vol.2, No.23

Fox A. (1966) *Industrial Sociology and Industrial Relations*, Royal Commission Research Paper No. 3, London, HMSO

Fox A. (1974) *Beyond Contract: Work, power and trust relations*, London, Faber

Gennard J. and Judge G. (2005) *Employee Relations*, 4th edition, London, CIPD

Guest D. and Conway N. (1997) Employee motivation and the psychological contract, *Issues in People Management*, 21, London, IPD

Guest D. and Fatchett D. (eds) (1974) *Worker Participation: Individual control and performance*, London, IPM

Hatch M. J. (1997) *Organisation Theory*, Oxford, Oxford University Press

Hiltrop J. M. (1995) The changing psychological contract, *European Management Journal*, 13 (3), pp286–94

Hollinshead G., Nicholls P. and Tailby S. (1999) *Employee Relations*, London, FT/Pitman Publishing

Hyman J. and Mason R. (1995) *Managing Employee Involvement and Participation*, London, Sage

IPD (1997) *Employment Relations into the Twenty-First Century: An IPD position paper*, London, IPD

Lewis P., Thornhill A. and Saunders M. (2003) *Employee Relations: Understanding the employment relationship*, London, FT/Prentice Hall

Marchington M. and Wilkinson A. (2005) *Human Resource Management at Work*, 3rd edition, London, CIPD

Marchington M., Wilkinson A., Ackers P. and Dundon T. (2001) *Management Choice and Employee Voice*, London, CIPD

Metcalf D. (2005) Highway to hell?, *People Management*, Vol.11, No.18, 15 September

Millward N., Bryson A. and Forth J. (2000) *All Change at Work*, London, Routledge

Mullins L. (2002) *Management and Organisational Behaviour*, 6th edition, London, FT/Prentice Hall

Patterson M. G., West M. A., Lawthom R. and Nickell S. (1997) Impact of people management practices on business performance, *Issues in People Management*, 22, London, IPD

Purcell J., Kinnie N., Hutchinson S., Rayton B. and Swart J. (2003) *Understanding the People and Performance Link: Unlocking the black box*, London, CIPD

Purcell J. and Gray A. (1986) Corporate personnel departments and the management of industrial relations: two case studies in ambiguity, *Journal of Management Studies*, 23 (2), pp130–7

Purcell J. and Sisson K. (1983) Strategies and practice in the management of industrial relations, in Bain G. S. (ed.) *Industrial Relations in Britain*, Oxford, Blackwell, pp95–120

Ramsay H. (1996) Involvement, empowerment and commitment, in Towers B. (ed.) *The Handbook of Human Resource Management*, 2nd edition, Oxford, Blackwell

Rose E. (2004) *Employment Relations*, London, FT/Prentice Hall

Salamon M. (2000) *Industrial Relations Theory and Practice*, 4th edition, London, FT/Prentice Hall

Schmidt W. H. (1974) Conflict: A powerful process for (good or bad) change, *Management Review*, 63, December, p39

Sparrow P. R. and Cooper C. (2003) *The Employment Relationship: Key challenges for HR*, Oxford, Butterworth-Heinemann

Thomas K. W. (1976) Conflict and conflict management, in Dunette M. D. (ed.) *Handbook of Industrial and Organisational Psychology*, Chicago, Rand McNally, pp484–528

Walton R. E. (1985) From control to commitment in the workplace, *Harvard Business Review*, March-April

Walton R. and Dutton J. (1969) The Management of Interdepartmental conflict: A Model and Review, *Administrative Science Quarterly*, Vol 14, pp73–84

# PART 3

# OPTIMISING AND SUSTAINING HIGH PERFORMANCE

# Leadership

*Linda Lee-Davies*

## LEARNING OBJECTIVES

- To define leadership
- To compare leadership theories and concepts
- To link effective leadership with performance
- To examine the creation and implementation of a leadership vision
- To isolate the different levels of group-based and shared leadership approaches

## INTRODUCTION

The study of leadership has evolved significantly over the last half century. In that time definitions have stemmed from the preceding studies of management techniques over a century before in containing scientific elements with a task-driven focus and moved right through many forms to the softer concepts of emotional and shared leadership theories today. This evolution has taken us from a more calculated approach of a pure productivity focus through to a focus on the traits and characters of the actual leaders themselves, and then on to assessing the followers and their effect on, and inclusion in, the whole leadership decision-making process.

## CONCEPTS AND THEORIES OF LEADERSHIP AND THE LEADERSHIP ROLE IN HIGH-PERFORMANCE ORGANISATIONS

From Sun Ztu (1991), whose leadership theories coloured warfare over 2,000 years ago, to a recent text written by the founder and Chairman of Reed Executive (Reed, 2001) which focuses on 'peoplism', and on to freshly published or about-to-be-published academic papers which research aspects of shared leadership, visioning and leadership links to performance, the selected literary range covers many aspects of leadership concept and theory.

Ancient leadership traits evolved under a life-and-death umbrella where the choice was win or die. Whether it is really that different in modern times is debatable. Some would argue the parallel of corporate death for the warfare analogy. Competitive advantage becomes the victory itself, with increased profits the gain. The people may not actually die but they can fail or leave – so they do so symbolically. It is clear that the practical issues and choices of yesteryear are still apparent in modern corporate warfare but emphasis on the more holistic aspects of the fight is more easily recognisable and in more plentiful supply in writings which cross this millennium. Science and art combine to produce a management/leadership mind which thinks outside the box to gain advantage but does not lose sight of the all- and ever-increasingly important individual.

## Early warfare (ballistics)

In the sixth century BC, Sun Tzu defined leadership as 'a matter of intelligence, trustworthiness, humaneness, courage and sternness'. With intelligence further defined as the ability to plan and know when to change, trustworthiness defined in terms of reliability and consistency, humaneness defined as compassion for people and appreciation of their toils, courage as the ability to seize opportunities without vacillation, and sternness as the ability to keep discipline in the ranks, Sun Tzu seemed to promote a rule of five for the ideal all-rounder. This definition of leadership was a part of probably one of the first management tools for strategic assessment. Again a rule of five – Sun Tzu suggested the following must be assessed: the way, the weather, the terrain, the leadership, and discipline.

Although Sun Tzu has a stern core to his military tactics and strategy, it is interesting and, indeed, refreshingly surprising to find such a large 'people' element to his thinking. Interpersonal skills were promoted as a means of victory and there is paradox in *The Art of War* in its actual opposition to and avoidance of war. Winning without fighting was best.

No such paradox exists when analysing the leadership tactics of General Patton (Axelrod, 1999). After practising his 'war face' in a mirror, General Patton faced war full on with the famous words, 'I want you men to remember that no bastard ever won a war by dying for his country. He won it by making the other dumb bastard die for his country.' His leadership sprang from a shower of verbal ballistics which cleverly ends in motivating the receiver by allowing them to make a vision of their own within the overall vision – thus giving each a personal stake in what is ahead. This is achieved with graphic references to the worst outcomes on the battlefield, metaphor, anecdote and extremely aggressive and rude language, but then taking each individual to their dotage in front of a fireplace with their grandson on their knee – asking what they did in the war. Thus visualising their own homes, future and pride, they each own a part of the overall vision.

Having started with ancient wisdom and having attempted to start linking it to the modern world, a dip into the recent text of the Dalai Lama (1999) reveals a cynical undertone regarding the military leaders of today.

His Holiness remarks on the evolution of generals. Having illustrated that previously rulers led their troops into battle and if they were killed, often the matter ended there, he states, 'Today they can be thousands of miles away in their bunkers underground conducting battles almost as if they were a computer game.' This begs the question as to whether they are really leading and is easily related to the business world where some leaders may be locked away in offices.

## People care (holistics)

Alec Reed, Chairman and founder of Reed Executive Plc, cites the seven stages of man from Shakespeare's *As You Like It*, and relates it to the seven-stage work cycle of attraction, recruitment, induction, career development and training, reward, retention and separation (Reed, 2001).

He introduces us to the new noun 'peoplism', stating that it is an economic state where individuals own and control the most important factor of production: their human ability. It very competently encourages readers to visualise their own thoughts in a Patton-like way as a manager/leader and to think how best to treat their own staff through the whole of the work–life cycle.

In the same spirit, the *Harvard Business Review* (HBR) on managing people (1998) contains two articles which outline the effect of leadership on how an individual feels in relation to his or her performance.

Stating that both enthusiasm and apathy are infectious, J. Sterling Livingston introduced the more holistic concept of 'Pygmalion in management' in the late 1960s. His research revealed that 'What managers expect of their subordinates and the way they treat them largely determine their performance and career progress.' The article puts emphasis on positive Pygmalion resulting in higher performance and links it to the level of faith the manager has in his or her own ability. This confidence and belief will then cascade through the performance ranks. This was supported by Bennis and Nanus (1985) 14 years later when they studied around 90 CEOs and commented,

> **Our study of effective leaders strongly suggested that a key factor was ... what we're calling ... positive self-regard. ... Positive self-regard seems to exert its force by creating in others a sense of confidence and high expectations, not very different from the fabled Pygmalion effect.**

The opposite of positive Pygmalion is acknowledged in the article, but most focus is on the positive. Nineteen years later Livingston reflected on his own work and commented that he wished he had spent more time investigating negative Pygmalion effects because these seemed to be in more prominence in business. He called this the 'dark side' and leaves us with the thought that

> **The difference between employees who perform well and those who perform poorly is not how they are paid but how they are treated.**

Jean-Francois Manzoni and Jean-Louis Barsoux introduced us to 'The Set-Up-To-Fail-Syndrome' in 1998. Staying along the same holistic lines they suggest that bosses can inadvertently have an 'in-group' and an 'out-group', and that this has a dramatic effect on performance and happiness in the job. To encompass the spirit at this stage they profess that bosses do not really realise that tight controls can end up negatively affecting performance by undermining motivation.

Again, the article hints that the origins of such treatment may lie within the level of security of the leader in the first place. We are returned to the theme that runs through these articles of different decades to the effect that the motivation within the leader himself or herself is pivotal to success. How the leader views the situation in the first place therefore has bearing on the outcome.

Among a wide-ranging set of articles on ethics, Peter Singer (1994) includes a view from Albert Camus (1969) on the myth of Sisyphus. Sisyphus is condemned to roll a rock up a mountain only to have it roll back again. Camus argues that this futile and hopeless labour is reframed by Sisyphus himself from within, and from the task he creates purpose and satisfaction. The self-motivation within him is enough to extract happiness.

## Competition

In further search of which leadership skills contribute to good performance, happiness, and hopefully have a causal effect – staff retention – a return is made to the area of direct competition. Having explored traits in the field of warfare, this is then investigated with corporate war in mind, with a view to evolving through to isolating more traits in the successful leader.

Competitive advantage has already been mooted as the modern 'win'. Michael Porter (1985) is well known for supplying management tools for isolating and developing this. His classic management text applies the term 'leadership' in a style different from all those noted above. Porter has a more scientific approach and applies his theories to activities rather than people. Leadership to Porter seems to imply that it is the company in the lead and it is the choice of generic strategy or activity that would determine this. Relationships and inter-relationships pertain to activities or departments/functions between value chains, and disappointingly there is no mention of the human value side of the business to achieve this.

Such science is important, though, and competitive advantage a key part of any leader role. The leader must make such crucial decisions for the business. Porter concentrates on what the scientific choices are for today's leader but does not go as far as suggesting the art of actually applying them or selling them in – especially from an internal marketing point of view. We can perhaps presume him more of a 'profitist' than a 'peoplist'.

Kenichi Ohmae (1982) offers a similar scientific route as he looks at the links between his 'three Cs'. Ohmae pivots directly on Customers, Corporation and Competitors, with little mention of the value of people (staff) until later in the book. He then introduces a favourite Japanese phrase, *hito-kane-mono*, meaning 'people, money, things'. He states that it is the balance of these which is necessary to successful performance, but the profit and people balance depends more on these elements being treated as a practical resource which can be trimmed or relocated within the company. The leadership of these elements is more statistical and logistical in his mind than holistical, and like Porter he stops short of providing a deeper insight into the 'how' and just deals with the 'what'.

This sound management balancing tool of *hito-kane-mono* from 20 years ago can be built on, though, to bring it into the new millennium. Using the same building-blocks as given by Ohmae in Figure 29 we can match *kane* 'money' with statistics [S], *mono* 'things' or 'buildings', etc, with logistics [L], and *hito* 'people' with holistics [H] to bring a new depth to findings. Although Ohmae does not actually say it, there is the intimation that success – or, if you like, good leadership – relies on the internal competition of the balance of the elements as illustrated in Figure 29.

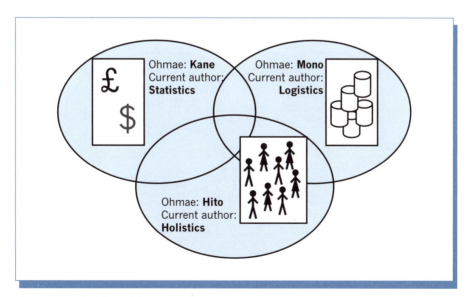

**Figure 29** *Kenichi Ohmae's hito-kane-mono balance (adapted by the current author to represent holistics-statistics-logistics)*
Adapted from K. Ohmae (1982) *The Mind of the Strategist*

---

## PAUSE FOR THOUGHT

How would you apply the balance in Figure 29 to yourself as you are now? What about your boss – would all areas be even, or would there be an imbalance between people and profit?

---

John Adair (1983) suggests a similar internal competition of elements but uses Task, Team and Individual in his pursuit of effective leadership. Two of these elements focus more on the people elements. Again it is the balance of the components which constitutes success. An equal balance of all three is reckoned to give the most likely combination for successful performance. The task could be matched with Ohmae's *kane* (Statistics), the team and the individual could match with *hito* (Holistics) but perhaps need splitting up for clarification, leaving the suggestion that Adair does not consider the management of the logistical side of the business a key feature in success.

Perhaps if one tool was overlaid on the other, a more comprehensive audit of leadership constrisution to business success could be made.

Figure 30 picks up on Adair's double dose of Holistics and evolves the work of Ohmae to expand on his use of people and form a new Japanese phrase – *hito-kane-mono-hito* – indicating that all touch on and affect each other, and that a balance is necessary for success, competitive advantage or leadership effectiveness.

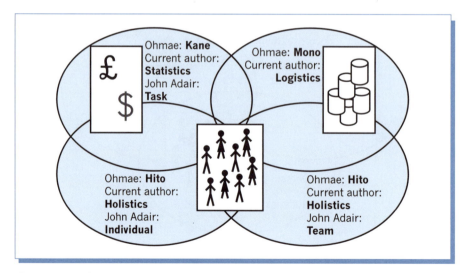

**Figure 30** *Kenichi Ohmae's hito-kane-mono balance merged with John Adair's Leadership functions (and adapted by the current author to include holistics-statistics-logistics balance)*
Adapted from K. Ohmae (1982) *The Mind of the Strategist*, John Adair (1983) *Effective Leadership*

## PAUSE FOR THOUGHT

As previously, how would you apply the balance in Figure 30 to yourself as you are now? What about your boss – would all areas be even, or would there be an imbalance between people and profit? What about individual and team focus – are they in balance?

David Smith (1998) illustrates how Blake and Mouton seem to pick up from this point and use this balancing mechanism for people and production with their famous grid (see Figure 31).

In fact Blake and Mouton developed this theory in 1969 before some of the theories above. According to them it appears that true 'team management' is achieved only when concern for production and people is balanced and high – so it is a theory similar to those which indicate that leadership style has an influence on success. Again, though, like Adair's, this theory does not include the context, background, surroundings: logistics.

## ACTIVITY . . .

Plot yourself and your boss on the Blake and Mouton grid.

Justify your positioning.

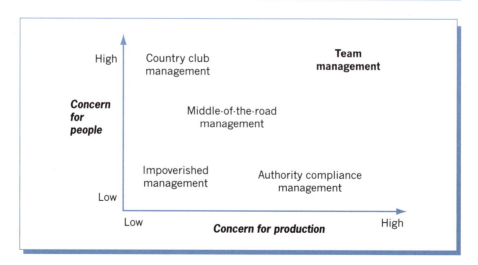

**Figure 31** *Blake and Mouton's managerial grid*
Source: D. Smith (1998) *Developing People and Organisations*

Bernard Bass (1985) built on many of these concepts by introducing transactional and transformational aspects to leadership.

The transactional elements of leadership could be held as the task/statistical and perhaps stretched to logistical, so covering the lower levels of Maslow's hierarchy of needs or McGregor's X factors. These would be the physiological needs or Herzberg's hygiene factors. The importance of transactional elements of leadership is in the balance of the day-to-day tasks towards the longer-term goals. Good leadership must essentially ensure the tasks are directed in the right way to complement and actually help make up the overall vision. The transformational element would appear to be the holistic element of the equation dealing with the higher levels of Maslow's hierarchy, such as self-esteem/actualisation and social needs, and McGregor's Y factor, which suggests that people want to contribute to meaningful goals they have helped establish, or equally Herzberg's 'motivators' such as recognition, achievement. Essentially this divided leadership into short-term practical obligations and longer-term inspirational and directional activities.

Thus, the search springs back to 'motivation' of the staff, and alongside this, that which is present in the leader/manager.

The competition within could be held to be as important as the competition without. Jane Cranwell-Ward *et al* (2002) completed an exciting study that used both.

The BT Global Challenge – a very competitive round-the-world yacht race – was used by the above as a parallel to a hostile and changing environment in the business world. The 14 skippers were interviewed as much for their holistic abilities as their statistical and logistical ones. Effectiveness was measurable by whether they won or not, and the particular traits of the podium winners put forward as the key leadership/management traits necessary for success.

A detailed breakdown of personal attributes, management skills and leadership attributes were measured and set against the position of the skippers in the race. This was monitored over 18 months and with over 500 interviews of the skippers and their respective 15-strong teams on each yacht.

This study does both management and leadership justice and heralds the value of both in the winners. The podium winners displayed both management and leadership qualities to win. The statistics and logistics were held to be as important as the more peoplist holistic side of things. Of note in the findings of this work was that all podium winners had self-belief, inner purpose and self-motivation, and that the lower-performing skippers distinctly lacked self-belief.

This study promotes the theory that a balance of personal, management and leadership qualities results in good performance culture and inspirational culture.

The competition of internal traits of leadership/management is followed through by Stephen Covey (1989) who suggests seven traits for highly effective managers including proactivity, a positive outlook and a focus on results. Covey clearly splits up leadership traits from management traits, but in that order. The traits end on the concept of 'self-renewal'. This could be interpreted as self-belief/motivation. Through this Covey then emphasises the importance of the individual and the team and uses the terms 'dependence', 'independence' and 'interdependence', suggesting that the balance is between self, the individual and the team. He uses Aesop's golden goose fable to promote his 2P/PC Balance. This stands for Production and Production Capability. The implication is that it is important to look after the goose laying the egg rather than focus solely on the egg itself. Perhaps it amounts to a simplistic translation of the Blake and Mouton theory above aimed at the pop market.

## Intuition

Daniel Goleman (1996) evolved these positive self traits into the concept of Emotional Intelligence (EQ) in leadership effectiveness. He travels from well known 1960s psychology asking the question 'nature or nurture?' as to character, through many modern-day anecdotes to find examples of the concept. He battles with IQ throughout the book, and at its expense cites the importance of emotions in decision-making and success. He believes that EQ includes self-awareness, impulse control and motivation, among other things. Cooper and Sawaf (1998) summarise it better:

> **Knowing one's own emotions and controlling them, recognising and understanding emotions in others, and self-motivation are the key dimensions of EQ.**

EQ is often iconised with a heart, and indeed the two texts explain that it constitutes the ability to use or see with the heart, that intuition would appear to be no accident, and that it is much the greater for a deliberate increase in attentiveness. They push EQ and associated softer, holistic traits at the total expense of other traits, and no attempt to balance is made. The message throughout regarding positive thinking and association is motivational in itself but mocks the intellectual and pays poor regard to using the head alongside the heart.

## Definition

Warren Bennis (1989) initially promoted leadership advantage very much at the expense of management. He served up these thoughts:

- The manager administers; the leader innovates.
- The manager is a copy; the leader is an original.

- The manager maintains; the leader develops.
- The manager focuses on systems and structure; the leader focuses on people.
- The manager relies on control; the leader inspires trust.
- The manager has a short-range view; the leader has a long-range perspective.
- The manager asks how and when; the leader asks what and why.
- The manager has his eye on the bottom line; the leader has his eye on the horizon.
- The manager imitates; the leader originates.
- The manager accepts the status quo; the leader challenges it.
- The manager is a good soldier; the leader is his own person.
- The manager does things right; the leader does the right thing.

This 'Bennis tennis' repeats the issue unnecessarily but does get the message across.

Here there is a more than definite split between what is leadership behaviour and what is management. More than citing leadership as the better of the two, Bennis makes management appear inferior. Some good points about the more holistic nature and value of leadership are lost in the aggressive attack on management itself. He defines the overall attack :

> **To survive in the twenty-first century, we are going to need a new generation of leaders – leaders, not managers. The distinction is an important one. Leaders conquer the context … while managers surrender to it.**

Although this 1980s differentiated definition seems rather clumsy and insulting now, it does go some way to encouraging deeper thought about what a leader is and what it takes to contribute to high performance.

The Kakabadses (A. and N. Kakabadse, 1999) explore the essence of leadership, suggesting that healthy narcissism must play a part in achieving leadership status. This element of the character of a leader can powerfully impress others and encourage his or her followers to follow. They warn, though, that there should be a dividing line between self-confidence and self-love.

Goldsmith and Clutterbuck (1997) comment constructively on the 'Bennis tennis'. They note that it is well-intentioned but that it may have done companies a disservice in making the two opposites in this way. They suggest that generations of managers could have striven to be good leaders in the belief that managers are second-class citizens. They think that the two are not separable and that a complement of both is key to success. They then suggest throughout the rest of the book that balance is important.

Bob Garratt (1996) thinks that 'The fish rots from the head' and calls leadership 'directing'. Although he too professes a balance of the two to be crucial to success, like Bennis, he also suggests that management is the lesser of the two, even suggesting that directing is a more intellectual activity than management. Progression through the book is technical and focused on scientific strategic assessment with little reference to the softer skills. Accountability is alluded to with illustrations of 'corporate killing' – in that if decisions by the top result in disaster, they should be held accountable – but it ends there with the dramatic example rather than the holistical implications of decisions within a normal business environment. One interesting term introduced in the book was that of 'malicious obedience', by which subordinates do what they are told/directed, but reluctantly, and therefore not as productively as they would if they owned the situation.

Alan Hooper and John Potter (2000) do devote a good deal of their text to the softer leadership skills. They split up the leadership traits and the management traits under the influence of John Kotter (1990) and Warren Bennis, but come to the conclusion, like many above, that:

> **For organisations to be successful in today's environment of constant change it is necessary to have some people who are good at both. While many organisations are well administered and well controlled, few have the appropriate vision, innovation and original thinking.**

Usefully, they then evolve this with a springboard from the original Bernard Bass theory. From transactional and transformational leadership, Hooper and Potter believe that 'intelligent leadership' is actually 'transcendent leadership' – a term they have coined themselves. This is the act of engaging the emotional support of the subordinate followers. The term 'holistic' crops up again as they outline their own set of leadership competencies, and they stress the importance of this 'motivation, empowerment, coaching and encouragement' to bring out the best in people.

Paul Taffinder (2000) reflects this, though with more operational focus. In his *Crash Course for Leadership* he builds through stages of gaining trust, etc, and towards the end of the book states that a decision must be made between commitment and compliance. He says,

> **Commitment engages the individual in willingness to take responsibility and to add value. ... Compliance secures the action intended by the leader, but the result is that it shifts the underlying**

> **responsibility straight back to the leader. Your people will be thinking and feeling: 'I'm doing this because I have to, not because I want to' [malicious obedience].**

With tests for 'inertia', tips for 'conflict protocol' and an overall aim to 'generate critical mass', the Taffinder Trail encompasses the balance of statistical targets, logistical restraints and holistical understanding to a point of synergy.

This fits with the thoughts of Alasdair White (1995), who states:

> **People only do something if they obtain a psychological or material benefit from doing it.**

Finally, Hamel and Prahalad (1996) turn the subject of leadership to the future. They do Adair, Ohmae and the statistics-logistics-holistics (SLH) theory considerable justice as they travel through resource management, strategic assessment and recognition of and valuing core competences. They intimate that balance is necessary, even if they do not demonstrate it vividly. Although quite scientific for most of the journey through the book, the authors do hint at more holistic aspects of leadership. They concentrate less on the differences between management and leadership and more on being prepared for the future, using a balanced mix of both skill types. They use the clever analogy of wolves.

> **In a wolf pack the leadership role is always clear, but often challenged, and is decided on capability and strength. The wolves are not all the same and not all equally capable. They maintain their individuality but are all members of the same team, and act in unison when on a hunt. The reality of mutual dependency is accepted by all members.**

So the task, team and individual are all in balance. Hamel and Prahalad evolve this to allow the individual to be individual within the team and task environment. They introduce the concept of 'community activists' who are not afraid to speak out but have the deep sense of community needed for the team. While they have a desire to improve their personal lot, they think of others in the team as well. The perfect balance may thus provide the perfect leader – or is it that the perfect leader needs to provide the forum for this to happen?

From the range of concepts and theories chosen, the majority would propose that performance success, and therefore leadership success, is achieved by maintaining a balance between task, team and individual, or *hito*, *kane* and *mono*, or statistics, logistics and holistics. It is interesting and encouraging to arrive at more or less the same recommendation for balance after following a wide variety of routes.

One thing that does seem to be clear and agreed by most in the various texts is the allocation of particular skills to the leader or manager categories. Management skills of an organisational nature and leadership skills of a directional/visional nature seem to be agreed in the main, and the real argument beyond that is over which is the better of the two or what balance of them is key to success.

## ACTIVITY . . .

Make a list of what you believe are management skills and what you believe are leadership skills.

## GROUP-BASED APPROACHES TO LEADERSHIP

Achieving any balance for more effective performance must lie in how leaders involve followers in the decision-making process and how they evangelise corporate strategies to them. Captivating the individual is one thing but achieving synergy out of the whole team is quite another. In addition, then, to ensuring individual buy-in, the leader must calculate the dynamics of the team and utilise them to full effect.

Any reasonably adept leader can achieve an output of four from a team of four. Of course a poor leader will achieve fewer outputs. An effective leader will not only achieve the four obviously available outputs but also one or two more invisible ones in the group by ensuring that the team work as well as possible together and are fully involved in the process.

There is a clear connection between people management and the performance in the organisation (Purcell *et al*, 2003). Increased involvement and consultation ensures group loyalty and not only enhances the commitment of the group as a whole as well as the individual members but also ensures that the group as a body learns continuously. So the group becomes a self-improving entity within the organisation and directly contributes to its performance – fully and willingly. Performance is linked directly to this employee commitment as well as corporate strategy and HR policies and practices (Purcell *et al*, 2003). This report unlocks the 'black box' of performance success and clearly illustrates through 11 studies that HR (and therefore any) strategy is a waste of time unless it is embraced by the actual line managers – the leaders within. In a more recent study the front-line managers or FLMs (Hutchinson and Purcell, 2005) are held to be the key link between the strategy and the staff, and performance success is therefore directly in their hands. The way they interpret ideas and information in either direction is crucial to success, and the very position they occupy puts them in a pivotal position of power and influence. Their ability to share, consult and participate becomes key to performance.

With greater demands on leaders in modern times from more informed stakeholders and shareholders it is more difficult to get things right and to pick out the one person who has the skills necessary to ensure performance success in increasingly competitive circumstances. The question arises as to whether it is indeed possible to arrive at that one person who has it all.

If no one individual can be everything, then a team of diverse individuals could stand a greater chance of providing what the organisation actually needs to gain competitive advantage and perform well. By cleverly harnessing the energy of the whole team and guiding it in the right direction, FLMs can share leadership and directly contribute to corporate performance. Their team members can also see their input and feel fully participative.

Valuing and handling such a diversity of input and opinion as well as the range of personalities requires a communication ability that not only collects the varied input but uses it wisely for the good of the organisation. This multiple dialogue is positively encouraged in a group-based approach to leadership (Kakabadse, Kakabadse and Lee-Davies, 2005). FLMs must be approachable and have the capacity to deal with such a shared leadership approach and the polylogue principles it operates.

Such group-based or shared leadership is a violent shift from a hierarchical focus or a hero-leader to a clear interactionist approach (Kakabadse, Kakabadse and Lee-Davies, 2005). Instead of instructions descending from one representative leader at the top through a series of dutiful followers who then enact their instructions with varying interpretation, the polylogue of the group-based leadership approach ensures the sharing and flow of new ideas, and this is fed back from customer to board level. Strategic planning then contains real and up-to-date information about the business, and so the organisation is more likely to perform appropriately to its market.

## CREATING AND IMPLEMENTING THE VISION

If vision is key in the leading of an organisation, successful leadership must incorporate its creation. Leadership in itself may be the art of creating the place to go – the direction to head – the long-term target to reach. If vision is 'an ideal and unique image of the future' (Kouzes and Postner, 1987), then vision is about looking ahead.

'Visioning' might then be a crucial leadership skill but must be more complicated than simply looking ahead where one can foresee events and, indeed, avoid catastrophes or even positively prepare for economic change (Kakabadse, Kakabadse and Lee-Davies,

2005). The creation of direction borne of foresight must also involve a full commitment to the whole strategic direction of the organisation and more detailed planning processes that accompany it. So rather than just predict and react to the future, visioning creates the future and creatively and proactively sets out to shape it.

Such dedication to creating the future direction is one of the seven sides of the great leader (Kakabadse and Kakabadse, 1999). With the first of these, then – conviction to craft the future, or visioning – goes the responsibility for all that it takes to get there. More than creating a long-term strategic direction, the vision is just the inspiring finishing-point, and it is necessary to map out a route all are happy to follow to get there.

This visioning process involves manageable and appropriate steps and follower involvement.

**PAUSE FOR THOUGHT**

What is your company's vision? How is it translated down the hierarchy?

The communication of the vision, the possession of a charismatic personality style to gain the following, and the taking of the various necessary actions intended to actually implement the vision (Baum *et al*, 1998) are, then, vital leadership skills. Making sense of the overall picture by breaking it down renders the leader a 'meaning-maker' (Conger, 1991) as he or she translates the created vision into real day-to-day action. These carefully considered actions then feed into the overall future goal. The leader also has a moral responsibility for ensuring that individuals get their own personal value out of their particular visioning journey, as well as ensuring that they believe that the vision is for the company good.

Creative transformation through vision is a risky business and success involves tuning into the workforce and understanding the practical actions and motivations necessary to head towards the overall desired goal as well as dealing with the unexpected along the way. The leader must be participative to gain employee commitment to the cause (Brabet and Klemm, 1994).

If all the employees are not heading in the same long-term direction, just what would be the effects of a more chaotic and multidirectional short-term approach?

In their study of leadership capabilities Kakabadse and Kakabadse (1999) identified the reasons some organisations fail as a lack of vision and visioning. Inner organisational chaos and division in the ranks at all levels divides the company and creates an internal war which causes distrust and a short-term mentality. Employee eyes are taken off competitor activity and focused on individual survival, so reducing competitive advantage and using precious employee energy in the wrong way. As employee input becomes meaningless to the overall corporate direction, employee output becomes restricted and there develops a divergence between the individual vision and the corporate one.

It would be naïve to expect in any organisation that the perfect visioning process exists, but it should be expected that senior management have the discipline to regard corporate wellbeing as paramount so that rather than fight over their differences they value, manage and respect them. The knowledge that any mismanagement of the internal negotiating process could seriously damage the fabric of the company over-rides potential disputes and, indeed, tempers any actual ones towards productive output (Kakabadse, Kakabadse and Lee-Davies, 2005). In the same academic paper Kakabadse, Kakabadse and Lee-Davies develop a 'visioning process model' which incorporates not only the elements of *not* visioning, as previously indicated, but also those which actually do make up successful visioning. They hold these to include a complete commitment and conviction from the 'visioneer' leader, his or her senior team, a fast feedback system and an ongoing creation of a visioning culture.

So having a vision is a part of and different from visioning. Visioning is the process required to achieve the final vision. Visioning or not can then come down to the individual choice of the leader, or perhaps even his or her actual ability.

So the choice of the leader, whether deliberate or otherwise, has a direct effect on the overall performance of the organisation in terms of visioning. Successful implementation of the vision or visioning means the employees are more likely to stick together and work for the overall purpose and direction. It is also likely that as this process develops it propagates a self-perpetuating cohesiveness and staff are more likely to buy into the overall vision from the positive example they are set. This could be especially attractive to the newly hired who buy into that vision from the beginning. Unsuccessful implementation of the vision or 'divisioning' (Kakabadse, Kakabadse and Lee Davies, 2005) means that the employees are less likely to stick together and will work for their own purposes rather than the overall one of the organisation. It equally propagates, but this time its own image is destructive and encourages division in the ranks. One vision becomes many confusing visions, and the confusion weakens the organisation. This could be especially unattractive to the newly-hired who find the division within the company too much to bear, and then the resulting high staff turnover rates cause cyclical problems and exacerbate the problem.

## EFFECTIVE LEADERSHIP AND ROLE MODELLING

Effective leadership, then, is that which directly and positively affects organisational performance. This cannot be for the short term but must contribute to long-term strategic planning. Effective leaders should be role models for leaders of the future and practise their craft in participation with the groups they work with. Individual and group involvement is key in performance success and the perpetuation of learning and good practice will result in more leaders continually evolving from the process. These leaders will be better and better tuned to working with others in the decision-making process and better able to value the input of all within the organisation without feeling threatened.

## KEY LEARNING POINTS

- By travelling through a leadership timeline it has been possible to isolate elements of successful leadership and begin to link this to organisational performance.
- Examining shared approaches to leadership which value the input of all and involve the whole team has brought to light the extra performance value available to a leader who correctly uses the synergy of a team to best advantage.
- This skill along with an ability to create and also implement a vision has a direct input on organisational success.

## Additional reading

Bass B. M. (1985) *Leadership and Performance Beyond Expectations*, New York, Free Press

Hooper A. and Potter J. (2000) *Intelligent Leadership – Creating a Passion for Change* [Foreward by Warren Bennis], Random House Business Books

House R. J. and Shamir B. (1993) 'Toward the integration of transformational, charismatic and visionary theories of leadership', in Chemers M. and Ayman R. (eds) *Leadership Theory and Research: Perspectives and directions*, San Diego, Academic Press, pp81–107

Kakabadse A. (1991) *The Wealth Creators: Top people, top teams and executive best practice*, London, Kogan Page

Kakabadse A, Kakabadse N. and Lee-Davies L. (2005) 'Leadership through polylogue', *International Journal of Leadership Education*

Kouzes J. M. and Postner B. Z. (1987) *The Leadership Challenge: How to get extraordinary things done in organisations*, San Francisco, Jossey-Bass

Westley F. and Mintzberg H. (1989) 'Visionary leadership and strategic management', *Strategic Management Journal*, 10, pp17–32

Willner A. R. (1984) *The Spellbinders: Charismatic political leadership*, New Haven, Yale University Press

Wilson I. (1992) 'Realizing the power of strategic vision', *Long-Range Planning*, 25 (5), pp18–28.

# REFERENCES

Adair J. (1983) *Effective Leadership*, London, Gower

Axelrod A. (1999) *Patton on Leadership, Strategic Lessons for Corporate Warfare*, London, Prentice Hall

Baum J. R., Locke E. A. and Kirkpatrick S. A. (1998) 'A longitudinal study of the relation of vision and vision communication to venture growth in entrepreneurial firms', *Journal of Applied Psychology*, 83 (1), pp43–54

Bennis W. G and Nanus B. (1985) *Leaders: The strategies for taking charge*, New York, Harper & Row

Bennis W. (1989) *On Becoming a Leader*, London, Arrow

Brabet J. and Klemm M. (1994) 'Sharing the vision: company mission statements in Britain and France', *Long-Range Planning*, 27(1), pp84–94

Camus A. (1969) *The Myth of Sisyphus, and Other Essays*, trans. Justin O'Brien, New York, Alfred Knopf

Conger J. A. (1991) 'Inspiring others: the language of leadership', *Academy of Management*, 5 (1), pp31–45

Cooper R. and Sawaf A. (1998) *Executive EQ*, London, Texere

Coulson-Thomas (1990) *Marketing Communications,* London, Heinemann Professional

Covey S. (1989) *The Seven Habits of Highly Effective People*, Franklin Covey

Cranwell-Ward J., Bacon A. and Mackie R. (2002) *Inspiring Leadership – Staying Afloat in Turbulent Times*, Thomson

(His Holiness the) Dalai Lama (1999) *Ancient Wisdom, Modern World*, London, Little, Brown & Company (UK)

Garratt B. (2003) *The Fish Rots from the Head: The crisis in our boardrooms – developing the crucial skills of the competentent board,* London, Profile Business

Goldsmith W. and Clutterbuck D. (1997) *The Winning Streak Mark II,* London, Orion Business Books

Goleman D. (1996) *Emotional Intelligence*, London, Bloomsbury

Hamel G. and Prahalad C. K. (1996) *Competing for the Future*, Boston, Harvard Business School Press

Hutchinson S. and Purcell J. (2005) *Bringing Policies to Life*, London, CIPD

Kakabadse A. and Kakabadse N. (1999) *Essence of Leadership*, London, International Thomson Business

Kakabadse A., Kakabadse N. and Lee-Davies L. (2005) 'Visioning', *European Management Journal*

Kotter J. (1990) *A Force for Change*, New York, Free Press

Livingston J.S. (1988) Pygmalion in Management, *Harvard Business Review* pp46–72

Manzoni J. and Barsoux J. (1998) The Set-up-to-fail Syndrome, *Harvard Business Review* pp197–226

Ohmae K. (1982) *The Mind of the Strategist*, New York, McGraw-Hill

Porter M. E. (1985) *Competitive Advantage: Creating and sustaining superior performance*, New York, Free Press

Purcell J., Kinnie N., Hutchinson S., Rayton B. and Swart J. (2003) *Understanding the People and Performance Link*, London, CIPD

Reed A. (2001) *Innovation in Human Resource Management*, London, CIPD

Singer P. (1994) *Ethics*, Oxford, Oxford University Press

Smith D. (1998) *Developing People and Organisations*, London, CIMA

Taffinder P. (2000) *The Leadership Crash Course*, London, Kogan Page

Tzu S. (1991) *The Art of War*, Boston and London, Shambhala

White A. (1995) *Managing for Performance*

# HRM and the management of strategic organisational change

## CHAPTER 11

## LEARNING OBJECTIVES

■ To discuss the nature and process of organisational change
■ To evaluate key features and characteristics of the change management process
■ To evaluate organisational and individual barriers to change, and the reasons behind resistance to change
■ To evaluate the concept and practice of flexibility in organisation and work design
■ To discuss the nature and scope of change interventions
■ To evaluate the nature and scope of the HR role in managing strategic organisational change

## INTRODUCTION

Change has been an enduring theme throughout the preceding chapters. Chapter 1 outlined the changing world of work and highlighted key environmental drivers of globalisation, technology, social and demographic change as forces of organisational change. Organisations do not operate in a vacuum, and subsequent chapters have drawn out the implications of environmental change for a range of HRM practices in the management of people at work. Rapid, discontinuous and far-reaching change has become an undeniable feature of industrial and commercial life. However, it would be wrong to over-emphasise the homogeneity of organisational change.

There are differences in the magnitude, rate and nature of change and the effectiveness with which organisations manage change. Change can be gradual, incremental and evolutionary. The use of new technology, for example, has driven requirements for new skills and working methods and employees have adapted to the use of technology. The ESRC Working in Britain Survey (2000) – part of the Future of Work Study – reported that two thirds of employees cited new technology as essential to job performance, compared with 35 per cent of men and 20 per cent of women in 1997 (Taylor, 2000: 16). Change can also be radical, revolutionary and transformational, involving the whole organisation in rapid, urgent and extensive restructuring and changes in job roles. Such change can be traumatic and stressful.

The CIPD (2004) Reorganising for Success study involved the experiences of 594 UK chief executives and directors across all industrial sectors and found that organisations were carrying out major restructuring – eg acquisition or divestment – every three years, and smaller-scale internal reorganisation virtually continuously. However, despite the volume of change activity, it is suggested that many change initiatives fail to realise their expected benefits. Holbeche (2005: 6) estimates that 75 per cent of all transformation efforts fail, as do 50–75 per cent of all re-engineering initiatives.

In mergers especially, companies that achieve short-term benefits fail to achieve longer-term potential benefits. The CIPD (2004) study reported that the majority of respondents admitted that changes failed to achieve their intended objectives in terms of financial return and competitive success measures. As the CIPD (2004: 2) report puts it,

> **reorganisations frequently fail to meet their objectives and both customer and employee relationships are prominent but avoidable casualties in the typical reorganisation process.**

The primary causes of failure in organisation change can be numerous and varied. However, there is growing recognition that the principal causes of failure are related to a lack of effective people management. As Holbeche (2005: 6) suggests, change is a profoundly human process requiring individuals to be willing and able to adapt behaviours and skills to respond to changing business needs. But as Chapter 1 has outlined, successive waves of organisational change incorporating restructuring, re-engineering and downsizing have served to severely damage the psychological contract, or the perceptions that employees and employers have of their mutual obligations.

Effective change happens when people commit to the change effort, but continuous, large-scale change has made it difficult for organisations to meet employee expectations and has served to fracture levels of trust that lie at the heart of the psychological contract. As Holbeche (2005: 6) suggests, low trust levels are one of the greatest barriers to effective organisational change.

The management of organisational change and the lack of a clear strategic vision and strategy for implementation has also impacted on the effectiveness of organisational change. As Brown (2004: 30) puts it,

> **The regrettably common approach [to organisational change] is for a narrow group of senior executives to come up with the change rationale and blueprint, which is heavily focused on financial**

**considerations and then rolled out by uninvolved managers across uncomprehending, demotivated employees, with the HR department often left to pick up the pieces.**

Against evidence of poor change management in organisations, due to a large extent to ineffective people management, the CIPD has conducted a research programme to inform the change process and analyse the capabilities required for effective restructuring and reorganisation. The research evidence suggests that HR plays a positive role in relation to every dimension of change management and is best placed to build organisational capability for sustainable change (Molloy and Whittington, 2005).

This chapter evaluates the process of organisational change and the HR role in managing strategic organisational change. It begins with an evaluation of conceptual approaches to the management of organisational change and considers key features of the change management process. It goes on to evaluate organisational and individual barriers to change and consider the HR role in addressing resistance to change and the HR contribution to managing strategic organisational change.

## ILLUSTRATION
### Back in black

With years of hierarchical structure, one of the worst industrial relations records in the UK, losses of over £1 million a day, with future cash flows in serious doubt, a disastrous rebranding, and constant media criticism … an opportunity for one of the biggest culture-change programmes in the UK or an HR director's worst nightmare?

Over the past three years, Royal Mail Letters has been through a massive renewal project. Launched in 2002, it was the biggest programme of change at the organisation for half a century.

Over the past 12 months, the results have begun to emerge. Last year, Royal Mail announced that its accounts were back in the black and proceeded to notch up a profit of £537 million for 2004–2005. In the last quarter of 2004 its letter delivery service showed its best performance in almost 10 years. Its December revenues were the highest ever. Absence levels fell from an average of 6.4 per cent between August 2003 and January 2004 to an average of 5.7 per cent over the same period the following year. Days lost to unofficial strike action fell from a peak of 86,000 in 2003 to 7,000 in 2004.

Source: Z. Roberts (2005) Back in black, *People Management*, 2 June, pp25–7

## CONCEPTUALISING ORGANISATIONAL CHANGE

Balogun and Hope-Hailey (2004: 3–6) suggest that there are two broad categories by which to view organisational change. The first sees change as continuous, with organisations evolving on a continuous and ongoing basis to keep pace with changes in the environment within which they operate. In this model, organisational change occurs through moderate but linked stages and the organisation adapts incrementally over a period of time to changed business conditions and pressures.

An alternative way of conceptualising organisational change is as a process of *punctuated equilibrium* where periods of adaptive and convergent change are interspersed by shorter periods of revolutionary change. Convergent change is adaptive and represents an extension of the past, whereas revolutionary change requires radically different ways of operating. In contrast to the incremental, continuous model, this approach sees change as both adaptive and radical.

The concept of 'strategic drift' is relevant here because as Balogun and Hope-Hailey (2004: 4) suggest, convergent change can result in inertia and resistance to change. Organisations may 'drift' away from addressing some of the forces at work in the environment and be faced with a severe crisis leading to the need for radical fundamental change in order to survive.

It is increasingly being recognised that change cannot be relied upon to occur at a steady rate and that there may be periods of incremental change sandwiched between more violent change. A good example of strategic drift, which has received a lot of recent media coverage, is that of the supermarket Sainsbury's. Once the UK's biggest supermarket chain, Sainsbury's has been overtaken by Tesco and Asda, and saw a huge drop in profits in 2004. It has been suggested that the retailer became complacent and ignored the need to change to respond to the needs of customers and suppliers in the face of fierce competition from rival supermarkets.

There are indications that Sainsbury's has responded to the need for change. The front cover of the 2004 annual report read 'What will it take to make Sainsbury's great again?', and the company has introduced a programme of structural change, improvements in product availability and quality, and the additional recruitment of 3,000 front-line staff. In the meantime, however, rivals such as Tesco and Asda have continued to grow their share of the market through price-cutting, store improvements and expanding their product ranges.

While conceptual models and frameworks may be helpful in understanding the nature of organisational change, there is limited empirical evidence to support either of these two broad models. As Balogun and Hope-Hailey (2004: 5) suggest, both models of change may be right and may apply to different types of organisation at different times and at different stages in the organisation's development.

Continuous change models may be appropriate to organisations operating within environments characterised by rapid and turbulent change and where continuous change is necessary for survival – eg high-tech industries. However, even in these environments, change may occur in certain areas while other areas and practices may remain unaltered. Moreover, situational factors may prevent an incremental approach. The punctuated equilibrium model may apply more to organisations operating in less turbulent environments where it may be possible to remain competitive without making fundamental changes in the way the organisation operates.

Balogun and Hope-Hailey (2004: 23) propose that it might be more appropriate to consider paths to change rather than types of change. As they suggest, an organisation may aim for transformation but may lack the resources, skills or finance to achieve radical change. Alternatively, the organisation may be in a crisis situation and need to take short-term action to address financial difficulties before longer-term change can be undertaken.

An alternative perspective on organisational change is offered by contingency approaches (Burnes, 1996) which suggest that different organisations face different situations and different levels of environmental complexity and need to respond accordingly. Contingency models of change emphasise the need for continuous environmental scanning in order to identify trends, probabilities and events that might impact on the organisation and suggest that the design and management of organisational change should take account of the specific situation or context of the organisation.

The CIPD Reorganising for Success study (2004: 38) suggested that

> **Although there are some common differentiators between highly successful and highly unsuccessful reorganisations, the precise mix of characteristics varies according to objectives. Reorganisation teams should not assume there is a standard formula for success, but should tailor their actions carefully to reorganisation objectives.**

There are a number of situational variables which might impact on the nature and scope of change processes, as illustrated in Figure 32.

## ACTIVITY . . .

Take an organisation with which you are familiar and consider how the contextual factors depicted in Figure 32 might impact on that organisation's ability to change.

Compare your findings with those of a colleague from a different organisation.

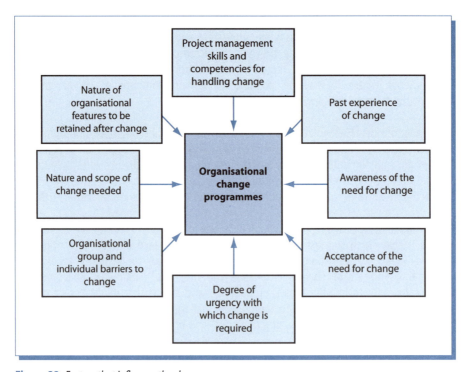

**Figure 32** *Factors that influence the change process*

Contingency approaches can also be broadened to include the concept of strategic choice or the view that organisations have some choice in the nature of the change process. The concept of strategic choice suggests that organisations do not merely respond to situational requirements but have a degree of choice over what and how to change. What is important is choosing appropriate responses in terms of structure, systems, culture, and style. Viewed in this way strategic choice represents a form of competitive advantage. As Burnes (1996: 16) puts it,

> **To ignore the presence of choice or not even to recognise its existence means taking decisions by default, and thus possibly missing major opportunities for increasing organisations' competitiveness.**

Studies (eg Goldsmith and Clutterbuck, 1998; Senior, 2002; Holbeche, 2006) have suggested that high-performing organisations are careful but deliberate innovators and balance the need for continuous change with the need to conserve core values. As Goldsmith and Clutterbuck (1998: 72) put it,

> They have a very strong preference for evolutionary change, for a whole variety of reasons; it gives time for both employees and customers to adapt; and it is less likely to disrupt people's attention to the core activities and values. They can, however, take rapid action when it is needed in response to unpredictable changes in their environment, because they usually have in-built nimbleness.

This view is supported by the CIPD (2004) Reorganising for Success study which found that successful reorganisations were conservative in that they followed processes and procedures used in previous reorganisations but innovative in terms of the organisation design and the processes adopted for improving people-related performance outcomes. Holbeche (2005: 123–48) also argues that high-performance organisations manage the human dimension when deciding on change levers and interventions through initiatives and practices such as genuine empowerment, extensive cross-functional teamworking, visionary leadership and clear communications.

The CIPD Reorganising for Success study (2004: 38) identified key systematic differences between successful and unsuccessful reorganisations related both to the organisational context and the team responsible for reorganisation and to the way in which the process was managed. The study summarises these differences as follows:

> Successful reorganisations are characterised by higher skill levels of the reorganisation management team, particularly with regard to political and communication skills; ... by greater levels of support by senior management, particularly political support; ... by more extensive changes in complementary aspects of the organisation (eg IS/IT, accounting and control procedures, career and reward systems, organisational culture); ... take place in organisations with greater previous experience of reorganising; ... typically have more substantial involvement of employees [which] goes beyond the dissemination of information to include more extensive consultation; ... demonstrate a close association with the efficient management of the reorganisation process and improvements in organisational performance.

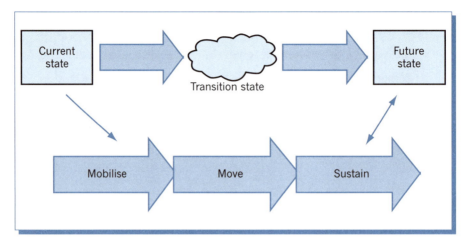

**Figure 33** *Three phases of organisational change*
Source: Balogun and Hope-Hailey (2004) *Exploring Strategic Change*, p139

## THE MANAGEMENT OF ORGANISATIONAL CHANGE

As the above discussion has illustrated, it is difficult to advocate one 'best way' of organisational change. Contingency approaches emphasise that different approaches to change may be adopted dependent upon the organisation's specific situation or context. Balogun and Hope-Hailey (2004) suggest a three-stage model of managing organisational change which is predicated on the need to fully understand the organisation's internal and external environment as a basis for determining the change process. The model is illustrated in Figure 33, and each stage is discussed briefly below.

### Analysing future state

Without a unifying vision, change initiatives can be unrelated, piecemeal and confusing. Balogun and Hope-Hailey (2004: 133) suggest that a vision encapsulates what the organisation is trying to achieve, a rationale for changes to be undertaken and a picture of what the future organisation will look like. This final aspect is likely to incorporate a statement of the values of the new organisation and what is expected of employees.

A unifying vision is also crucial in embedding and sustaining change. As Purcell *et al*'s (2003) work has shown, in assessing the connection between people management and organisational performance, successful companies have strong values which express beliefs and norms about what is important, appropriate and valued behaviour. Purcell *et al* (2003: 8) say that

> **the Big Idea ... is a simple way of expressing some basic assumptions about what the organisation is and how it works.... If it is embedded, enduring and connects the inside with the outside, it is very likely to be habitual – that is, seen as normal shared practice.**

## ILLUSTRATION

### Selfridges

The Selfridges story is one of reinvention and growth. Once seen as the embodiment of Grace Brothers, the fusty old department store depicted in *Are You Being Served?*, Selfridges now markets itself as the 'House of Brands', with its own strong image. Selfridges embarked on a programme of corporate renewal in an explicit effort to model the underlying stakeholder values required in its dealings with customers, employees and the local community, suppliers and other stakeholders. These values were expressed under four goals; to be 'aspirational, friendly, accessible and bold'. For each goal, it asked the following questions:

- Employee values – how does this make me want to work here?
- Customer values – how am I encouraged to shop here?
- Shareholder values – why should I invest in the store?
- Community values – how does Selfridges reflect the spirit of the city?
- Supplier values – what makes Selfridges an interesting proposition?

The aim was to turn values into value by acting out those values.

Source: Purcell *et al* (2003) They're free!, *People Management*, 15 May, pp34–5

The cultural web represents a useful tool for preparing a picture of the future organisation state. According to Johnson *et al* (2005: 201) the cultural web is 'a representation of the taken-for-granted assumptions, or paradigm, of an organisation and the physical manifestations of organisational culture' which can be used to identify the behaviours and taken-for-granted assumptions about the organisation. Johnson *et al* (2005: 203) depict the cultural web as a series of overlapping circles, as illustrated in Figure 34 on page 309.

The cultural web allows for a consideration of the positive aspects of the organisation which need to be retained. It also allows for the identification of possible barriers to change.

## ACTIVITY . . .

Produce a cultural web for your organisation or an organisation with which you are familiar. Consider the organisational history embedded in stories about the organisation; identify key symbols – eg logos, offices, car-parking facilities, style of dress and language used; assess the power structure and where the dominant coalition of the organisation lies; review organisational control systems or the mechanisms to measure what the organisation values and feels should be rewarded; evaluate the organisational structure and the nature and degree of hierarchy; identify routines and rituals of the organisation or specific activities or events that are important. Finally, consider the paradigm of the organisation or the fundamental taken-for-granted assumptions about the organisation and what it stands for.

Produce a hypothetical future cultural web for the same organisation. If the organisation is to anticipate future environmental challenges and pressures, what should the component elements of the cultural web look like?

Identify areas of mis-match between the existing and future webs. What aspects of the current way in which the organisation functions would need to change? What factors might inhibit the proposed changes?

Systematically analysing the future state enables consideration of an integrated approach to the implementation and management of change. As Molloy and Whittington (2005: 13) suggest,

> There are many drivers of change including technology, competition, regulation and government policy. Organisations have to define how best to organise themselves to effectively respond to these challenges, and build in capability for future change. More importantly, they need to define how best to realise benefits from the management of change. Change should integrate structures, processes, job design, capabilities and behaviours, in line with overall strategy. In short, this requires a vision of where the organisation means to get to and a path to get there.

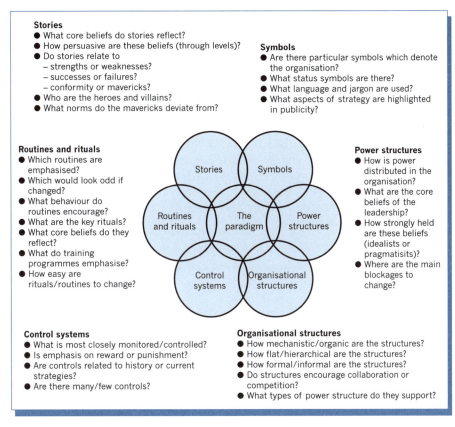

**Stories**
- What core beliefs do stories reflect?
- How persuasive are these beliefs (through levels)?
- Do stories relate to
  – strengths or weaknesses?
  – successes or failures?
  – conformity or mavericks?
- Who are the heroes and villains?
- What norms do the mavericks deviate from?

**Symbols**
- Are there particular symbols which denote the organisation?
- What status symbols are there?
- What language and jargon are used?
- What aspects of strategy are highlighted in publicity?

**Routines and rituals**
- Which routines are emphasised?
- Which would look odd if changed?
- What behaviour do routines encourage?
- What are the key rituals?
- What core beliefs do they reflect?
- What do training programmes emphasise?
- How easy are rituals/routines to change?

**Power structures**
- How is power distributed in the organisation?
- What are the core beliefs of the leadership?
- How strongly held are these beliefs (idealists or pragmatisits)?
- Where are the main blockages to change?

**Control systems**
- What is most closely monitored/controlled?
- Is emphasis on reward or punishment?
- Are controls related to history or current strategies?
- Are there many/few controls?

**Organisational structures**
- How mechanistic/organic are the structures?
- How flat/hierarchical are the structures?
- How formal/informal are the structures?
- Do structures encourage collaboration or competition?
- What types of power structure do they support?

**Figure 34** *The cultural web*
Source: G. Johnson, K. Scholes and R. Whittington (2005) *Exploring Corporate Strategy*, p203

## ILLUSTRATION

### Creating the vision and path for change

The transition from being a government department to becoming a competitive commercial organisation required substantial organisation-wide change. In particular, there was key challenge in communicating the immediate, medium- and long-term strategic vision for the organisation. With an established history of stability and a clear sense of purpose, the move to becoming a leading technology enterprise in a tough market environment was characterised by a shift to more project-based ways of working.

Following extensive and thorough consultations with all levels of employees in the organisation and intensive strategic planning workshops with the senior management team, facilitated by external consultants, an organisational journey was charted. The metaphor of a railway journey was developed. We put this plan together, represented by a railway journey. It's a single-track railway, a one-way journey, because we wouldn't be going back. It didn't have a starting-point because change has been going on forever, and we couldn't say when we would finish.

Along the route were 'stations' – key milestones in the organisation's development that could easily be identified. Each of these points had specific actions, inputs and outcomes associated with it, and these had to be completed before the organisation could progress along its journey. The railway journey set out the future vision of the organisation and the means of realising it in a way that was easily communicated throughout the organisation, enabling alignment of the objectives of the new projects with the overall strategy.

Source: a respondent to the CIPD (2005) *HR: Making Change Happen* survey, pp15–16

## Analysing the current state

Analysis of the organisation's current context allows for diagnosis of the need for change, the organisation's competitive position and factors within the organisation's external and internal environment that might be driving or inhibiting change. In addition to determining the reason for change it allows for consideration of the content of change – ie what needs to change in order for the future state to be achieved. Lynch (2000: 144) identifies seven key stages of external environmental analysis:

- general consideration of the nature of the environment and the degree of turbulence
- general analysis of the factors that will affect many industries
- growth characteristics or stage in the life cycle of organisational development
- identification of key factors for success
- examination of buyers, suppliers, new entrants, substitutes and competition in the industry
- study of direct competitors
- study of customers.

As outlined in Chapter 1, a useful way of identifying, categorising and evaluating the impact of environmental factors on the organisation is through the use of frameworks such as PEST, PESTLE and SWOT. Within a SWOT analysis, the Strengths and Weaknesses relate to internal aspects of the organisation's functioning, whereas Opportunities and Threats relate to consideration of external factors and their possible impact on the organisation.

Continually analysing the environment within which it operates allows the organisation to identify factors of strategic significance which may represent opportunities or threats. Scanning the environment is a wide-ranging but practical activity which allows the organisation to keep abreast of changes in the wider context which might constitute threats to the current business or provide opportunities for the future.

## ACTIVITY . . .

Many organisations are using scenarios as a long-term planning tool to detect major discontinuities or fractures which might de-rail trends in their industry or sector. A scenario is a picture of a possible future environment for the organisation of which the strategic implications can then be investigated. It is less concerned with prediction and more involved with developing different perspectives on the future.

1 Using the approach to scenario-construction outlined below, build two alternative scenarios for an organisation with which you are familiar.
2 Through environmental scanning, identify key aspects of the political, economic, social and technological environment within which the organisation is operating.
3 Identify factors which represent major areas of risk and uncertainty for the organisation. It is those factors which constitute high risk but about which there is a great deal of uncertainty that form the basis for scenarios.
4 Using the information from steps 1 and 2, develop stories about future possible events for the organisation and how they may unfold.
5 Use these stories to develop two plausible alternative futures. Aim to be creative and produce genuine alternative futures for the organisation rather than a development of past trends. One scenario could feature the best possible outcome, the other could outline the worst-case scenario
6 Identify the HR implications of each scenario. What would be the consequences for people if these scenarios were to take place?

Analysing the current state also requires diagnosis of the internal context or consideration of factors such as existing leadership style, culture, structure, people, politics, task and technologies. The 7-S framework (Peters and Waterman, 1982) represents a useful analytical basis for examining the organisation and the relationship between component elements.

The superordinate goals at the centre of the framework reflect the values, beliefs and vision of the organisation while the remaining elements of strategy, structure, style, systems, staff, style and skills reflect other aspects of the functioning of the organisation. The framework emphasises the need for coherence between these various elements and suggests that 'soft' issues such as style, skills and staff are as important as 'hard' elements such as strategy, structure and systems, although they may be less tangible and difficult to assess.

Analysing the features and characteristics of the internal context further contributes to identifying potential barriers to change. Barriers to change can arise from individual resistance (see the next section, *Transition state*) and wider organisational factors. As Mullins (2005: 914) suggests, despite having to adapt to their environment, organisations become comfortable operating within the systems and structures that have served them well in the past and tend to set up defences against change.

Principal reasons for organisational resistance to change can stem from a variety of causes. The organisational strategy may represent an inappropriate response to environmental pressures and challenges. Structural deficiencies arising from a lack of effective co-operation and co-ordination may inhibit the organisation from responding to changing circumstances. An organisation's culture or ways of doing things might be deeply embedded and result in inertia and resistance to change. In particular, the informal aspects of organisational functioning may undermine or even de-rail change initiatives. Change can represent threats to the power and influence of certain groups within the organisation and may become diluted through organisational politics. The effectiveness with which past change programmes and initiatives have been handled can also influence the adoption of new initiatives. Past agreements – eg with suppliers and customers – can also act as a brake on the nature and scope of change.

## Transition state

The transition state involves the process of moving from the current to the desired state and implementing the necessary changes. Balogun and Hope-Hailey (2004: 13) suggest that this stage is often overlooked as implementation is conceived in terms of the planning for change rather than the process of managing the transition itself. They go on to suggest a three-phase approach to the transition stage – mobilise, move and sustain.

This is built upon an original model developed by Lewin (1951) which referred to three stages of unfreezing, moving and refreezing. *Unfreezing* relates to creating a readiness for change by establishing an awareness of the need to change and dissatisfaction with the status quo; *moving* is concerned with the implementation of necessary changes and the development of new behaviours and attitudes; and *refreezing* involves stabilising and embedding changes throughout the organisation.

Although vision statements, plans and goals are important aspects of effective change, they will not make change happen, especially if the change involves requiring employees to adapt to new working systems and practices. As Balogun and Hope-Hailey (2004: 140) suggest, organisations only change if the individuals within them change, and it is important therefore to consider individual responses to change and transition.

It has been suggested that individuals pass through a cycle of emotions and reactions when dealing with change, a psychological process that has been compared to that of bereavement and mourning (Kubler-Ross, 1969). Individuals may differ in terms of the timing and depth of their emotional responses but tend to follow a similar pattern, as illustrated in Figure 35.

*Immobilisation* refers to the initial feeling of shock that individuals experience when they are faced with the need for change; *denial* is a stage where individuals may attempt to rationalise the change as of limited significance for them – those who disagree with the changes may spend longer in the denial stage; in the change cycle model, *anger* reflects an awareness of the need to change; the *bargaining* stage suggests acceptance of the change and a willingness to let go of old behaviours and attitudes and consider alternatives; *depression* reflects a nostalgia for old ways of doing things and with extensive and radical change this stage may take time to pass through; *testing* relates to the stage where individuals start buying in to the change and trying out new behaviours in new situations; *acceptance* is the stage at which new behaviours become integrated and embedded into everyday working.

## OVERCOMING BARRIERS TO CHANGE

As suggested earlier, individuals may pass through the change cycle at a different rate and in different ways. The cycle illustrates a typical pattern of responses that individuals are likely to demonstrate and shows that resistance to change is a natural and inevitable part of the change process.

Individuals may resist change for a variety of reasons. Holbeche (2005: 52–3) identifies a range of factors contributing to employee resistance which can in turn block change:

■ *change-weariness*: employees become disheartened and cynical as a result of considerable activity but little progress

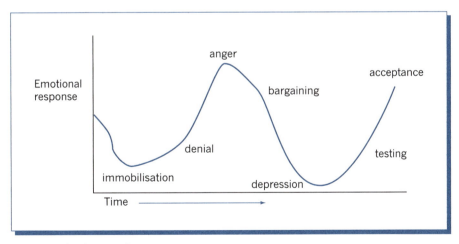

**Figure 35** *The change cycle*
Source: Molloy and Whittington (2005) *HR: Making Change Happen*, p37

- *lack of inspiring purpose*: where change efforts are focused on cost-cutting rather than revenue enhancement or where shareholder interests are put before employee well-being and security
- *lack of leadership*: where senior managers fail to take ownership of change or lose interest once a change effort is under way
- *tokenism*: where a 'change director' may be appointed in lieu of real ownership from the top
- *legacy of failure*: where previous changes have failed, employees may develop the ability to passively resist new change initiatives
- *lack of support*: where change results in increased workloads and lack of support, employee anxiety and stress levels may rise
- *poor communication*: where 'mushroom management' prevails – ie keeping employees in the dark about the results of change programmes.

## ACTIVITY . . .

Identify a specific change initiative that you have experienced that was met with resistance. This might have been a change in organisational structure, systems or working practices, or it might have involved change in technology or a combination of factors.

Discuss with a colleague *what* the change(s) involved; *who* resisted; *why* they resisted; *what form* the resistance took; and *how* the resistance was dealt with.

The change cycle and consideration of the psychological and organisational barriers to change underscores the crucial role of HR in making change happen and supporting individuals through the change process.

Effective communications strategies can help minimise the shock of change, address resistance to change and get people to accept the need for change. Support mechanisms such as coaching, counselling services, the provision of feedback, together with training and development programmes can enable individuals to test out new behaviours in a supportive environment. Continuing support, long-term investment in learning and development together with wider initiatives to celebrate success can help embed new behaviours and ways of working.

## ILLUSTRATION
### Coping with change

Introducing radical change in this specialised education agency was an extremely sensitive matter. Faced with an increasingly aggressive and competitive marketplace, as well as tightening regulation, ways of working that had been in place for 40 years had to change. A loyal, unified and local workforce was the strength of the organisation although it had always had an adversarial relationship with management. People were deeply anxious about job reallocation. Persuading staff that change was not about redundancy but about re-training, career development and the survival of the organisation was key to the success ... but a very difficult process.

When I came in, it was all positive, positive, positive. We all want this change. Everyone was singing from the same hymn-sheet. But in reality, what really surprised me was the depth and severity of how resistant people were. They were paying lip service in terms of commitment, but the underhand tactics and the backstabbing politics that came through were really quite frightening and quite staggering.

Source: a respondent to the CIPD (2005) *HR: Making Change Happen* survey, p39

The CIPD (2004) Reorganising for Success study found that employee-related issues were the most problematic aspects of change resulting in increased levels of employee complaints, higher levels of employee turnover and the loss of essential staff. The study went on to identify six key characteristics typically associated with successful reorganisations, several of which are directly linked to the HR role.

According to the study (CIPD, 2004: 3–5), successful reorganisations require:

1 *organisation-wide, holistic change* – changes set within coherent change programmes that recognise the implications of change for the organisation as a whole rather than piecemeal approaches
2 *project management* – the incorporation of project management skills and disciplines
3 *employee involvement* – real, rather than symbolic, involvement which provides employees with opportunities for feedback and questions within a context of defined milestones and rigorous project management
4 *Effective leadership* – management support in terms of resources, organisational politics and the clear setting of objectives in conjunction with skills of managing organisational culture, organisational design, project management and political astuteness
5 *communication with external stakeholders* – keeping key customers and stakeholders informed
6 *internal and external experience* – successful reorganisations stem from collective experiences of reorganisation often drawn from outside the organisation's specific sector.

## ACTIVITY . . .

*'We trained hard, but it seemed that every time we were beginning to form into teams we would be reorganised. I was to learn later in life that we tend to meet any new situation by reorganising, and a wonderful method it can be for creating the illusion of progress while producing confusion, inefficiency and demoralisation.'*

Gaius Petronius, AD 66, quoted in Mullins (2005) p654

Identify an example of organisational change which has taken place within an organisation you are familiar with.

What have been the main implications of that change for the organisation and for employees?

Could the change process have been handled differently, and if so, how?

## THE HR ROLE IN MANAGING STRATEGIC ORGANISATIONAL CHANGE

The characteristics of successful reorganisations underscore the prominent role of HR professionals in managing strategic organisational change. In particular, they highlight the following aspects of HR involvement and expertise:

- to ensure that people issues are comprehensively integrated into overall change programmes
- to insist that employee involvement is truly substantive
- to ensure that the necessary reorganisation skills are available to the organisation
- to participate directly in the change process
- to be ready to seek out a broad range of experience in relation to reorganisations.

As the discussion above has shown, HR can play a crucial role in successful reorganisation and effective organisational change. The CIPD (2005) survey of organisational change drew on two surveys and in-depth case studies of eleven organisations over a period of two and a half years. The research identified seven key areas of activity associated with successful change, which were termed the 'seven Cs' of change:

- choosing a team: being a team – key skills of the leadership team involve the management of organisational culture, organisational design, project management and political astuteness
- crafting the path and the vision – setting realistic and achievable objectives and using project management techniques

- connecting organisation-wide change – synchronising 'hard' change in structure and systems with 'soft' people and culture-related change
- consulting stakeholders – ensuring that employees, unions and other stakeholders are meaningfully consulted and involved
- communicating – accurate, meaningful, regular, consistent, transparent, up-to-date and cascaded throughout the organisation
- coping with change – putting in place mechanisms to enable people to cope with change
- capturing learning – capturing and disseminating knowledge and experience internally and externally.

The survey found that HR played a positive role in relation to every dimension of making change happen and was best placed to build organisational capability for sustainable change. The change agent role is one of the four key HR roles identified by Ulrich (1998). As Ulrich (1998: 38) suggests, HR's role in managing change is 'to replace resistance (to change) with resolve, planning with results, and fear of change with excitement about its possibilities.' The research evidence suggests that the HR function must be fully involved in the change process to ensure that the issues identified above are fully and effectively addressed.

## ILLUSTRATION

### Spirit of co-operation

When Helen Sweeney walked into the headquarters of the Co-operative Insurance Society (CIS) in 2003, she felt as though she had stepped back in time. Sweeney, HR director at Co-operative Financial Services (CFS), moved from the Co-operative Bank as part of a change management team. The team's brief was to help bring together the CIS, the Bank and the Internet bank under common leadership, sharing vision, focus, processes and goals. But the cultures of the Bank and the insurance company couldn't have been more different. The Bank was people-focused and customer-driven, with a flat structure and an empowered workforce. The CIS was technically-focused and process-driven, run by actuaries who were promoted from within according to length of service, and the culture was very traditional, male-dominated, hierarchical and status-oriented. High heels were banned in the boardroom and the mostly male workforce used 'Mr' when addressing each other.

In 2004, CFS announced a major change programme, the most important part of which was to change the culture of the company in order to empower employees to deliver the kind of performance the CFS team required. The results of a climate survey provided the basis for a roadmap of change and determined its priorities. A Development of Potential programme was introduced for directors and extended to team leaders in order to identify talent and develop an understanding of people's strengths and development needs. HR's challenge was to help people accept the need for change and prepare for it. Change agent workshops were organised for 1,000 middle managers aimed at helping managers understand their own preferences for dealing with change and to break down barriers to change.

The most difficult challenge was to make change happen. HR facilitated workshops with each leadership team in order to clarify objectives and identify ways of translating these into meaningful actions. Key goals were established and translated into daily activities with measures and targets. Alongside the change process, HR set itself the task of retaining and attracting high performers and improving people performance.

Source: *People Management*, 11 August 2005

## ILLUSTRATION

### Making change happen

HR played a transformational role in the planning and delivery of a merger of two very large service businesses over a two-year period. HR supported strategic, operational and transactional aspects at each stage. The organisation was fortunate in that it had significant project management experience and resources in-house. However, HR provided a critical role in helping strike the optimal balance between the more operational aspects of reorganisation and the people issues.

The danger was that our project managers – very good at the nuts-and-bolts stuff – managed the projects but ignored some of the softer issues. As HR, we built in a dedicated people stream for the appointments activity and the communications activity. Changing the organisation system and processes has to be done alongside addressing the people issues of transition.

Source: a respondent to the CIPD (2005) *HR: Making Change Happen* survey, p49

## KEY LEARNING POINTS

■ Change has become a key feature of organisational life and organisations embark on a range of change programmes in relation to changes in their business environment. Despite the volume of change activity, it is estimated that the majority of change initiatives fail to achieve their potential benefits because of people-related issues.

- Change can be conceptualised as a three-stage process involving analysis of the future state or a vision of where the organisation wants to be; analysis of the current state or the existing internal and external environment of the organisation; and the transition state or the process of moving from the current to the future state.
- Barriers to change can result from a range of organisational and individual factors. Barriers may be structural, cultural, political and psychological.
- Key characteristics of successful change programmes emphasise the crucial role of HR in managing change and supporting employees through the change process.

## Additional reading

CIPD (2005) *Change Management* Factsheet, available at **www.cipd.co.uk**

Carnall C. (2003) *Managing Change in Organizations*, 4th edition, Harlow, FT/Prentice Hall

Iles K. and Sutherland K. (2001) *Organizational Change. Managing Change in the NHS: A review for healthcare managers, professionals and researchers*, available at **http://www.sdo.lshtm.ac.uk/pdf/changemanagement_review.pdf**

Mabey C. and Mayon-White B. (eds) (1993) *Managing Change*, 2nd edition, London, Open University/Paul Chapman Publishing

Paton R. and McCalman J. (2003) *Change Management. A guide to effective implementation*, 2nd edition, London, Sage

Whittington R. (2005) *HR's Role in Organising: Shaping change*, Research Report, London, CIPD

### Web-based sources of information

**www.managementfirst.com/changemanagement**
**www.businessballs.com/changemanagement.htm**

## REFERENCES

Balogun J. and Hope-Hailey V. (2004) *Exploring Strategic Change*, 2nd edition, Harlow, FT/Prentice Hall

Brown D. (2004) Early intervention, *Personnel Today*, 8 June, p30

Burnes B. (1996) *Managing Change: A strategic approach to organisational dynamics*, 2nd edition, London, Pitman

CIPD (2004) *Reorganising for success. A survey of HR's role in change.* Survey report, available at **www.cipd.co.uk/surveys**

ESRC (2000) *Working in Britain Survey*, available at **www.esrc.ac.uk**

Goldsmith W. and Clutterbuck D. (1998) *The Winning Streak Mark II*, Orion Business Books

Holbeche L. (2005) *The High Performance Organization. Creating dynamic stability and sustainable success*, Oxford, Elsevier Butterworth-Heinemann

Holbeche L. (2006) *Understanding Change. Theory, implementation and success*, Oxford, Elsevier Butterworth-Heinemann

Johnson G., Scholes K. and Whittington R. (2005) *Exploring Corporate Strategy*, 7th edition, Harlow, FT/Prentice Hall

Kubler-Ross E. (1969) *On Death and Dying*, New York, Collier, Macmillan Publishing

Lewin K . (1951) *Field Theory in Social Science*, New York, Harper & Row

Lynch R. (2000) *Corporate Strategy*, 2nd edition, Harlow, FT/Prentice Hall

Molloy E. and Whittington R. (2005) *HR: Making Change Happen*, Executive Briefing, London, CIPD

Mullins L. (2005), *Management and Organisational Behaviour*, London, FT/Prentice Hall

*People Management* (2003), 15 May, pp34–5

*People Management* (2005), 11 August

Peters T. and Waterman R. (1982) *In Search of Excellence: Lessons from America's Best Run Companies*, New York, Harper and Row

Purcell J., Hutchinson S., Kinnie N., Swart J. and Rayton B. (2004) *Vision and Values: Organisational culture and values as a source of competitive advantage*, Executive Briefing, London, CIPD

Roberts Z. (2005) Back in black, *People Management*, 2 June pp25–7

Senior B. (2002) *Organisational Change*, 2nd edition, Harlow, FT/Prentice Hall

Taylor R. (2000) *Britain's World of Work – Myths and Realities*, ESRC Future of Work Programme Seminar Series

Ulrich D. (1998) HR with attitude, *People Management*, 13 August, pp36–9

# Index

# Membership has its rewards

Join us online today as an Affiliate member and get immediate access to our member services. As a member you'll also be entitled to special discounts on our range of courses, conferences, books and training resources.

To find out more, visit www.cipd.co.uk/affiliate or call us on 020 8612 6208.

## Also from CIPD Publishing . . .

# Business Environment:

## Managing in a strategic context

John Kew and John Stredwick

Business environment has become an established and growing part of most business courses. Having knowledge of the key environmental influences – economic, social, and legal – is essential to developing an understanding of business strategy at every level.

Written in an easy to use format, for students with little or no prior knowledge of the subject area, practical implications of theories are emphasised and examples clearly set out.

The text also includes chapter objectives, student activities, definitions, case studies, lists of further reading and a tutor support site.

**Order your copy now online at www.cipd.co.uk/bookstore or call us on 0870 800 3366**

**John Kew** was Principal Lecturer in Management Studies and Head of the Business School at Harlow College until 1993, teaching Business Environment and Strategic Management on CIPD and DMS programmes. Since 1993 he has been an educational consultant, and has also written Flexible Learning material for the CIPD's Professional Development Scheme.

**John Stredwick** spent 25 years as a Human Resource Practitioner in publishing and shipbuilding before joining Everest Double Glazing for 11 years as Head of Personnel. In 1992, he joined Luton University as Senior Lecturer and has directed the CIPD programmes since that time. *Business Environment* is his sixth with the CIPD. He is a national moderator for the CIPD and has run several CIPD short courses on reward management.

| Published 2005 | 1 84398 079 7 | Paperback | 304 pages |
|---|---|---|---|

The Chartered Institute of Personnel and Development is the leading publisher of books and reports for personnel and training professionals, students and all those concerned with the effective management and development of people at work.

## Also from CIPD Publishing . . .

# Equality, Diversity and Discrimination

Kathy Daniels and Lynda Macdonald

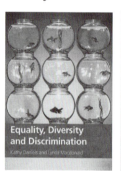

Equality, Diversity and Discrimination
Kathy Daniels and Lynda Macdonald

This text is designed specifically for the increasing number of students taking a module in Equality and Diversity, including those students taking the CIPD specialist elective, Managing Diversity and Equal Opportunities. It will also be relevant on many equality, diversity and equal opportunities modules that are part of general business or HR degrees.

The text contains a range of features, including:
- learning objectives – at the beginning of each chapter summarising the content
- interactive tasks to encourage students to research around the subject
- case studies
- legal cases
- key points and summary at the end of each chapter
- examples to work through at the end of each chapter.

### Order your copy now online at www.cipd.co.uk/bookstore or call us on 0870 800 3366

**Kathy Daniels** teaches at Aston Business School and is a tutor for ICS Ltd in Employment Law and related topics. She is also a tutor on the Advanced Certificate in Employment Law for the Chartered Institute of Personnel and Development. A Fellow of the CIPD, she is a lay member of the Employment Tribunals sitting in Birmingham. Prior to these appointments she was a senior personnel manager in the manufacturing sector.

**Lynda Macdonald** is a freelance employment law trainer, adviser and writer. For fifteen years prior to setting up her own business, she gained substantial practical experience of employee relations, recruitment and selection, dismissal procedures, employment law and other aspects of human resource management through working in industry. With this solid background in human resource management, she successfully established, and currently runs, her own business in employment law and management training/consultancy.

| Published 2005 | 1 84398 112 2 | Paperback | 272 pages |
|---|---|---|---|

The Chartered Institute of Personnel and Development is the leading publisher of books and reports for personnel and training professionals, students and all those concerned with the effective management and development of people at work.

## Also from CIPD Publishing . . .

# Organisational Theory

David Crowther and Miriam Green

This new text is designed to provide a theoretical framework for students, so that they can place organisational practice in a theoretical context. This text provides a solid knowledge base in organisational theory and its application for both undergraduate students and those on postgraduate and MBA programmes studying organisational theory or organisational behaviour.

*Organisational Theory* explains the development of theory in the social, cultural, political and ideological contexts in which organisations develop in different societies. It evaluates the theories critically using different theoretical approaches; analysing the interpretation and application of these theories to organisations, their reception and implementation by people in different types of organisation and at different levels; and their influence.

## Order your copy now online at www.cipd.co.uk/bookstore or call us on 0870 800 3366

**David Crowther** is Professor of Corporate Social Responsibility and Director of Research at The Business School, London Metropolitan University. Prior to his time at London Metropolitan University he worked at Aston University for six years. He also has over 20 years experience in industry, commerce and the public sector as an accountant, consultant and general manager.

**Miriam Green** is a Senior Lecturer in Organisation Studies and Programme Leader for the Higher National Certificate in Business Management at the Business School of London Metropolitan University. She has been a college/university lecturer for over 30 years.

| Published 2004 | 0 85292 999 4 | Paperback | 224 pages |

The Chartered Institute of Personnel and Development is the leading publisher of books and reports for personnel and training professionals, students and all those concerned with the effective management and development of people at work.

# Also from CIPD Publishing . . .

# People Resourcing

## 3rd Edition

Stephen Taylor

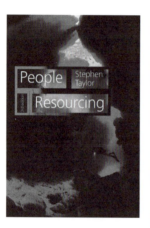

*People Resourcing* (formerly *Employee Resourcing*) addresses fundamental management issues such as attracting the best candidates, reducing staff turnover and improving employee performance. It provides a comprehensive overview of and a theoretical underpinning to the subject, while giving practical guidance to students and practitioners alike.

Key areas covered include human resource planning, recruitment, selection, absenteeism, dismissal, grounds for dismissal and best practice, the law and its implications, flexibility, and vital current issues such as emotional intelligence and knowledge management.

The text is also referenced with the latest legislation and research findings. It contains detailed sources of further information, and frequent questions and case studies to enable readers to place theories firmly in a practical context. Each chapter has a clear overview and concise summary, providing ideal points for revision and reference.

**Order your copy now online at www.cipd.co.uk/bookstore or call us on 0870 800 3366**

**Stephen Taylor** is a senior lecturer at Manchester Metropolitan University Business School and the CIPD's examiner for the Managing in a Strategic Business Context paper. He teaches and researches in HRM, employee resourcing, reward management and employment law. He has written and co-written several books about HR and regulatory issues.

| Published 2005 | 1 84398 077 0 | Paperback | 528 pages |
| --- | --- | --- | --- |

The Chartered Institute of Personnel and Development is the leading publisher of books and reports for personnel and training professionals, students and all those concerned with the effective management and development of people at work.

# Also from CIPD Publishing . . .

# Personal Effectiveness

Diana Winstanley

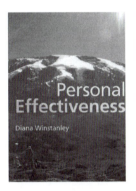

Written by a leading author in this field, this new text on Personal Effectiveness is designed to give students a basic understanding of study skills and management skills, and to give context to other studies.

Suitable for use on a range of undergraduate and postgraduate modules, including those relating to self development, personal skills, learning and development, management skills, study skills and coaching modules, and as part of general business or HR degrees, this text seeks to be both comprehensive and accessible through the use of learning aids.

Each chapter includes:
- learning objectives and a synopsis of content;
- vignette examples to illustrate key points;
- exercises with feedback;
- a self-check exercise and synopsis at the end of the chapter; and
- references and further sources of information.

## Order your copy now online at www.cipd.co.uk/bookstore or call us on 0870 800 3366

**Diana Winstanley** has over 15 years experience of training staff, students and managers in personal effectiveness, as well as in human resource management, and is already a well respected author of a number of books and articles. She has also led, designed and supported a number of PhD and postgraduate programmes in transferable skills and personal effectiveness, and is currently Professor of Management and Director of Postgraduate Programmes at Kingston Business School. Previously she has been Senior Lecturer in Management and Personal Development, Deputy Director of the full-time MBA programme and Senior Tutor at Tanaka Business School, Imperial College London. She also has professional qualifications as a humanistic counsellor.

| Published 2005 | 1 84398 002 9 | Paperback | 256 pages |
| --- | --- | --- | --- |

The Chartered Institute of Personnel and Development is the leading publisher of books and reports for personnel and training professionals, students and all those concerned with the effective management and development of people at work.